British Autobiography
in the
Seventeenth Century

British Autobiography
in the
Seventeenth Century

PAUL DELANY

1969

LONDON

ROUTLEDGE & KEGAN PAUL

NEW YORK

COLUMBIA UNIVERSITY PRESS

Published 1969
in Great Britain by
Routledge & Kegan Paul Limited
and in the United States of America by
Columbia University Press

Printed in Great Britain

Copyright © Paul Delany 1969

Library of Congress Catalog Card Number: 69-19285

Printed in Great Britain

Contents

Contents

*

To my
Father and Mother

Preface

I HAVE tried in this book to give an orderly account of a somewhat obscure and unwieldy mass of seventeenth-century British literature; I am all the more grateful, therefore, to those who have offered skilful guidance and encouragement, especially Professors Wayne Shumaker and G. A. Starr of the University of California at Berkeley. Thomas Barnes, of the University of California, John N. Morris, of Washington University, and C. A. Patrides, of the University of York, also gave me the benefit of their scholarship and wise counsel.

I am indebted to the Council for Research in the Humanities, Columbia University, for a summer fellowship which enabled me to work at British libraries in 1966.

My greatest debt is to my wife, Sheila, for her sympathetic criticism and constant support.

Paul Delany

Columbia University
New York

I
Introduction

IN WRITING this study of British autobiography in the seventeenth century I have been impressed by the risks, and the problems, involved in attempting to impose modern habits of thought and literary definitions on the past.[1] For the educated Englishman of that time, a recognized literary genre entitled 'autobiography' did not exist, any more than the word itself (which seems to have been coined by Southey in 1809). From our perspective, on the other hand, we see in seventeenth-century literature many kinds of auto-biographical writings, to which their authors gave such titles as 'Journal of the Life of Me', 'History of the Life and Times', 'Adventures', 'Confessions' and so forth. The critic's first task is to decide which works, among a great mass of more or less personal or self-revelatory writings, should be singled out for inclusion in a history of autobiography. He must commit himself to some kind of formal definition of the genre, even though it is bound to give rise to anomalies in practice—especially in the literary culture, so rich in eccentricities, of seventeenth-century Britain. My own concern has been to frame a definition which excludes the bulk of random or incidental self-revelation scattered through seventeenth-century literature, but does not impose on the autobiographies of the period rigid rules and conventions invented by the modern critic for his own purposes.

To specify: the term 'autobiography' as used hereafter will designate literary works (1) *primarily* written to give a coherent account of the author's life, or of an extensive period or series of events in his life, and (2) composed after a period of reflection and forming a unified narrative. The distinction often made between 'autobiography'

[1] 'British' autobiography should be understood in a geographic rather than a linguistic sense: autobiographies in any language by inhabitants of the British Isles are included, whereas those from continental North America are not. The chronological scope includes autobiographies written, though not necessarily published, between 1600 and 1699; plus a few works written after the turn of the century but dealing entirely with seventeenth-century events.

and 'memoirs'—the former defined as an analytical and introspective life-record, the latter as one more concerned with external events—will be used sparingly, since it too easily lends itself to confusion in a Renaissance context. We contribute little to the cause of clarity when we define as 'memoirs' what Benvenuto Cellini called his 'life' and everyone nowadays calls his autobiography. Since the amount of explicit self-analysis in a seventeenth-century autobiography may vary so widely it is easier and clearer to distinguish between mainly objective and mainly subjective narratives. To the objective type of autobiography in its pure form as a bald record of the external events in the author's life we may give the convenient label of *res gestae*—a more precise tag than 'memoirs'.

Difficulties in applying a definition of autobiography such as the one above arise mainly when an author writes either too personally, or not personally enough. Some authors are determinedly reticent about their own affairs, and speak only of the historical events they have witnessed or of the famous people they knew; they may reinforce their self-effacement by adopting the third-person form of narrative. For example, Bishop Burnet's *History of his Own Time*, in which his personal affairs count for very little, is clearly not an autobiography; William Lilly's *History of his Life and Times* clearly is, in spite of the historical anecdotes embedded in it.[1] At the other extreme from *res gestae* are works so subjective as to be rhapsodies or intimate essays rather than true autobiographies; for example, Browne's *Religio Medici* or Cowley's discourse 'Of Myself'. I have taken such works into account only in so far as they help to illuminate the more central problems of seventeenth-century autobiography. Finally, I have rather stringently excluded autobiographical passages which are part of larger works. From Milton's writings, in particular, enough autobiographical passages can be extracted to fill a substantial book;[2] but Milton always used his self-revelations as aids to the fulfilment of some other aesthetic or controversial end. He never chose to write a complete and independent autobiography. Though much is lost by excluding autobiographical segments of longer works, such a policy imposed itself. The scope of this study would otherwise have been expanded to unmanageable proportions; moreover, the problem of truth or sincerity in autobiography becomes hopelessly confused when an autobiographical statement is inextricably linked to some larger and extraneous aesthetic design, and the critic finds himself enmeshed in such insoluble questions as the precise degree of

[1] To avoid confusion, I should note that Burnet did write an authentic autobiography; he planned it as an appendix to his *History*, but it was suppressed by his executors and did not appear until 1902.

[2] See *Milton on Himself*, ed. J. S. Diekhoff.

identification between Milton and the hero of *Samson Agonistes*.

Within the limits of my study I have identified nearly two hundred autobiographies, published and unpublished, and undoubtedly many have eluded my search. They are an extraordinarily mixed group of works, with some relevance to many fields of scholarly investigation both in English literature and in other disciplines, especially history. This heterogeneity has driven me to use a somewhat eclectic blend of historical, critical and psychological approaches in the discussion of individual autobiographies, and to divide the book into sections on religious and secular autobiography. The rationale for these choices should be briefly explained.

One of the most important aims of this study is to provide the scholar with a guide to what the term 'British seventeenth-century autobiography' really designates; for even specialists in the literature of the period are unlikely to have read more than a few of the works here discussed. Such neglect can largely be blamed on the absence of any comprehensive, full-length study of the subject.[1] Since I have not been able to assume that my readers will be familiar with many of the works considered, I have been fairly generous with summaries and quotations. I have also recorded sources, influences and personal acquaintances between autobiographers where these seemed relevant; though this task has been a minor one because of the independent, even secretive working habits of most autobiographers, and because of the scarcity of published autobiographies before 1700. So far as I have been able to discover them, I have recorded the essential historical details of each work, usually in the bibliographical appendix, with the aim of providing a concise but useful reference guide for the student and scholar. Apart from these historical aims, I have stressed two further ones: to analyse critically the autobiographies as literary works, and to suggest relationships between them and the culture and society of their time.

The division of this book into sections on 'religious' and 'secular' autobiography perhaps requires justification. No doubt virtually all seventeenth-century Englishmen held some kind of religious belief, and were as a rule more devout than all but a handful of moderns; but, none the less, many autobiographers narrate their worldly careers rather than the progress of their souls. Clarendon, for example, may have been a faithful Anglican, but this is not directly

---

[1] The two chief scholarly studies are a chapter in Stauffer's *English Biography before 1700* and Margaret Bottrall's *Every Man a Phoenix*, supplemented by sections of Starr, *Defoe and Spiritual Autobiography* and J. Morris, *Versions of the Self*. I have also consulted the unpublished dissertations of A. W. Brink and I. D. Ebner (see bibliography, part II).

relevant to our judgement of his autobiography, which is an essentially political and secular record. Englishmen of that time were much more prone than we to define their roles in life rather narrowly—usually in terms of their social rank or profession. A veteran of the Civil War would write his autobiography from the viewpoint of a professional soldier, with accounts of battles and sieges; an aristocrat would tell of his adventures at court or in diplomacy; neither would be likely to write a spiritual autobiography, since they would probably not consider their soul-histories to be as distinctive as what they had done in their worldly capacities. They might also consider religion to be a field in which a layman had small claim to authority, and in fact almost all the religious autobiographies of the period were written by priests, ministers or preachers of the various denominations.[1]

Within the category of religious autobiography, a distinction may be made between objective accounts of religious life and more introspective soul-histories, 'spiritual autobiographies'. The former type of work was written, typically, by Catholics and Anglicans; the latter by Presbyterians and even more by members of the various radical sects. I have arranged the discussion of religious autobiographers according to the denominations to which they belonged, this being a generally more objective and reliable means of classification; the correlation between the sectarian loyalties of autobiographers and the kind of expression they chose will emerge clearly enough.

Secular autobiographies form such a diverse group that no obvious scheme of arrangement immediately suggests itself. Works in the *res gestae* convention, dealing with their authors' experiences of travel or of military or political life, are relatively unimportant as literature and have been segregated in a short chapter. A miscellaneous group of more subjective autobiographies remain. I have chosen to classify them according to the rank or occupation of their authors. This system would certainly be open to criticism if applied to a collection of published works in a recognized literary genre; but most secular autobiographies of the time were not published until long after their composition, and individual works usually show little awareness of any autobiographical tradition. Moreover, the autobiographer's social position tends to have a dominant influence on everything from style and structure to the raw material of the life he describes. Autobiography is linked more directly than any other literary genre to the particular culture or sub-culture which moulded the lives of

[1] Browne's *Religio Medici* shows in many places the diffidence of a layman in discussing religion; he called it 'a private Exercise directed to my self' and did not release it for publication until forced to do so by counterfeit and corrupt editions.

4

the men who wrote it. The arrangement of my discussion of secular autobiography is designed to bring out the significance and the specific nature of this cultural link.

Autobiographies by women, whether secular or religious in emphasis, merit separate treatment. In general, female auto-biographies have a deeper revelation of sentiments, more subjectivity and more subtle self-analyses than one finds in comparable works by men. The sociological reasons for this difference are obvious, and have existed since antiquity; yet it is not until the seventeenth century that what we now call the 'feminine sensibility' enters the main stream of English literature—before then it was usually ignored by the male writers who dominated literary life, or obscured by a narrow and stereotyped anti-feminism. The expression of this sensibility in seventeenth-century autobiography deserves study both in its own right and for the light it may shed on the appearance of the novel soon after.

Before the main discussion begins, something needs to be said about the vexing problem of 'Renaissance individualism' and the relevance of this famous (or notorious) abstraction to the development of autobiography. The following chapter, then, touches on some of the cultural trends which may have influenced auto-biographers, from Petrarch onwards, in Western Europe.

II

The Renaissance and the Rise of Autobiography

'THE RENAISSANCE' has too often been conceived as a kind of intangible force which had an effect on men of that time additional to, or separate from, the usual motives of human conduct, and which produced in some automatic fashion varied expressions of individuality. To avoid such misconceptions, I have used the term simply as a chronological tag: by 'Renaissance Italy' is meant the Italy of about 1341-1600, while the Renaissance period in Northern Europe is taken as 1494-1643.[1] During these periods autobiographies began to be written in significant numbers for the first time in each area; this chapter will suggest some changes in man and society which seem to have contributed to the new popularity of autobiography as a means of self-expression. I will discuss here changes in concepts of history, in forms of self-consciousness, and in class structures; new developments in religion will be discussed in Chapter III.

Since we will be dealing with broadly European trends, modified in greater or less degree by national peculiarities, we should first make allowance for the relative weakness of Britain's cultural ties with the Continent. When Cellini refers casually to 'those brutes of Englishmen',[2] he is expressing the quite normal reaction of a Renaissance Italian to a nation which was, by his standards, small, poor, remote, and intellectually backward.[3] New developments in art or literature

[1] Because of the limited sense in which I use the term 'Renaissance' it seems unnecessary to enter into a long justification of these particular dates; 1341 is the year of Petrarch's crowning with the laurel, 1494 the year of Charles VIII's invasion of Italy and Durer's first journey there, 1643 marked the accession of Louis XIV.

[2] *Autobiography*, tr. George Bull, p. 30.

[3] See, for example, the amusing account by Aeneas Sylvius of his journey to Scotland and England in the 1430s; in Northumberland 'all the men and women of the village came running as if to see a strange sight and as our people marvel at Ethiopians or Indians, so they gazed in amazement at Aeneas, asking the priest where he came from, what his business was, and whether he was a Christian.

6

did not usually take root in Britain until long after they had been adopted in the wealthier and more sophisticated Continental states; the late appearance of autobiography in Britain was in accordance with this rule. We cannot, however, ascribe this delay to the failure of British autobiographers to respond to the inspiration of Continental models; for many of the most significant Continental autobiographies were not published at all until long after their authors' deaths— Cellini's, for example, did not appear until 1728.[4] Moreover, literary history has amply demonstrated that a genre cultivated in one country will not achieve success in another until time and circumstances there are favourable; the Petrarchan sonnet, to take an obvious case, did not become popular in England until some hundred and fifty years after Petrarch's death. In Renaissance Europe, autobiography tended to develop independently in each country, with Italy the leader both in time and in quality.[5] Most British autobiographies written before 1700 show little trace of foreign literary influences; by their extraordinary diversity these works bear witness to the isolated workings of their authors' imaginations.

We may now consider some of the conditions which encouraged men of Renaissance Europe to write autobiographies, after the dearth of such works in the medieval period and in antiquity.

Concepts of History

The lack of a sense of their own individuality among members of primitive tribes has often been noted. Autobiography cannot be written until this primitive community breaks up, or at least becomes sufficiently loosened that some men can live in partial independence of it. A feature of this dissolution of communal bonds is the emer-

---

Aeneas, having learned of the scanty entertainment to be found on his journey, had obtained at a certain monastery several loaves of bread and a jug of wine and when he brought these out, they excited the liveliest wonder among the barbarians, who had never seen wine or white bread. Pregnant women and their husbands kept coming up to the table, touching the bread and sniffing the wine and asking for some, so that he had to divide it all among them.' *Memoirs of a Renaissance Pope*, tr. Florence Gragg, pp. 34-5.

[4] Cardano's *De Vita Propria*, published in 1643 at Paris, sixty-seven years after his death, seems to have influenced Herbert of Cherbury's autobiography, which he wrote around 1645.

[5] The desultory spread of literary genres in Renaissance Europe contrasts with the extraordinarily rapid dissemination of such technical inventions as printing— 'within fifteen years after Gutenberg's death in 1468 printing presses had been set up in every country of western Christendom from Sweden to Sicily and from Spain to Poland and Hungary.' S. H. Steinberg, *Five Hundred Years of Printing*, p. 27.

gence of a sense of history, which Georges Gusdorf has identified as one of the vital preconditions of autobiography:

Il faut d'abord que l'humanité soit sortie, au prix d'une révolution culturelle, du cadre mythique des sagesses traditionelles, pour entrer dans le règne périlleux de l'histoire. L'homme qui prend la peine de se raconter sait que le présent diffère du passé, et qu'il ne se répètera pas dans l'avenir; il est devenu sensible aux différences plutôt qu'aux ressemblances; dans le renouvellement constant, dans l'incertitude des événements et des hommes, il croit que c'est chose utile et valable de fixer sa propre image, vouée sans cela a disparaître comme toutes choses en ce monde.[6]

However, the autobiographer requires a more sophisticated sense of history than a simple awareness of the difference between past and future. The scarcity of autobiographies during the Middle Ages may be at least partially attributed to the rather undeveloped sensitivity to change, in both their own and others' lives, which seems to have characterized the men of that time. They were aware, for example, that the ancients were different from themselves; but the difference was mainly thought of as quantitative—the ancients were merely superior, they lived in an unhistoric, ideal realm. Medieval historians tended to see earlier societies in terms of their own, and hence to lack a real sense of the past. Not the least important innovation during the Renaissance was the rise of a more relativist concept of historiography: 'the development of a sense of perspective on the past, the ability to place oneself in time with respect to an age as a whole, the awareness of historic distance, all this was a contribution essentially of humanist thought'.[7] The improvement in historical methods was accompanied by a great increase in the quantity and variety of historical writing as monastic chroniclers lost their monopoly of the profession. One feature of this new interest in history was the writing of many family histories, to which their authors, as the most recent representatives and chroniclers of family tradition, often added sketches of their own lives and opinions. Histories of this kind first became popular in Italy, and the opening of the Florentine Buonaccorso Pitti's chronicle illustrates the spirit in which they were undertaken:

NEGLI ANNI DOMINI Mccccxij

Io Bonacorso di Neri di Bonacorso di Maffeo di Bonsignore d'un altro Bonsignore de' Pitti nel detto anno di sopra cominciai a scrivere in su questo libro per fare memoria di quello ch'io ò potuto trovare e

---

[6] 'Conditions et limites de l'autobiographie,' in G. Reichenkron, ed., *Formen der Selbstdarstellung*, p. 107. Hereafter cited as Gusdorf.

[7] Myron P. Gilmore, *The World of Humanism 1453-1517*, p. 201.

sentire di nostra anticha progienia e de' parentadi nostri antichi e moderni e che a' miei dí sono fatti o faranno; e ancora ci farò su alquanti ricordi della vita e modi d'alcuni de' detti nostri progienitori e per ispeziale di quelli ch'io ò veduti.[8]

Pitti focuses his attention here on family tradition; though he does, by placing a special emphasis on the deeds of those members 'ch'io ò veduti', suggest something of the importance of his own role in family affairs. At the beginning of the next section of his chronicle, however, he shifts to a directly autobiographical mode: 'Io Bonaccorso di Neri faro qui apresso ricordo de l'andare per lo mondo ch'io o fatto dipoi che io rimasi sanza padre' (p. 34). In early British autobiographies we often find similar transitions from genealogy to autobiography; by placing his own story in the context of family tradition the writer could invoke filial piety as a motive for composition and could avoid giving the appearance of an unseemly egotism.

An obvious external cause for the increase in family histories was the improved literacy of the upper classes. It is well known that many medieval noblemen could not read or write in the vernacular, not to mention Latin. They were dependent on clerks for their written records; and although a clerk might commemorate the deeds of a noble house to which he was attached, he would scarcely be so presumptuous as to add to the work his own autobiography.[9] Another reason for the proliferation of family histories lay in the difference of status between, say, the English feudal lords of the twelfth century and the gentry of the sixteenth century. Because of the dissolution of the feudal bond, the latter group included a far larger number of autonomous family units; and each unit had a history of its own, instead of merely reflecting the fortunes of its seigneur. Literacy and autonomy, both of which were first achieved widely during the Renaissance, were the two prerequisites of the type of family history which could provide a springboard for autobiography. Beyond these minimum requirements, however, we must look to a closer analysis of individual cases in which family history and personal history are linked. This analysis will be limited to British authors.

British historiography did not begin to match the advances made by such men as Commines and Machiavelli until the seventeenth

---

[8] *Cronica di Bounaccorso Pitti*, ed. A. B. Della Lega (Bologna, 1905), p. 7.

[9] Einhard begins his *Life of Charlemagne* with an account of the Merovingian dynasty, but says nothing of his own life, though he was a foster-son of Charlemagne. For the extent of literacy in ninth to eleventh century Europe see Marc Bloch, *Feudal Society*, tr. L. A. Manyon, pp. 75-81. 'But north of the Alps and the Pyrenees at least the majority of the small or medium lords who exercised most authority at this time were illiterates in the full sense of the word.' (p. 80).

century.[10] However, interest in family or 'private' history did increase steadily in the course of the sixteenth century, perhaps mainly because of the remarkable vicissitudes experienced by the aristocracy, and the high turnover in their membership, during the Wars of the Roses and the reign of Henry VIII. By the early seventeenth century Francis Markham appends a brief autobiography to his family history, and a remarkable number of the country gentry pursue antiquarian and genealogical interests. Throughout the century secular autobiographers regularly link their own lives with those of their forebears, in genealogical introductions which range from a few sentences to Herbert of Cherbury's extensive survey of almost two hundred years of family achievements. At the end of the century Roger North excels both in family history and in autobiography, with his *The Lives of the Norths* and his *Autobiography*.

A further contribution to the development of autobiography came from the interest aroused by the extraordinary political disturbances of the seventeenth century, which created in many men an urge to record their own participation in important events. William Lilly's *History of His Life and Times* (written 1667) is mainly auto-biographical, despite a title which promises even-handed treatment of his own and other people's affairs; once men set out to record history from a strictly personal viewpoint, the influence of natural egotism could easily turn their chronicles into autobiographies. The Civil War especially, like no previous national upheaval, made a powerful impression on the imaginations of virtually everyone who had sufficient education to understand the ideological issues over which the war was fought. In addition to the numerous military or political memoirs which were based directly on their authors' labours for Crown or Parliament, the war had the indirect effect of bringing to many autobiographers a heightened awareness of their particular convictions and predispositions. If 'the Elizabethan discovery of England'[11] was mainly inspired by the nationalist and Protestant zeal of those antiquaries, chroniclers and topographers who so thoroughly surveyed the past and present of their homeland, the seventeenth century discovered that more than one kind of zeal could be at large within the bosom of a single state—'Zeal-of-the-land-Busy', for example, represented a powerfully disruptive new force. Awareness of the internal tensions of England's social structure undoubtedly contributed to the development of a more sophisticated sense of

[10] Commines died *c.* 1511, Machiavelli in 1527. Bacon's *History of the Reign of Henry VII* (1622) is usually considered the first fruit of the 'new history' in England.

[11] Title of Chapter II of A. L. Rowse's *The England of Elizabeth*; see pp. 31-3 for the development of Tudor interest in English history.

10

history during the seventeenth century. This deeper understanding of historical forces, through the insight it offered into the origins and significance of personal actions and allegiances, was an important factor in the rise of autobiography.

Renaissance Self-consciousness

> To the discovery of the outward world the Renaissance added a still greater achievement, by first discerning and bringing to light the full, whole nature of man.
> This period, as we have seen, first gave the highest development to individuality, and thus led the individual to the most zealous and thorough study of himself in all forms and under all conditions.[12]

This *locus classicus* of Burckhardt (though in the first sentence he was paraphrasing Michelet) may serve as a starting-point for our inquiry into the growth of more subtle kinds of self-consciousness during the Renaissance and their expression in autobiography. Burckhardt points to the individual's 'zealous and thorough study of himself'; but self-study was hardly a Renaissance invention. St. Augustine, after all, studied himself; though scarcely, it is true, in what we think of as the Renaissance spirit—he wished to exhibit his life as a case of pathological development, from the evil effects of which he was saved by the grace of God. His aim was not self-assertion: 'L'auteur des *Confessions* veut donc parler de Dieu plutôt que de lui-même. Son but est de témoigner non en sa propre faveur, mais en faveur de Dieu qui l'a sauvé, Dieu, le "médecin intérieur" (*medice meus intime*). Il espère ainsi pouvoir être utile à son prochain.'[13] Self-study, though again not for its own sake, must have been a routine duty for medieval Catholics in the form of the examination of conscience. Even Petrarch, whether or not he was the first 'Renaissance man', continued the Augustinian tradition in his self examination, as can be abundantly documented.[14]

A more novel feature of Renaissance individualism, I would argue, lies elsewhere: in the emergence of men who are able to imagine themselves in more than one role; who stand as it were outside or above their own personalities; who are protean. Medieval thought personifies conflicting mental tendencies in the *psychomachia*—the good and bad angels may fight over man's soul, but the essence of his personality remains intact. The new man, conversely, succumbs to a

---

[12] Jacob Burckhardt, *The Civilization of the Renaissance in Italy*, tr. S. Middlemore, p. 184.
[13] Gusdorf, *La Découverte de Soi*, p. 19.
[14] See, e.g., *Secretum Meum*, which consists of three dialogues between the poet and Augustine. Tr. W. H. Draper, *Petrarch's Secret*.

more or less destructive schizophrenia in the same circumstances; his core of self-hood splits and his very identity becomes doubtful. The great symbol and epitome of this new state of being in the Renaissance is Hamlet. His consciousness of playing a part which is in some sense alien to his real self finds innumerable echoes in contemporary literature; in fact, the dominant metaphor for human existence is now the stage, replacing the medieval figure of the 'Pèlerinage de la vie humaine'.[15] Montaigne is especially aware of the connection between role-playing and the autobiographical persona:

> Many yeares are past since I have no other aime, whereto my thoughts bend, but my selfe, and that I controule and study nothing but my selfe. And if I study any thing else, it is immediatly to place it upon, or to say better, in my selfe. ... I impart what I have learn't by this, although I greatly content not my selfe with the progresse I have made therein. There is no description so hard, nor so profitable, as is the description of a mans owne life; Yet must a man handsomely trimme-up, yea and dispose and range himself to appeare on the Theatre of this world. Now I continually tricke up my selfe; for I uncessantly describe my selfe.[16]

Montaigne was not content to merely re-create his historical, external self in the *Essays*; he sought a role or persona which would convey something of the subtle, internal motions of his personality— 'I write not my gests, but my selfe and my essence' (II, 60). Yet the origins of this division and its accompanying search for the inner or 'authentic' self remain obscure.

Gusdorf, in his audacious and stimulating essay on autobiography, attributes the 'discovery of self' in large part to the invention of good mirrors towards the end of the Middle Ages.[17] Improved mirrors were certainly a factor in the proliferation of self-portraits from the later fifteenth century onwards; and there is a close correlation between the development of self-portraiture and autobiography in the various European countries. The first substantial English auto-

---

[15] I would suspect that this shift from the essentially linear pilgrimage to the three-dimensional stage reflects the same tendencies which were responsible for the roughly concurrent shift from 'flatness' to perspective in the graphic arts. See Pierre Francastel, *Peinture et Societé*; discussed in Z. Barbu, *Problems of Historical Psychology*, p. 35 ff.

[16] *Essays*, tr. J. Florio, II, 58-9. I have quoted Montaigne in this translation because of its great influence in seventeenth-century Britain. Even Florio's inaccuracies are instructive; comparison with the original of the passage quoted will show that Florio develops the theatre metaphor more fully and specifically than Montaigne himself.

[17] Gusdorf, 'Conditions et Limites,' pp. 108-9. Venetian glass mirrors were first produced in quantity from the early sixteenth century onward; before this polished metal was used—a material with obvious limitations.

biography and the first self-portrait by a native Englishman were produced within a year of each other, so far as we can tell.[18] Dürer gives us the best example of how an early-Renaissance artist, exploring new inner realms, could use the mirror as an accessory to introspection. His first recorded work, made at the age of thirteen in 1484, is a drawing of himself with the inscription 'made out of a mirror'.[19] At least eight more self-portraits followed in which Dürer showed himself in an extraordinary variety of roles, from the self-assured and handsome young man (holding a good-luck charm) of 1493 (Panofsky, Fig. 30) to the nude 'Man of Sorrows', with whip and scourge, of 1522 (Panofsky, Frontispiece). Another portrait, from 1498, is more directly self-assertive:

> the Prado picture was painted without any ulterior purpose and is thus perhaps the first independent self-portrait ever produced. It was, in a sense, a challenge to the world at large, claiming for the artist the status of a 'homo liberalis atque humanus', or, to use Dürer's own word, of a 'gentilhuomo'. In Italy, this claim had long been granted— in Germany, it had yet to be raised. But it could be raised only by an artist become 'self-conscious'—in every possible sense of the word— through his providential encounter with the Italian *rinascimento*. There is undeniably an element of vanity and pride in Dürer's attitude, quite natural in an artist who had already won the confidence of great men and achieved international fame at the age of twenty-six. But this personal element is outweighed by the gravity of a more than personal problem—the problem of the 'modern' artist as such. (Panofsky, p. 42)

Dürer's self-portraits change radically as he pursues his elusive core of selfhood through various costumes, settings, and expressions. The brooding self-portrait at the age of twenty seems to suggest an anxious search for a lost identity; (Panofsky, Fig. 25). This search becomes obsessive in the more than a hundred self-portraits of Rembrandt, the presiding genius of seventeenth-century art.[20] In literature, Montaige describes the elusiveness of that inner self which he wished to present to the world:

> And though the lines of my picture change and vary, yet loose they not themselves. . . . I cannot settle my object; it goeth so unquietly and

[18] Thomas Whythorne wrote his *Autobiography* about 1576; Nicholas Hilliard painted a miniature self-portrait in 1577, when he was thirty. For the overall development of self-portraiture, see L. Goldscheider, *Five Hundred Self-Portraits*.

[19] E. Panofsky, *Albrecht Dürer*, p. 15. Durer draws his body almost to the waist, which suggests that a fairly large mirror, and hence probably one of glass rather than metal, was used.

[20] Cf. Gusdorf, 'Conditions,' p. 109 and R. Pascal, *Design and Truth in Autobiography*, p. 18.

staggering, with a naturall drunkennesse. I take it in this plight, as it is at th'instant I ammuse my selfe about it. I describe not the essence, but the passage; not a passage from age to age, or as the people reckon, from seaven yeares to seaven, but from day to day, from minute to minute. My history must be fitted to the present. I may soone change, not onely fortune, but intention. (III, 23)

Others gifted with the kind of protean nature I have been trying to define could be cited—Donne, for example, with his lyrics in different voices and his portrait in the shroud. However, they should not be thought of as providing norms for the typical 'Renaissance man'; rather, they were men of exceptional sensibility who extended the boundaries of personality while the mass of their contemporaries stuck to age-old habits. Yet how did these superior men transcend their origins and reach a new and higher level of self-awareness? The answer must come from the still rudimentary science of historical psychology, and an almost insuperable difficulty arises at once: we know practically nothing about the childhood and adolescence of most Renaissance men, even quite famous ones.[21] A few scholars have tried to penetrate this obscurity, notably Erik Erikson in his bold speculations on the psychological origins of Luther's revolt against Rome. In a more general application of his approach, Erikson suggests that breakthroughs into new fields of human activity are likely to occur when society causes its young people to pass through especially complex or painful 'identity crises':

In some young people, in some classes, at some periods in history, this crisis will be minimal; in other people, classes, and periods, the crisis will be clearly marked off as a critical period, a kind of 'second birth', apt to be aggravated either by widespread neuroticism or by pervasive ideological unrest. Some young individuals will succumb to this crisis in all manner of neurotic, psychotic, or delinquent behaviour; others will resolve it through participation in ideological movements passionately concerned with religion or politics, nature or art. Still others, although suffering and deviating dangerously through what appears to be a prolonged adolescence, eventually come to contribute an original bit to an emerging style of life: the very danger which they have sensed has forced them to mobilize capacities to see and say, to dream and plan, to design and construct, in new ways.[22]

We will be examining in detail later some of these 'second births', which in seventeenth-century Britain usually sprang from crises in adolescent religious belief. Even those autobiographers who did not

[21] This statement should be qualified: we know a good deal about the *general* circumstances of child-rearing in the Renaissance, but very little about particular persons. See P. Ariès, *Centuries of Childhood.*

[22] *Young Man Luther*, pp. 14-15.

14

radically change their outlook at any one stage, and who seemed to have achieved an impressive mental firmness and maturity, often displayed in later life the kind of self-absorbed narcissism typical of adolescence. They were not willing to accept entirely at face value the narrow and stereotyped roles which society was still attempting to impose on its members. They were aware of the potential for change in themselves and others, and sought in their autobiographies to commemorate the particular destiny that chance or inclination had given them.

A false impression of the trends of the age might be created if we did not make some mention of the very considerable intellectual opposition to self-study and self-assertion during the Renaissance. Norman Nelson has commented on the paradox that the Renaissance, the age which is said to have fostered the development of individuality, was also the age of humanism—an intellectual movement fundamentally opposed to individualism and singularity.[23] It was from this perspective that Pascal mocked Montaigne—'le sot projet qu'il a de se peindre!'[24]—and that Donne deplored the pride and presumption of his contemporaries:

> 'Tis all in peeces, all cohaerence gone;
> All just supply, and all Relation:
> Prince, Subject, Father, Sonne, are things forgot,
> For every man alone thinkes he hath got
> To be a Phoenix, and that then can bee
> None of that kinde, of which he is, but hee.[25]

However, these two critics of individualism seem to oppose in others tendencies which they sensed in themselves, but tried to suppress; Donne says as much, with his anguished outcry 'Take mee to you, imprison mee, for I | Except you'enthrall mee, never shall be free' (Holy Sonnets, XIV). Moreover, in Britain it was not until the eighteenth century that humanism, now garbed in neo-classicist robes, was able to mount a thorough and successful offensive against individual singularity.

To what extent do early British autobiographers display new and imaginative forms of self-consciousness? Those writers who are content to define themselves rigidly and exclusively by their rank or calling seem to have remained quite medieval in their self-concepts—

---

[23] 'Individualism as a Criterion of the Renaissance,' *JEGP*, XXXII (1933), 316-34.
[24] *Pensées*, ed. C.-M. des Granges, p. 85.
[25] 'An Anatomie of the World. The first Anniversary,' ll. 213-18.

the military and political purveyors of *res gestae* often fall into this category. But a new spirit can be discerned in the *Autobiography* of Thomas Whythorne (*c*. 1576); and more strongly in the amusing and flamboyant self-presentation of Simon Forman the alchemist, who composed his fragmentary autobiography in about 1600.[26] A taste for role-playing reappears in a more extreme form a generation later with Sir Kenelm Digby's *Loose Fantasies*, a fictionalized auto-biography in which Digby disguises himself as the pastoral hero 'Theagenes'.[27] Herbert of Cherbury, who wrote in the 1640s, had perhaps more opportunity than any other British secular auto-biographer of the time to produce an early masterpiece in the genre. In fascination with himself he was the equal of Cardano (whom he probably read); he shared the intellectual openness of Montaigne and the forceful, unmediated egotism of Cellini. Unfortunately Herbert, despite his intelligence and advanced philosophical thinking, was too invincibly complacent to produce an autobiography which advanced the art of introspection.

Herbert's achievement, though real, was limited; and his failure to exploit fully the resources at his disposal was all too typical of the broad development of autobiography as a genre in seventeenth-century Britain. The complex and self-aware 'Renaissance man'—as epitomized in such highly-developed personalities as Leonardo, Dürer, and Montaigne—began to appear in Britain around the beginning of the seventeenth century. Moreover, from about 1600 the language and vocabulary of introspection became much more refined and searching than they had ever been; Donne's Holy Sonnets and *Devotions upon Emergent Occasions*, Browne's *Religio Medici*, and the soliloquies of Shakespeare's mature plays give ample testimony of this improvement. But the most talented self-students failed to commit themselves to the writing of formal autobiographies, choosing rather to express the results of their introspection in other ways. One reason for this shying away from autobiography may be discerned in Sir Kenelm Digby's stricture on *Religio Medici*: 'What should I say of his making so particular a Narration of personal things, and private thoughts of his own; the knowledge whereof cannot much conduce to any mans betterment?'[28] Autobiography, except for such particular species of it as military memoirs, was simply not respect-able. The seventeenth-century Englishman was even more careful of

---

[26] *The Autobiography and Personal Diary*, ed. J. O. Halliwell.

[27] *Private Memoirs of Sir Kenelm Digby*, ed. Sir N. H. Nicholas.

[28] *Observations upon Religio Medici*, p. 331. At this time, Digby had the guilty secret of having written an autobiography himself, though at the time he wrote it he gave instructions for it to be burnt after his death; see *Private Memoirs*, p. 327.

his 'public face' than his modern counterpart, and if he published any personal revelations he would rarely allow himself to appear as a man of less than scrupulous conventionality and probity; unless, of course, he wrote in the accepted genre of religious confessions, in which case he would probably go to the opposite extreme and claim to have been the chief of sinners.[29] Even Rousseau, the first man to display unabashedly his naked, 'self-centred self', entitled his autobiography *Confessions*; though his virtual glorification of individuality for its own sake would have been condemned by all shades of British opinion in the seventeenth century. Although we find in the autobiographies of this period many strong personalities, and a good deal of individual eccentricity or self-scrutiny, the prudent Englishman usually placed his essential self in a social and subordinate relation to God, state and community. This habit of self-effacement has been typical of British autobiographers up to the present century.

Autobiography and Social Class

The questions to be investigated here are, first, which classes were most productive of autobiographies in our period and, secondly, what was the relation between an autobiographer's class and the type of work he wrote? However, these questions raise such delicate problems of literary sociology that we must restrict our enquiry to Britain, and even then can do no more than suggest some tentative solutions. Religious autobiographers can be dealt with briefly, since with them social class was a less crucial factor, and after a quick survey of their social origins we will pass on to the knottier problems of secular autobiography.

Religious autobiographers—given the obvious precondition of literacy, which excluded the lowest classes—came from all levels of society.[30] More important than social origin was the status they claimed both within their church and among the general mass of Christians; for the overwhelming majority of religious autobiographers were priests, ministers, elders, or persons holding some other kind of clerical office. They were a militant elite who often braved persecution for their faith, practised heroic self-denial, or

---

[29] To display one's sins to the public in this way was, to be sure, considered rather ill-bred by the gentlemen of the Establishment; though the title of 'chief of sinners' had little enough meaning—Cromwell himself was one of many who claimed it.

[30] Even literacy was not always necessary; some religious testimonies were delivered orally and recorded by literate members of the congregation. For a survey of the mainly middle-class origins of the Puritan clergy see M. Walzer, *The Revolution of the Saints*, pp. 135-9.

spent their lives on endless and often hazardous missionary journeys.[31] In this sense they constituted a spiritual aristocracy—though sometimes only in their own estimation. Among Protestants, entrance into this aristocracy was often earned by laying claim to a conversion-experience; sometimes a written testimony concerning the way in which one came to see the light was required for entry into a particular church or sect.[32] Catholic autobiographers tended to give conversion less prominence and to rely on the traditional dignity of the priesthood.

To undertake an autobiography, the author must have a sense of his own importance; in the religious sphere, men of all ranks could claim the dignity of being equal candidates for salvation. But when they gave testimony of their spiritual experiences, the works they produced naturally differed in accordance with the writers' background and education. Men of good birth, or with aristocratic ties, such as Arthur Wilson or Thomas Ellwood, still used a courtly literary style in autobiographies written after their conversion to sects whose members were predominantly middle-class in outlook and expression. Class origin, in these cases, had a direct and distinctive effect on literary form. We should remember that the lower the social class of an autobiographer, the more restricted his reading would tend to be, reaching an irreducible minimum with Bunyan's favourites: the Bible and Foxe's *Book of Martyrs*. There would naturally be corresponding effects on his style; William Chappell for example, who was an Anglican bishop, wrote his autobiography in Vergilian hexameters; Lodowick Muggleton, the son of a horse-doctor, imitated the Bible to the extent of dividing his life into chapter and verse. Perhaps because of the readily-available and concentrated stimulus of certain autobiographical sections of the Bible, those sects which drew numbers from the lower and lower-middle classes produced many autobiographies; Anglicans, on the other hand, were more influenced by genteel inhibitions against self-revelation, and those who did write their life-histories usually left them in manuscript for posthumous study or publication. The contrast extended to tone: the Anglicans, usually gentlemen's sons and also in a sense 'gentry' among ministers of religion, tended to write with measured, objective soberness; the Baptist ministers, of more plebeian and

[31] Calvinism, apparently a belief with particular appeal to the autobiographical temperament, included all its faithful in an elite group set apart from the unregenerate mass of humanity; 'by founding its ethic in the doctrine of predestination, it substituted for the spiritual aristocracy of monks outside of and above the world the spiritual aristocracy of the predestined saints of God within the world.' Weber, *The Protestant Ethic*, p. 121.

[32] For examples of such testimonies see Charles Doe, *A Collection of Experience of the Work of Grace.*

uninhibited stock, coupled heaven and hell in their spiritual out-pourings from the tub.

In this book I have arranged my discussion of secular auto-biographers in rough accordance with their social position. Such a division, though convenient for purposes of exposition, cannot readily be justified conceptually. The connection between a literary genre and a particular social class can sometimes be convincingly demon-strated, as with Restoration comedy or the eighteenth-century novel. But the rise of secular autobiography in the seventeenth century is distinguished precisely by the peculiarity that authors from all social classes made significant contributions to the genre. One must assume either that class factors did not exert a significant influence on the genre's development, or that some social force was acting diffusely on men of all classes, bringing them to a higher level of self-awareness and moving some to express that self-awareness through the medium of autobiography. Anyone who has read at all widely in seventeenth-century autobiography will, I think, accept the second alternative as being closer to the truth. Some deep change in British habits of thought must have occurred between the early sixteenth century, when virtually no autobiographies were being written, and the late seventeenth, when they had become commonplace.

My thesis here will be that the spur to increased self-awareness among seventeenth-century Englishmen was not the developing fortunes of a specific class but rather the unprecedented general social mobility of the period—the very existence of widespread and violent change which could, like Marvell's Cromwell, 'ruine the great Work of Time, | And cast the Kingdome old | Into another Mold'.[33]

'They that are not touched with a sense of the present distractions, and divisions of Church and State are either somewhat more or some thing less than men.' So wrote Arthur Woodnoth, a pious Anglican and friend of George Herbert, in 1645.[34] A modern sociologist generalizes this observation on the effects of civil disturbances:

> there is a type of knowledge which can never be conceived within the categories of a purely contemplative consciousness-as-such, and whose first assumption is the fact that we come to know our associates only in living and acting with them. . . . We are dealing here with a dynamic process in man, in that his characteristics emerge in the course of his concrete conduct and in confrontation with actual prob-lems. Self-consciousness itself does not arise from mere self-contempla-tion but only through our struggles with the world—i.e. in the course of the process in which we first become aware of ourselves.

[33] 'An Horatian Ode upon Cromwell's Return from Ireland,' ll. 34-6.
[34] *Autobiography*, p. 118.

19

Here self-awareness and awareness of others are inseparably inter-twined with activity and interest and with the processes of social interaction.[35]

Because of the turmoil and instability of the seventeenth century, it was by the end of the period normal for an intelligent, intro-spective man to enquire into the sociological or psychological origins of his own and others' beliefs, and to see himself and his class, in Lukacs' phrase, 'both as an object and a subject in the social pro-cess'.[36] He would be aware that, with different formative influences, his social status or opinions could have turned out differently; and he would tacitly accept that he had become what he was more by the action of understandable social forces than by the vagaries of chance or the inscrutable decisions of divine providence. Thomas Hobbes, in a famous instance, attributed his timorous nature and love of order to the great Armada scare of 1588, which caused his mother to give birth to twins, himself and fear; his scorn for democracy he attributed, less fancifully, to his reading and translation of Thucydides. Roger North, as he speculated in middle age on the origins of his Tory bias, suggested that his excitement when seven years old at the Restoration celebrations was the cause. In these examples, individual thought and opinion are viewed as being conditioned by, and contingent on, particular currents of social opinion. No doubt the wide dissemina-tion of moral relativism by Montaigne and his successors helped make it possible for educated Englishmen to take a more detached view of their own prejudices.

Modern work on social change in Renaissance England has pro-vided systematic corroboration for the belief of contemporary observers that theirs was an age of great social mobility. Lawrence Stone, in a recent study, contends that 'between 1540 and 1640 English society experienced a seismic upheaval of unprecedented magnitude.'[37] For our present purpose, we are mainly interested in individual rather than group mobility. Individual horizontal mobility—movement from one place to another, or between occupa-tions of roughly equal status—must have been extremely high in 1500-1700, judging by the rapid rates of urbanization and emigration which prevailed. For example, the population of London was in 1700 about nine times as large as in 1500; one Englishman in ten was a Londoner at the later date, as against one in fifty in 1500.[38] The move

[35] Karl Mannheim, *Ideology and Utopia*, p. 169.

[36] Quoted in Mannheim, p. 127.

[37] 'Social Mobility in England, 1500-1700,' *Past and Present*, no. 33 (April 1966), p. 16.

[38] The rate of increase in London is even more impressive when set against the high death-rates there; in both 1603 and 1625 it is estimated that some 15 per cent of the population of London died of the plague. See Stone, pp. 29-33.

to London was an especially significant one, and we find that more than half of the secular autobiographers discussed in Chapter IX took this step—a strikingly high proportion. External emigrants who found their metiers, and wrote their autobiographies, overseas include Richard Norwood of Bermuda and Richard Boyle, the 'Great Earl of Cork', who went to Ireland. However, vertical mobility seems to have been an even more effective excitant of the self-awareness requisite for autobiography.[39] This can be seen clearly enough in an autobiographer like Richard Boyle, who wrote specifically to commemorate his rise from poverty to enormous wealth and power; but some cases of more indirect influence are worth citing.

A period of rapid social change arouses anxieties about status even among people whose own position is fairly secure. One kind of response to these anxieties may be regression: 'a reversion to forms of behaviour characteristic of earlier stages in the life of a community, or even of earlier stages in the mental development of individual members of the community'.[40] A classic example of regressive response is documented in the autobiography of Herbert of Cherbury. A wealthy and intellectually gifted aristocrat, he attempted to present himself as the embodiment of the chivalric ideals of the twelfth century, despite the Quixotic absurdities which inevitably followed from his choice of such a role. In real life, his weak-kneed capitulation to the Parliamentary forces in the years before his death in 1648 demonstrated his continued failure to find a psychologically consistent and satisfying role as a member of the contemporary aristocracy. Later in the century, another group of gentleman-autobiographers reveal a consistent pattern of withdrawal from a turbulent, acquisitive, and Whig-dominated urban society, in order to assume roles based on Stoic renunciation of ambition or Horatian rural virtue (see Chapter IX below, pp. 229 ff).

An opposite response to social change can be seen in a more adventurous group of autobiographers who abandoned their childhood homes to find a new role for themselves; they entered vocations with scope for opportunists, such as soldiering, astrology, international trade or upper-class parasitism (pp. 133 ff). One of them called his autobiography *Fortune's Uncertainty or Youth's Unconstancy*—a typical expression of the mingled hope, fear, and self-doubt with which they faced the increasingly fluid social structure of

[39] Boyle, of course, was both horizontally and vertically mobile; but he wrote his autobiography mainly to commemorate his (vertical) rise to fame and fortune. For Stone's evidence of greatly increased vertical mobility in about 1550-1650 see op. cit. pp. 33-6.
[40] Barbu, *Problems of Historical Psychology*, p. 52.

seventeenth-century Britain.[41] At the beginning of the century, sensitive observers might fear widespread anarchy or psychological breakdown as a consequence of increased social mobility and class strife. But autobiographies show that a wide variety of adaptive or defensive responses were available to men of any imagination; moreover, they could respond with the choice of a new role in real life (as did the multitude of London-bound adventurers), or else only in the fantasy-life (Herbert of Cherbury, and others).[42] In either case they sought to come to terms with their worldly condition by means of a temporal and secular adaptation, unlike medieval men who, when faced with similar unrest and social dislocation, typically looked for an other-worldly solution—some cataclysm or millennium—which did not require them to readjust their individual roles or personalities.[43]

Once an autobiographer had settled on a role, the form and style of his autobiography would of course be conditioned by his social position and by his knowledge of possible literary models. Thus Sir Kenelm Digby's prose might be influenced by the *Arcadia*, Charles Croke's by the French romance (popular in the 1660s), Thomas Raymond's by the irony he had cultivated as a defence against the miseries of his childhood. But the choice of style was generally subordinate or auxiliary to the mode of self-presentation. In any case, one could not expect to find a powerful and normative *stylistic* tradition for secular autobiography in an age when few contributors to the genre wrote for publication. The effects of the latter reticence were two: first, autobiographers did not usually have the opportunity to adjust their works to a particular model accepted as appropriate for men of their class; second, this freedom from precedent was matched by freedom from the constraints imposed by the demands or expectations of a specific class of readers.[44] As a result seventeenth-

[41] It should be noted here that Stone postulates a decline in social mobility and a general raising of barriers between classes at the end of the seventeenth century, foreshadowing the stable and oligarchical power structure of eighteenth-century England (op. cit. p. 51).

[42] The choice of role often involved the assumption of a suitable name, usually with romance overtones; thus, Sir Kenelm Digby called himself 'Theagenes', Richard Boyle took 'Philaretus', and Charles Croke 'Rodolphus'.

[43] It might be argued that seventeenth-century religious autobiographers continued the medieval pattern of behaviour; but they too characteristically reacted to spiritual anxiety by assuming a role—they tried, often strenuously, to convince themselves that they were acting and feeling like one of the elect. The effort might include the adoption of special clothing, deportment, and speech-habits; much to the disgust of the unregenerate, as we can see in Jonson's *Bartholomew Fair* and *The Alchemist*.

[44] However, autobiographies were often addressed to a private audience, usually the authors' family or friends; the effects of this orientation will be considered in the discussion of individual works.

century autobiography, in Britain at least, had a greater variety of individual forms than any other genre, and in fact drew on most other genres for inspiration, according to each autobiographer's social position and literary taste. Instead of the writer's usual problem of how to express himself within the confines of an accepted genre, the autobiographer would consider which established form would best fit the self-concept he wished to develop: did his life have the texture of romance, or of an exemplum; was he himself an Aeneas, or an Augustine? The forces involved in these decisions were as complex as the entire social nexus which had formed the individuals making them; but in an autobiographer's choice of role or stylistic convention we can often discern the influence of a move from one social class to another, or of a perceived change in the status of the class to which he belongs.

Religious Autobiography

III
The Origins of Religious Autobiography

VERY FEW religious autobiographies were written in Britain before 1600; yet during the next century the number of such works runs well over a hundred. In this and the three following chapters I attempt to describe and to account for the rapid efflorescence of this literary form in seventeenth-century Britain. The task is simplified by dividing autobiographies according to the denominations or sects to which their authors adhered, for striking differences between each group, in both quantity and type, soon become evident. Works by Catholics, Anglicans, and even Presbyterians are comparatively scarce; works produced by members of the dissident sects[1] are correspondingly plentiful, with the Quakers easily the most prolific group. This lopsided distribution of autobiographers across the range of doctrinal belief makes the critic's task of analysis easier than it might otherwise be. Autobiographers from the more conservative denominations usually worked independently of each other, and produced well-differentiated autobiographies; autobiographers from the sects, on the other hand, tended to conform, sometimes slavishly, to the traditions and conventions of their particular group. These conventions might derive either from the specific doctrines of the group, such as the emphasis on childhood wickedness among Calvinists, or from the example of a particularly strong personality, such as that of the founder of Quakerism, George Fox. But before entering in detail into the differences between various schools of religious autobiography, we should first examine some elements of the Judaeo–Christian tradition which provided inspiration for the rise of autobiography; this will be followed by an explanation of the scheme of exposition to be used in the three following chapters.

[1] The word 'sects' in this and the following chapters is used to designate the many religious groups which after 1642 grew up outside the Anglican or Presbyterian churches, and which laid claim to freedom from any central clerical or secular authority; the most successful sects were the Baptists and the Quakers.

27

Scriptural Origins

(a) *Old Testament.* For our present enquiry the most important book of the Old Testament is *Psalms.* Its description of a passionately intimate relationship between God and man had an enormous influence, especially among Protestants, on the practice of religion in the sixteenth and seventeenth centuries.[2] Moreover, Renaissance divines read *Psalms* autobiographically; the Presbyterian autobiographer Henry Burton, for example, considered the book to be a literal description of David's own life, and cited Psalm lxvi, 16 as proof: 'Come and hearken, all ye that fear God, and I will tell you what he hath done for my soule.'[3] John Donne found in *Psalms* a paradigm for every Christian's life:

> The Psalmes are the Manna of the Church. As Manna tasted to every man like that that he liked best, so doe the Psalmes minister Instruction, and satisfaction, to every man, in every emergency and occasion. David was not onely a cleare Prophet of Christ himselfe, but a Prophet of every particular Christian; He foretels what I, what any shall doe, and suffer, and say.[4]

The emotionalism and the intimate, dramatic relationship with God which are typical of *Psalms* were well calculated to appeal to the zealous seekers after the Lord who abounded in Britain after 1600, and it is in the autobiographies of members of the more radical Protestant sects that the psalms are most frequently invoked, and their tone imitated. Bunyan's *Grace Abounding* is the most famous representative of the numerous spiritual autobiographies in which the relationship of the writer to God is so close as to include even voices from heaven, and providential interventions of Divine power:[5] the alternate despair and exaltation of the Psalmist, and the intensity of his conversations with the Lord, create a dramatic confrontation between man and God which spiritual autobiographers from Augustine onward strove to emulate.

After *Psalms,* the books of Job and the major prophets probably had the most influence on religious autobiography. These books, written in a later and more complex period of Jewish history than the time of the Pentateuch, are much concerned with the plight of the individual who attempts to live justly and holily in a corrupt and

---

[2] In the *Institutes* Calvin cites *Psalms* twice as often as any other book of the Old Testament (Isaiah comes next), and more frequently than any book of the New Testament.

[3] *A Narration of the Life of Mr. Henry Burton* (1643), Preface, sig. A2ᵛ.

[4] *The Sermons of John Donne,* ed. Simpson and Potter, VII, 51.

[5] See, e.g., *Grace Abounding,* ed. G. B. Harrison, p. 12. Bunyan cites *Psalms* four times in his brief preface.

confusing society. The springs of justice have been poisoned; yet God does not intervene, or comes tardily, and man must learn to live with evil. Whether he resists by stoicism, like Job, or by denunciation, like Isaiah, he must dissociate himself from the community in order to seek his individual salvation; he thus becomes a potential model for the scripturally-inspired autobiographer. In seventeenth-century Britain many religious autobiographers felt themselves alienated from the workaday society around them, and reacted by adopting the role of men singled out for special attention by the Lord. Some went so far as to proclaim themselves successors to the Old Testament prophets, and to disseminate their private revelations—Arise Evans and Lodowick Muggleton were two of the most famous such pseudo-prophets (and autobiographers). Scripture had an inordinately strong influence on half-educated men of this kind, because they read little else; we shall see some of the bizarre results of this single-mindedness in Chapter VI.

(b) *New Testament*. For the religious autobiographer, St. Paul was the great exemplary figure of the New Testament. To imitate Christ was an undertaking which only the deranged or the mystic could undertake in full literalness; and St. Peter, though nominally Paul's superior, was a shadowy figure who lacked Paul's vividness and force of character. The Reformation brought with it a great revival of interest in Paul. Both Luther and Calvin were strongly attracted to him, and were in many ways similar to him in temperament.[6] Paul's influence on Protestant autobiographers may be considered under three heads: his use of autobiographical testimony in the *Acts* and elsewhere, his conversion (which became the archetype for later narratives of spiritual awakening), and his contribution to Christian doctrine.

Paul, unlike Jesus at *his* trial, was ready with an articulate and systematic defence of his beliefs. It was a trait which Bunyan remarked on in the preface to *Grace Abounding* (p. 4): 'It was Paul's accustomed manner (Acts xxii), and that when tried for his life (Acts xxiv), ever to open, before his judges, the manner of his conversion,

---

[6] This could be demonstrated at length; but, to take only one point, Luther's 'Thurmerlebnis' and Calvin's sudden conversion to the cause of the Reformation in 1533 were psychologically equivalent to Paul's vision on the road to Damascus. The most striking feature of the conversions of all three men is their devoted, lifelong struggle against their earlier loyalties.

Luther's preference for Paul over St. Peter was also connected with his war against the Papacy: 'The caus (said Luther) why the Papists boast more of St. Peter than of St. Paul, is this, St. Paul had the Sword, St. Peter the Keyes: They esteemed more of the Keyes (to open the Coffers, to filtch and steal, and to fill their thievish purs) then of the Sword.' *Colloquia Mensalia*, p. 367.

he would think of that day, and that hour, in the which he first did meet with grace; for he found it support unto him.' Bunyan himself had been imprisoned for several years when he wrote these words, and a remarkable number of seventeenth-century spiritual auto-biographers seem to have shared his experience; so that Paul's behaviour in front of his accusers provided a dramatic example to those who had good reason to identify with his predicament. Arise Evans, beginning his autobiography, shows how Paul's example could be invoked: 'But I suppose such an account as St. Paul some-time gave to the people, is expected from me, that is in some measure a Narration of my whole life, & specially of my calling to his work, Acts 22, Acts 27.'[7] *Acts* xxii suggested to later autobiographers both a means of justifying their works and a style of self-presentation.

The substance of Paul's autobiographical statements was even more influential than the circumstances in which they were made. His account of his conversion on the road to Damascus, brought about by a voice from heaven, was an inspiration to all spiritual seekers. The conversion became such a *locus classicus* among the more extreme and Calvinistically-inclined Protestants that, in their auto-biographies, they tried to make their early misdeeds seem as heinous as possible, attempting in this way to approximate Paul's dramatic change from a persecutor to a follower of Christ. The voice which spoke to Paul from Heaven speaks again to St. Augustine, and to the sectarian visionaries of the English Commonwealth. Imitation of Paul becomes slavish in Francis Bamfield's *A Name, an After-one; or a Name, a New-One, In the Later-day Glory*, which is sub-titled:

> Or, An Historical Declaration of the Life of Shem Acher [i.e. Bamfield], Especially as to some more eminent Passages of his Day, relating to his more thorow lawful Call to the Office and Work of the Ministry, for about Twenty Years last past.
> Wherein Paul is propounded for an Example, and the Case, so far as it doth run Parallel, is set down before it; tho the Prehiminence is given unto Paul.

A similarly close parallel to Paul's experience is claimed in the *Recollections* of Sir William Waller, the Parliamentary general.

These attempts to imitate Paul by seventeenth-century auto-biographers undoubtedly cramped the development of religious autobiography. Autobiographers commonly distorted the true pattern of their lives by trying to fit every detail into the Pauline archetype, and spiritual autobiography was forced into an unduly rigid convention which was all too easy for men of small literary talent to employ without imagination.

---

[7] *An Eccho to the Voice from Heaven*, 'To the Reader'.

Doctrinally, Paul always claimed to be a strictly orthodox follower of Christ. His message, he proclaimed, was a simple one: 'And I, brethren, when I came to you, came not with excellency of speech or of wisdom, declaring unto you the testimony of God. For I determined not to know any thing among you, save Jesus Christ, and Him crucified' (1 Cor. ii, 1-2). Nevertheless, Paul did add an emphasis of his own to Christ's teachings, and it was one which appealed especially to the more militant Protestants, who admired Paul's determined asceticism and his sharp distinction between the carnal and the spiritual man. William Haller notes this elective affinity: 'the pattern to which, under the formula given by Paul in the eighth chapter of Romans, the life of the elect conformed was exemplified by the preachers and set forth in the story of their lives'.[8] This passage provided the inspiration for that civil war in the soul which is so endlessly fought and re-fought in the autobiographies of Bunyan and his school: 'for they that are after the flesh do mind the things of the flesh; but they that are after the Spirit, the things of the Spirit. For to be carnally minded is death; but to be spiritually minded is life and peace' (Rom. viii, 5-6). In the same chapter, vs. 28-34, we find Paul's famous statement on predestination and justification; we will frequently encounter this doctrine in Chapters V and VI, for it was a perennial cause of self-scrutiny among autobiographers who held Calvinist views.

From Augustine to the Seventeenth Century

(a) *Augustine*. At a critical point in his conversion, Augustine turned to the apostle with whom he had most in common:

> Most eagerly then did I seize that venerable writing of Thy Spirit; and chiefly the Apostle Paul. Whereupon those difficulties vanished away, wherein he once seemed to me to contradict himself, and the text of his discourse not to agree with the testimonies of the Law and the Prophets. And the face of that pure word appeared to me one and the same; and I learned to rejoice with trembling.[9]

The line of descent from Paul to Augustine is clear enough; but it did not continue uninterrupted down to the British spiritual autobiographers of our period. Instead, they returned to the fountainhead of the Pauline epistles and, with a few exceptions, were remarkably little influenced by the *Confessions*.[10] The reasons for this neglect

---

[8] *The Rise of Puritanism*, p. 108. Hereafter cited as Haller.

[9] *The Confessions*, tr. E. B. Pusey, p. 141.

[10] However, a few British autobiographers did take their main inspiration from Augustine; see the discussion of Sir Tobie Matthew (Ch. IV) and of Richard Norwood and Robert Blair (Ch. V).

seem to have been mainly sociological. Conservatives in religion, who would have known Augustine's works, tended to write restrained autobiographies in which Augustinian fervour and self-accusation were carefully avoided. The Baptists and other enthusiastic sects were closer to the spirit of the *Confessions*; but his works were probably too scholarly and expensive for them, since he is very rarely mentioned in their writings.[11] It was on the Continent, rather than in Britain, that his true disciples appeared—notably those oddly-assorted geniuses, St. Teresa and Jean-Jacques Rousseau.

(b) *Medieval Tradition and Autobiography.* The Medieval period must be passed over briefly, in part because it was a time when few important autobiographical works were written, and in part because the majority of our seventeenth-century autobiographers were either hostile to, or ignorant of, medieval culture. Such works as Abelard's *Historia Calamitatum* or *The Book of Margery Kempe* might as well not have existed for all the influence they had.[12] The main link between medieval religious writings and seventeenth-century autobiography came from sermons and other commentaries on the workings of God's providence in everyday life; in particular, the medieval *exemplum* survived into the Renaissance in modified form. We may take as an example an anecdote in the autobiography of Samuel Clarke, a nonconformist preacher. He tells how 'a Lusty young Woman' insisted on dancing on Sunday in defiance of his remonstrances; 'but as she was dancing, it pleased the Lord to strike her with a sudden, and grievous Disease, whereof she died within three days'.[13] This manifest judgement greatly increased his authority in the village, and he went on to a successful career. When we com-

---

[11] The first English translation of the *Confessions* was by the Catholic Sir Tobie Matthew (1620); this translation, and others, were reprinted five times in the course of the century.

W. Y. Tindall (*John Bunyan Mechanick Preacher*, p. 230, n. 2) mentions a reference to Augustine by a friend of Bunyan's. The 'mechanick preachers' were fond of boasting, in somewhat anti-intellectual vein, that they drew their inspiration solely from the Bible and from the Holy Spirit; but they probably read also cheap devotional literature, romances, chap-books, and the like. Bunyan may have read Spenser and Milton, as well as Foxe's *Book of Martyrs*; see Tindall, Ch. IX.

[12] The *Historia Calamitatum* was translated into French by Jean de Meun in the thirteenth century, and also appeared in *Petri Abaelardi . . . Opera* (Paris, 1616). In about 1501 Wynkyn de Worde printed *A Shorte Treatyse of Contemplacyon . . . Taken Out of the Boke of Margerie Kempe of Lynn*. This was reprinted in 1521, but then Margerie and her book were virtually forgotten for almost four hundred years.

[13] Samuel Clarke, ed. *The Lives of Sundry Eminent Persons in this Later Age* (1683), p. 7.

pare this anecdote to a similar medieval tale, which tells of the punishment meted out to the 'Dancers of Colbek', we find that the moral drawn is a more general one:

> Þys tale y tolde ȝow to (make) ȝow aferde
> Yn cherche to karolle, or yn chercheȝerde,
> Namely aȝens þe prestys wylle:
> Leueþ whan he byddeþ ȝow be stylle.[14]

The former story is presented as proof that God was on Clarke's side at a time of moral crisis for him, whereas the latter is simply a fable that any priest could use in his sermon.

In religious autobiographies published after 1600 we often find the author using his personal sins and struggles as *exempla*. Richard Coppin, a frequently imprisoned itinerant preacher during the Commonwealth period, shows how autobiography and pulpit oratory could be mingled:

> Hearken my beloved brethren, come behold, and see the race which you are to run, the way which you are to come, and the price that is to be won, as I will here shew unto you, by setting before you the race that I have run, the way that I have gone, and the price that I have won; wherein if the Lord will, you may behold the manner and course of my life . . . that you by comparing with it the manner and course of your life, and the dealings of God with you, may see how near a progress you have made to this price, the fathers Kingdom.[15]

In the Protestant autobiographer's use of the *exemplum*, the emphasis has shifted away from the article of doctrine which the medieval preacher sought to make more vivid by means of an illustration. Now the stress is laid, not on dogma, but on the autobiographer's search for salvation, and on the vital relevance of this search to the reader's own struggles—the autobiographer himself incarnates the example. In the Protestant community, now that there is no authoritarian priest to lay down the law for everyone, each member should, ideally, be an example of the devout life to his fellows; instruction is given by deeds and testimony instead of by parables.

(c) *The Reformation and After.* Religious autobiographies were not commonly written in Britain until more than a hundred years after Henry's break with the Pope; this delay reflects the slowness with which the true Reformation spirit was assimilated into English religious life (Scotland was a little more advanced). Luther had a

---

[14] Robert Mannyng of Brunne, *Handling Synne* (begun 1303); I quote from the extract in *Fourteenth Century Verse and Prose*, ed. K. Sisam (Oxford, 1955), p. 12.
[15] *Truth's Testimony*, pp. 9-10.

hearty contempt for Henry's revolt, which he considered half-hearted, and denounced him as roundly afterwards as he had before: 'That King is still the old Hintz, as in my first book I pictured him; hee will surely finde his Judg: I never liked his resolutions, in that hee would kill the Pope's bodie, but preserv his soul; that is, his fals Doctrine.'[16] The antagonism between Luther and Henry ensured that the initial impact of Lutheran devotional practices in England would be relatively slight. But Luther's dominant concern with the 'inner man', rather than with man in his external and social roles, gradually made itself felt. His emphasis on the personal dialogue between man and God, and his basing of Christian life on the rock of individual conscience instead of the rock of Papal dogma, had the effect of internalizing many religious observances which formerly had been acted out publicly in sacraments and ceremonies. As Erasmus put it: 'without ceremonies perhaps thou shalt not be a Christian; but they make thee not a Christian'.[17]

Luther's internalization of religion was given a particular tone (which became an integral part of Protestant tradition) by the anguish and neurotic conflicts which accompanied his struggles with the doctrine of salvation by faith:

> The content of the depressions was always the same, the loss of faith that God is good and that he is good *to me*. After the frightful *Anfechtung* of 1527 Luther wrote, 'For more than a week I was close to the gates of death and hell. I trembled in all my members. Christ was wholly lost. I was shaken by desperation and blasphemy of God.[18]

Despairing episodes of this kind entered into the standard emotional repertoire of seventeenth-century spiritual autobiographers.

Luther's vulnerability to attacks of doubt and depression was an individual weakness which he attributed to the devil's anger against him for defying the Pope—the devil's representative on earth. Calvin, however, institutionalized the believer's inner anxiety and made it into a vital component of his theological system. His *Institutes of the Christian Religion* opens with a discussion of what one might call 'Christian psychology': 'Our wisdom, in so far as it ought to be deemed true and solid wisdom, consists almost entirely of two parts: the knowledge of God and of ourselves.'[19] After a discussion of the 'miserable ruin' into which Adam's fall cast man, Calvin extols the perfections of God as contrasted with man's ignorance and corrup-

---

[16] *Colloquia Mensalia*, p. 464.
[17] Quoted by H. Chadwick in J. Hurstfield, ed. *The Reformation Crisis* (London, 1965), p. 39.
[18] R. Bainton, *Here I Stand; A Life of Martin Luther*, p. 361.
[19] Tr. Henry Beveridge. Hereafter, I cite the *Institutes* by the original Book, Chapter, and Section divisions, as used in the Beveridge edition.

tion. The Christian should cultivate in himself an awareness of this depravity:

> indeed, we cannot aspire to Him in earnest until we have begun to be displeased with ourselves. For what man is not disposed to rest in himself? Who, in fact, does not thus rest, so long as he is unknown to himself; that is, so long as he is contented with his own endowments, and unconscious or unmindful of his misery? Every person, therefore, on coming to the knowledge of himself, is not only urged to seek God, but is also led as by the hand to find him. (I, i, 1)

In this first chapter of the *Institutes* we find a capsule prescription for Calvinist self-analysis, the difficulties and triumphs of which will be exhaustively described in the spiritual autobiographies of Calvin's followers. Book III of the *Institutes* tells in more detail how the Christian should conduct his inner war against sin and despair. Calvin first refutes the Catholic practice of auricular confession; in Scripture 'one method of confessing is prescribed; since it is the Lord who forgives, forgets, and wipes away sins, to him let us confess them, that we may obtain pardon. He is the physician, therefore, let us show our wounds to him' (III, iv, 9). However—and this advice had an important effect on Calvinist autobiography—members of the congregation are allowed to assist and console each other in spiritual tribulations. If a believer 'is so agonized and afflicted by a sense of his sins that he cannot obtain relief without the help of others' (III, iv, 12) he may confess such sins as he pleases to the minister—though Calvin adds the qualification that man can never know or describe the full extent of his own wickedness.

The Calvinist obsession with the enemy within exemplifies the Renaissance tendency to internalize the struggle of conflicting mental forces instead of allegorizing and externalizing it as the medieval *psychomachia* did. Calvin in fact put the devil within man himself: instead of the bogey-man of preceding centuries who 'walked to and fro upon the earth', the devil is now in full possession of every man's mind:

> Let it stand, therefore, as an indubitable truth, which no engines can shake, that the mind of man is so entirely alienated from the righteousness of God that he cannot conceive, desire, or design anything but what is wicked, distorted, foul, impure, and iniquitous; that if some men occasionally make a show of goodness, their mind is ever interwoven with hypocrisy and deceit, their soul inwardly bound with the fetters of wickedness. (II, v, 19)

Convinced that he was possessed by evil, the Calvinist naturally clutched at some kind of reassurance within himself, since no external observances—such as good works or sacraments—could avail a whit towards his salvation. His normal reaction was to embark on a complicated, even devious process of rationalization which always seemed to culminate in a semi-mystical assurance that *he*, at least, was enrolled among the elect: 'now had I an evidence, as I thought, of my salvation from heaven, with many golden seals thereon, all hanging in my sight'.[20] The period of spiritual turmoil which led up to his achievement of a settled faith in God's favour towards him was the most significant phase of a Calvinist's life, and the one in which he was most dependent on his unaided inner resources. When he emerged from this experience he would naturally be inclined to describe it to his spiritual brethren, perhaps drawing on a diary or other written record of his struggle; accounts of successful 'convincements' would be especially useful to those believers who were still enmeshed in the agonies of doubt over their own wickedness and uncertainty of election. From this kind of mutual help and encouragement it was a relatively small step to the writing and publication of formal spiritual autobiographies.

Calvinism did not become a force in English religious life until the return of the Marian exiles at Elizabeth's accession; for a long time thereafter it was confined mainly to intellectual circles, and it was not until the 1630s that Calvinist principles achieved mass support.[21] The triumph of Puritanism in the following two decades was accompanied by the writing of religious autobiographies in significant numbers, for the first time in Britain. The intimate relation between the English Revolution and the rise of autobiography will be amply documented in the following chapters.

Luther had begun his work as a participant in a strong and widespread movement for reform of the Catholic Church from within, and the work of those Catholics who wanted reform without Reformation continued after his departure. Two movements which formed part of the general current of Catholic reform seem to have had particular relevance to the rise of autobiography: the flowering of mysticism, with its great representatives St. Teresa and St. John of the Cross; and the emergence of the Jesuit order as a disciplined and militant spiritual elite.

St. Teresa stands out in her own right as author of a classic autobiography and by virtue of her place in the tradition which derives from Augustine. Like Petrarch before her, she felt a close personal kinship with the saint:

[20] Bunyan, *Grace Abounding*, p. 41.
[21] In Scotland, of course, Calvinism was dominant some seventy years earlier; but few religious autobiographies were written there until about the middle of the seventeenth century.

When I began to read the *Confessions* I seemed to see myself portrayed there, and I began to commend myself frequently to that glorious saint. When I came to the tale of his conversion, and read how he heard the voice in the garden, it seemed exactly as if the Lord had spoken to me. So I felt in my heart.[22]

However, Teresa's mysticism has no counterpart in the auto-biographies of British Catholics who, under the Elizabethan and Stuart persecutions, were preoccupied with severely practical neces-sities.[23] The Society of Jesus had a more direct influence, for all the British seventeenth-century Catholic autobiographers were members at one time or another. The Jesuits formed a spiritual aristocracy rivalled only by the intellectual leaders of Calvinism, and the auto-biographies written by each group present a striking and informative contrast. Jesuit works resemble intelligence reports: they are sober narratives of persecutions suffered, traps avoided, and souls won for Christ. The Jesuit missionaries to Britain wrote for the information and encouragement of their fellows in the order; that is to say, for an audience already indoctrinated and convinced of the truth. For this reason, we do not find in them the frightful inner struggles recorded in both private and public Calvinist autobiographies. To gain con-verts, the Jesuits used their bravery and their skill in apologetics; whereas the Calvinists depended more on personal testimony of their own spiritual wrestlings and final convincement of salvation. The Jesuit was trained in obedience, discretion and self-effacement; the Calvinist minister strove to project himself as a vivid exemplar to his hearers. The natural autobiographical form for the Jesuit was *res gestae*; for the Calvinist, history of his soul.

(d) *Conclusion.* Religious autobiography, unlike the secular variety, was well established as a genre before the Renaissance, but it under-went unusually rapid growth and change after 1500. The dominant trends were, first, the placing of more emphasis on inward events and self-scrutiny, and, secondly, an enormous increase in quantity of confessions, testimonies, relations, and spiritual autobiographies of all kinds. This increase was undoubtedly linked to the proliferation of rival Protestant sects, though we should not think of spiritual autobiography as a sole product or invention of Puritan groups: members of all denominations contributed to the genre.

[22] *The Life of Saint Teresa*, tr. J. M. Cohen, p. 69.
[23] This is not to say that the Jesuit missionaries to England were ignorant of the mystical tradition. Teresa's *Life* was first translated into English (Antwerp, 1611) by M. Walpole, a confidential servant to Fr. Gerard—who wrote, in an essentially objective mode, the best English Catholic autobiography of the seventeenth century. Fr. William Weston had mystical experiences, but was reticent about them in his autobiography. See Chapter IV.

As usual, England lagged behind the Continent in these developments. Only a handful of religious autobiographies were written in the Tudor period; Jesuit autobiographers began to write in the early seventeenth century, followed soon after by Anglican prelates and, from about 1640, by the Presbyterians. The autobiographies written by the two former groups were objective in style, histories of events in the religious sphere of social life rather than histories of the progress of a soul. Not until Richard Norwood wrote his *Journal* in 1639-40 do we find a clearly-defined spiritual autobiography; though diaries and religious meditations were commonly written, by men whose piety took an introspective turn, from the last decades of the sixteenth century onward.

In each denomination autobiographers seem to have been moved to write especially in response to the challenge to their faith of religious oppression or persecution. Thus, at the beginning of the seventeenth century the most significant autobiographies were written by Catholics, who were at that time being harried almost to the point of extinction. The next generation of autobiographers were mainly Presbyterians, such as Henry Burton who had his ears clipped for his opposition to episcopacy. Among Anglicans, Bishops Hall and Chappell wrote after they had been driven from their dioceses by the Revolution. In 1650-70 the Baptists and other sectaries were most productive; and for the remaining years of the century the Quakers surpassed all competitors, quantitatively at least, with autobiographies for which their various sufferings at the hands of the law provided much of the subject-matter.[24] It would seem that Catholic, Calvinist, or other ideas did not usually find expression in autobiographical form until the shock of some external stimulus, such as a persecution, had moved men to testify concerning their beliefs; the ideas, by themselves, did not provide sufficient cause for the rise of religious autobiography in Britain. From this it follows that the existence of successive waves of religious autobiography in the seventeenth century, each with its own pattern of growth and decline, must be recognized and related to the broad movements of social history which impinged on the autobiographers' lives. In the next three chapters I have tried to keep in focus this relation between religious autobiography and contemporary society by discussing individual autobiographers in the context of the nature and fortunes of the

[24] This scheme of successive waves of religious autobiographers must, of course, be qualified in many details. Actual publication of the autobiographies followed a different rhythm; the sectaries, for example, published their works much more promptly than members of less radical groups—Bunyan's *Grace Abounding* (1666) appeared thirty years before the posthumous *Reliquiae Baxterianae*, though Baxter was the older man by thirteen years.

particular denominations to which they gave their allegiances. An institutional framework of this kind is especially helpful for analysis because so many seventeenth century autobiographies were not published until long after they were written; this tendency to private composition meant that autobiography did not develop as regularly, continuously, or openly as other literary genres. In the three following chapters, therefore, the discussion of religious autobiography will work across the spectrum of Christian belief, from Catholics and Anglicans to the radical sects spawned by the English Revolution.

IV

Catholic and Anglican
Autobiographers

ALMOST ALL British Catholic autobiographers wrote during the first half of the seventeenth century, before increased apostasy and natural attrition reduced the Catholics to an insignificant minority. The three most significant autobiographies were produced by Jesuits: John Gerard, William Weston, and Sir Tobie Matthew; the remaining works, either fragmentary or uninspired, will be given brief notice later on.

Both Gerard and Weston wrote their autobiographies (in Latin) at the request of their superiors in the Jesuit order.[1] Gerard's preface (p. xxiv) extols the virtue of obedience, echoing the self-effacing spirit of his order's motto, *Ad majorem Dei gloriam*, which he puts at the head of the page:

> The precepts of Superiors are from God 'from whom all power proceeds'. It is at their orders that I am setting down in a simple and faithful narrative all that happened to me, under God's providence, during the eighteen years I worked on the English mission. And it must not, then, be thought an unusual or remarkable thing to do.
>
> What I achieved was insignificant, when it is compared with the work of others, who were fitter instruments of Christ. Besides, it is a 'praiseworthy thing to make known the works of God', and, on this account too, I need have no bashfulness in recording the results of my own poor efforts.
>
> With few talents or natural gifts my endowment was slender, and my store of virtue more slender still. . . . What was done, was done by God. And, I believe, He chose to do it through me, because I was a member—an unworthy one, I admit—of that body which has received from Jesus its head a remarkable outpouring of His Spirit for the healing of souls in this last era of a declining and gasping world. This is how I account for anything that God has been pleased to work in and through me.

[1] *John Gerard; The Autobiography of an Elizabethan*, tr. Philip Caraman. Weston, *An Autobiography from the Jesuit Underground*, tr. Caraman.

His superiors probably wished to use Gerard's narrative for the edification and instruction of Jesuit novices who were being trained for the dangerous task of becoming missionaries to England. We must assume, therefore, that Gerard is giving us a highly selective account of his past history; that he does not write to inform the general reader 'what really happened', but to inspire Jesuit novices to imitate his feats of endurance and cunning. The son of Catholic parents, he has no conversion to anatomize; his devotion is taken for granted as he tells of his adventures with Elizabeth's prisons and secret police. He describes in great detail methods of tricking and evading spies, as well as how to deal with the subtle interrogations to which captured priests were subjected. He had, no doubt, an intense inner spiritual life, regulated by the precepts of St. Ignatius according to the model to which all Jesuits conformed; but though he mentioned his use of Ignatius's *Spiritual Exercises* he says little about his internal struggles.[2]

Gerard came under Jesuit influence as a youth, and when he was about fifteen 'first heard God in His infinite mercy and goodness call me from the crooked paths of the world to the straight road and to the perfect following of Christ in the Society' (p. 2). At eighteen he was imprisoned in Marshalsea as a recusant for a year, and had to remain in England for three more years on bail before he could leave for France. Two years later, having been ordained at Rome, he set out for home as an underground missionary in August, 1588, refusing to wait until the popular rage against Catholics caused by the Armada had died down. He landed in Norfolk with three other priests, all of whom were later captured and executed. Separating from his companions, he made his way inland, pretending to be a gentleman whose falcon had strayed:

> Whenever I saw anybody in the fields I went up to him and asked my usual questions about the falcon, concealing all the time my real purpose, which was to avoid the villages and public roads and get away from the coast where I knew watchers guarded the thoroughfares and kept out strangers. Most of the day went like this and in all I managed to cover eight or ten miles, not, of course, walking in a straight line, but diagonally, even turning back now and again the way I had come. (p. 11)

After having been arrested once and released without his mission

[2] See, e.g., p. 25: 'In this period also I gave the *Spiritual Exercises* to a number of persons with good effect.' Caraman notes that 'The Spiritual Exercises are planned to occupy an entire month and the meditations are divided into four "weeks". In the first week the purpose of creation, sin and hell are considered, in the second the ministry, in the third the passion and in the fourth the risen life of Our Lord.' (p. 221.)

being discovered, Gerard made his way to Norwich, from where he was able to reach London. There his superior, Fr. Henry Garnet, briefed him and sent him back to East Anglia. For nearly six years he moved from one country house to another, making many converts.[3] In 1594 a servant betrayed him; the pursuivants searched for four days while he crouched in an ingeniously constructed 'priest's hole', but were unable to find him. However, Gerard did not realize the identity of his betrayer, and so was finally trapped three weeks later in London. In prison, he had a dramatic confrontation with the anti-Catholic inquisitor, Richard Topcliffe. Topcliffe—'old and hoary and a veteran in evil', as Gerard describes him—tries to trick him into signing an incriminating statement. When outwitted, he flies into a murderous rage:

> 'I will see that you are brought to me and placed in my power. I will hang you up in the air and will have no pity on you; and then I shall watch and see whether God will snatch you from my grasp.' He spoke from the cesspool of his heart. But his effect on me was the opposite of what he wanted: he raised my hopes. . . . I answered in a few words:
> 'You can do nothing unless God allows it. He never abandons those who trust in Him. God's will be done!' (p. 70)

But Gerard could not be convicted of anything except being a priest, and so was left for three years in relatively comfortable imprisonment. In 1597, it was learnt that he had been in secret communication with the Continent and a commission, which included Francis Bacon, was appointed to question and, if necessary, torture him. He was stubbornly silent, and was hung up by his wrists from a pillar for several hours. On the second day, he almost died on the pillar and had to be revived with hot water. He still refused to confess:

> 'Very well, then, we must hang you up again now, and a second time after dinner.'
> He spoke as though he were sorry to have to carry out his orders.
> '*Eamus in nomine Domini*,' I said. 'I have only one life, but if I had several I would sacrifice them all for the same cause.'
> I struggled to my feet and tried to walk over to the pillar but I had to be helped. I was very weak now and if I had any spirit left in me it was given by God and given to me, although most unworthy, because I shared the fellowship of the Society.
> I was hung up again. The pain was intense now, but I felt great consolation of soul, which seemed to me to come from a desire of death. . . . And my heart filled with great gladness as I abandoned myself to His will and keeping and contemned the will of men. (pp. 113-14)

[3] Gerard almost succeeded in converting Penelope Rich, Sidney's 'Stella'; but at the last moment he was thwarted by her lover Charles Blount, Lord Mountjoy, who made a hobby of theology.

Gerard was saved from death by the mercy of the Governor of the Tower, and six months later he escaped from prison. He spent nine more years at large and finally left for Rome when the aftermath of the Gunpowder Plot made life in London too dangerous for him. His autobiography was written three years later.

The contrast between Gerard's work and spiritual autobiographies of the *Grace Abounding* type is instructive. Whereas Bunyan agonizes over such childish sins as playing 'cat' on Sunday, Gerard is tempted only in extreme situations—when he is tortured, for example:

> The pain was so intense that I thought I could not possibly endure it, and added to it, I had an interior temptation. Yet I did not feel any inclination or wish to give them the information they wanted. The Lord saw my weakness with the eyes of His mercy, and did not permit me to be tempted beyond my strength. With the temptation He sent me relief. (p. 109)

Even here, we never learn what the actual temptation was; and Gerard seems to mention it only to show that God would always help in such a crisis.

Although Gerard cultivates the virtue of humility he is never oppressed by any Calvinistic sense of inexpiable sinfulness. Consequently, his actions are not paralysed by guilt or excessive introspection—he could scarcely have survived in England for eighteen years without unusual vigour, initiative, and decisiveness. The Jesuits were experts at staying out of prison; their mission was to save souls, and that could best be achieved when they were at liberty. The Nonconformists who were persecuted after 1661, on the other hand, were usually unable to escape imprisonment and on occasion even courted it: for oppression by the sons of Belial could be taken, by the victim, as a sign of his own righteousness. Gerard shows no fear of martyrdom, but neither does he need it in order to reassure himself that God looks with favour on his work. He has other sources of strength: his fanatical devotion to the Society, his eagerness to save souls at any cost, and his serene confidence in the heavenly reward promised to those executed for the faith. His well-defined spiritual tasks—to save souls and live a holy life—contrast with the Calvinist's lucubrations over his own election, and his endless pondering of a question that only death can decide. Despite the frightful external dangers which they describe, the autobiographies of Gerard and Weston convey a sense of tranquillity which is rare among religious autobiographies of the century.

William Weston's autobiography is less skilfully presented than Gerard's, but is similar to it in purpose and form. Weston wrote at Seville in 1611, while he was convalescing from the hardships of twenty years of missionary labour in England. His narrative opens in 1584, when he lands in East Anglia and soon reaches London; one of his first missions there is to visit Fr. Jasper Heywood in the Tower, aided by Heywood's sister, the mother of John Donne. Weston travels from one country-house to another, preaching and casting out devils. After two years he is arrested in London, but escapes torture. He disputes, indecisively, with Lancelot Andrewes (pp. 128-30), and later is sent off to a special prison at Wisbech Castle, where he remains for eleven years.

Weston, who was not as ingenious at preserving or recapturing his liberty as Gerard, spent seventeen of his twenty years in England in prison. The ordeal almost broke him, both mentally and physically: 'I was much weakened by failing sight and sleeplessness. My days seemed to hold no contentment, my nights no respite. Mind and senses were worn by constant preoccupation and wakefulness, and death appeared to me as something more desirable than life' (p. 219). His sanity was endangered, and devils frequently appeared to him, bringing him ropes and knives with which to commit suicide (p. 227). The autobiography is full of uncritically offered stories of devils, relics, miraculous cures, and so forth. Weston's credulity and love of pious old wives' tales contrast sharply with the acute and vigorous intellect of Gerard; but that he retained his sanity during long years in an Elizabethan jail, and lived to write the tale, was perhaps achievement enough.

Sir Tobie Matthew's autobiography, unlike those of Gerard and Weston, is in the form of a conversion narrative.[4] It was written in 1640 for Mary Gage, a Benedictine nun:

> At your request, or rather upon your commandment, I will here declare that, in brief manner, which passed between God and me, in order to my conversion to the Catholic faith. Remember you, on the other side, the faithful promise, which you have made me of keeping it wholly to yourself; and upon that consideration I will instantly deliver you from any further suspense. (p. 1)

Matthew, who was the son of an Anglican archbishop, had gone to Italy to learn the language in 1604. He fell into the company of Fr. Persons, rector of the English College at Rome, and with him studied scripture and the Church Fathers. But Matthew was not yet convinced of the truth of Catholicism, being still engrossed by wordly affairs:

> I frequented plays, and worse places. I went equally to the mountebanks and to preachers. I read also books of all kinds, and very often

[4] *A True Historical Relation of the Conversion of Sir Tobie Matthew to the Holy Catholic Faith*, ed. A. H. Mathew.

44

such as were of the lightest air; as comedies whose matter not affecting the mind much, the words would both come quicklier, and stick closer to it. For the language was that mistress which I resolved most to court at that time. (p. 35)

The tone of his self-accusation, it may be noted, is rather mild, and he makes no serious attempt to present himself as a great sinner. Soon after this period of frivolity he was convinced by Augustine's *De Unitate Ecclesiae* of the authority of the Catholic Church. He wrestled with temptations that he would lose his worldly goods, and with fears of being hanged at Tyburn; but by the intercession of the Virgin his doubts were resolved and he was admitted into the Church (pp. 53-54). The remainder of the *True Relation* describes Matthew's difficulties after his conversion, and the controversies in which he was involved; he was imprisoned on his return to England, after he had refused to abjure his new faith, and while in jail he disputed with various scholars and divines, including Albericus Gentili and Lancelot Andrewes (pp. 88-93).[5] He was eventually released, but had to leave England when he refused to take the oath of allegiance to James I. After the events described in his autobiography he became a priest, returned to England and entered the Society of Jesus (probably on his deathbed).

Matthew made the first English translation of Augustine's *Confessions*.[6] But although he makes some rather half-hearted attempts to imitate Augustine's fervent repentance, the *True Relation* is basically a calm and factual narrative whose emphasis is on apologetics rather than on spiritual transformation. This lack of passion no doubt reflects the conditions under which the work was composed: Matthew was writing some thirty-five years after the events he described, and for the private information of a friend, without thought of publication. However, Gerard, Weston, and other British Catholic autobiographers all tended to shun emotionalism in their works. We should not assume from this that the Jesuits led less intense spiritual lives than the sectarians did. The Society prescribed in detail a form of meditation for its members; all were expected to adhere to this norm, without fuss or self-dramatization, in order that they might be more efficient and selfless soldiers in the cause of God and Rome. The Jesuit autobiographers accordingly stressed their roles in the

[5] Also with his friend Francis Bacon (on other occasions), though he found him a poor opponent: 'he was quickly and very easily to be answered; for he was in very truth (with being a kind of monster both of wit and knowledge also in other things) such a poor kind of creature in all those which were questionable about religion, that my wonder takes away all my words.' (p. 112.)

[6] Printed at St. Omer in 1620 and distributed clandestinely in England. The second edition (Paris, 1636) has a preface by Sir Kenelm Digby.

'holy war' of the Counter-Reformation, rather than their individual wrestlings with the Holy Spirit.

Other English Catholic autobiographers may be dismissed briefly. Gilbert Blakhall's *A Breiffe Narration of the Services Done to Three Noble Ladyes* is a substantial but dull work by a Scottish priest who, as his title indicates, was too fond of the nobility for his own good. John Ogilvie's *Relatio Incarcerationis* was sent to his Jesuit superior a few days before Ogilvie was executed at Glasgow; his fragmentary narrative of his interrogation is in the tradition of Gerard and Weston. Fr. Robert Persons' *Memoires* are incomplete and unimaginative. James Wadsworth was a Jesuit who converted to Protestantism and became a counter-spy; his *Memoires* of his days in the Jesuit seminary at St. Omer offer crude but vigorous propaganda. Richard Carpenter's *Experience, Historie and Divinitie* is an apostate work in the same vein as Wadsworth's, except that Carpenter was an ex-Benedictine. Finally, Thomas Stapleton may be mentioned; his autobiographical poem, written in 1598, is for the most part a description of the theological works which he wrote to refute Whitaker, Calvin, and Beza.[7] It will be noted that every autobiographer mentioned in this section was a priest or an ex-priest; Catholic laymen produced no religious autobiographies during the seventeenth century.

There is a certain barrenness and holding-back of emotion in the group of autobiographies I have been describing; but given the desperate political plight of the British Catholic Church it is hardly surprising that the great devotional and meditative Catholic tradition bore little fruit in Britain at this time. Robert Southwell's penetrating and fervent self-analysis promised much, but he died a martyr and found his successors in Donne and Herbert rather than among his co-religionists.[8] From Gerard to Newman, we find the energies of British Catholic autobiographers devoted more to hard labour of apologetics than to Augustinian and Teresan dialogue between God and man.

In the seventeenth century, religious autobiographies by Anglicans are relatively scarce and usually unimpressive; this weakness is all the more striking when one takes into account the dominant position of Anglicanism as an established church, with its corresponding control of the largest source of patronage for intellectuals. Moreover, Anglican spirituality achieved its most refined development in this period, inspiring several of the century's literary masterpieces. There can be no doubt, then, that Anglican autobiography fell far short of its potential; but before we try to account for this deficiency it would

[7] *Compendium Breve, et Verum, Studiorum Thomae Stapletoni S.T.D.*, in *Opera*, vol. I. The poem has only ninety-two lines.
[8] See Martz, *The Poetry of Meditation*, Ch. 5.

be well to examine the qualities and defects of the works we do have, taking them in the approximate order of their authors' births.

A first group includes three bishops: William Cowper, Joseph Hall, and William Chappell. *The Life and Death of William Cowper* seemed a sufficiently edifying narrative to Samuel Clarke that he included a version of it in his Puritan martyrology, *The Marrow of Ecclesiastical Historie* (1650). One can easily see why Clarke endorsed it, for although Cowper rose to be Bishop of Galway he had definite Puritan[9] leanings; and his *Life*, though more decorous in tone than the later work, conforms to the pattern of spiritual development described in Bunyan's *Grace Abounding*. For example, Cowper reproaches himself for 'the vanities and ignorance of youth' (p. 3), in spite of the fact that he was already noted for his piety when he was eight years old. Later, when a minister near Perth, he is granted a vision which foreshadows his transfer to Stirling. He endures continual temptations and spiritual conflicts until comforted by a second vision, after which his troubles abate; in this account of his inner trials we recognize one of the earliest adaptations of the Pauline and Augustinian spiritual crisis in a British religious autobiography. However, Cowper, as befits a bishop, still preserves both his dignity and a certain objectivity in narrating his spiritual development; his tone is much milder than the self-accusatory outcries indulged in by later, more radically Calvinist autobiographers. But the publication of Cowper's autobiography in 1619 (the year of his death) marks the emergence of a theme which came to be handled with less and less restraint in the course of the seventeenth century.

Joseph Hall, best known for his *Characters* and for a defence of episcopacy which provoked Milton into writing his anti-prelatical tracts, was also an autobiographer. He felt the decline in his fortunes after 1642 so keenly that he wrote two quite different narratives: one, entitled *Some Specialties of Divine Providence in his Life*, describes the pre-1642 period, the other, *Bishop Hall's Hard Measure*, his arrest and imprisonment by the Parliamentary forces.[10] In his introduction to the first work Hall minimizes his own importance, perhaps following the example of Augustine:

> Not out of a vain affectation of my own Glory, which I know how little it can avail me, when I am gone hence; but out of a sincere desire to give glory to my God, (whose wonderful Providence I have noted in

[9] Here, and elsewhere, I use the word 'Puritan' in the sense defined by Haller, *The Rise of Puritanism*, pp. 3-18; in brief, a Puritan may be considered one who wanted further reform of the established church, in the direction of greater simplicity and stricter discipline, and who was a Calvinist sympathizer—though he might, like Milton, reject the strict Calvinist position on predestination.

[10] Both are included in *The Shaking of the Olive Tree. The Remaining Works of . . . Joseph Hall, D.D.*

all my wayes) have I recorded some remarkable passages of my fore-
past life: what I have done is worthy of nothing, but silence and
forgetfulness; but what God hath done for me, is worthy of everlasting and thankfull Memory. (p. 1)

God's 'wonderful Providence' shines favourably on Hall during his
early career. He becomes a fellow of his college at Cambridge, and
later is appointed rector to the Lady Drury, where he is embroiled in
an episode distressingly typical of the religious mentality of the time.
He finds that Lord Drury is under the ungodly influence of 'a
dangerous Opposite to the Success of my Ministry, a witty and bold
Atheist, one Mr. Lilly'. Happily, God intervenes by arranging for
Lilly to die in the epidemic of plague then afflicting London; Hall,
delighted by this answer to his prayers, comments 'now the coast was
clear before me' (pp. 13-14). He thrives in his mission, is able to
marry 'a comely and modest Gentlewoman', and rises to the fine
bishopric of Exeter. In *Bishop Hall's Hard Measure*, however, fortune
has turned against him; with the other Anglican bishops he is
imprisoned in the Tower and harassed by the Parliamentarians. This
part of his autobiography is a mere hodge-podge of complaints and
self-justification, lacking any but historical interest. By and large,
both parts of Hall's work use the *res gestae* convention, with a
corresponding absence of intimate revelation or emotional fervour.
He did not write as a troubled soul-searcher working out his salvation in fear and trembling, but as an imposing, and more than a little
self-righteous, prelate. His autobiography would probably not have
been written if he had not been cast down from his bishop's seat and
thereby induced to take stock of the vicissitudes of his life.

William Chappell, Bishop of Cork and Ross, was of Hall's generation and the two men had similar careers; Chappell's autobiography,
however, is a very odd production when compared with Hall's.[11] In
1641 Chappell was driven from his diocese by the Irish rebellion and
was forced to spend the remaining eight years of his life in England.
During these years he composed a *Vita* in Vergilian hexameters,
ending it with a lively account, in the style of *Aeneid I*, of his storm-
tossed flight from Dublin in 1641. For incident, the *Vita* has only a
rather dull enumeration of *res gestae* to offer; but the work is
redeemed by Chappell's fine gift for the bathetic:

> Subinde climactera nova vitae meae
> Famosa morte Heroum, et heroica cluet,
> Incipit, & excutit reliquias dentium
> Ante putrium, monetque mortis sim memor. (p. 264)[12]

[11] *Vita Guilielmi Chappel*, in Thomas Hearne, ed., *Joannis Lelandi Antiquarii . . .
Collectanea*, editio altera, V, 261-8.
[12] Thereupon a new climacteric, infamous for the death of heroes and called

The autobiographies of two bishops of a later generation, Symon Patrick and Gilbert Burnet, are more conventional.[13] Patrick wrote his 'brief account' of his life in 1706, his eightieth year, and the sober dignity of an ancient bishop pervades the story. He carefully shields his inner spiritual and emotional life from scrutiny, while giving a clear and full presentation of his successful and productive public career. As we shall see many times later, personages of this kind—of mature age and eminent social position—seem to have considered that a decent reticence concerning their personal affairs was a duty they owed to their status as pillars of the Establishment. Burnet's autobiography is somewhat livelier than Patrick's, though its tone is also one of mature self-possession. It is a thoroughly competent literary performance—if no more—covering the intellectual and familial influences on Burnet's youth, his career, in which piety and opportunism were curiously combined, and the plan of education he laid out for his children. He was particularly concerned with this latter scheme because of his keen sensitivity to the unhappiness inflicted on him by his own father, who gave him . . .

> much severe correction, in which how much soever I might deserve it by manny wild frolicks yet I think he carried that too farre, for the fear of that brought me under too great an uneasynes and sometimes even to a hatred of my Father. The sense of this may have perhaps carried me in the education of my children to the other extream of too much indulgence. (p. 454)

Burnet's autobiography is given an additional piquancy by his constant embroilment with enemies of every stripe; though from the information he gives us we are hard put to account for his unpopularity, and must make the most of such occasional hints as his description of himself as a young man: 'I loved solitude and silence and so I avoided manny tentations, but I was out of measure conceited of my selfe, vain and desirous of fame beyond expression.'[14]

After this succession of worldly prelates one turns with some relief to the sublimer aspirations of Henry More, as recorded in the 'Praefatio Generalissima' to his collected Latin works.[15] Other auto-

---

"heroic", begins; it strikes out the rest of my teeth before they are rotten, and warns me to be mindful of death.

[13] Patrick, *Autobiography* in *Works*, ed. Rev. Alexander Taylor, vol. IX. Burnet, *Autobiography* in *A Supplement to Burnet's History of My Own Time*, ed. H. C. Foxcroft.

[14] pp. 474-5. We may note here the three reasons Burnet gives for his having undertaken the work: (1) to give 'usefull instructions' to his children; (2) to give the true story of his life, forestalling less well-informed biographers; (3) to follow the example of Thuanus (J. A. de Thou).

[15] *Henrici Mori Cantabrigiensis Opera Omnia*, I, i-xxiv.

biographers of the time show how their mature character has been moulded by childhood impressions; More, on the other hand, is unique in his eagerness to demonstrate that he became a Platonist and latitudinarian in spite of the influence of his parents, relatives, and tutor—all of whom were dedicated, even bellicose, Calvinists. Speaking of the occasions and motives of his books, More tries to prove that his intellectual development refutes the theory that human personality is determined by environmental influences:

> paulo altius res repetenda est, & pauca de eis quae in prima etiam nostra adolescentia si non pueritia acciderunt, praelibanda; quo plenius constet quae scripsi nulla esse ascititia mutuatitiave quae educationi librorumq; lectioni debeantur dogmata, sed sensa Animi propria ex intimis meis visceribus hausta ac deprompta, nec omnem Animam humanam abrasam esse Tabulam, sed innatos habere sensus ac notiones boni & mali, turpis ac honesti, veri ac falsi, easdemq; vividas vegetasque.[16]

He goes on to show that as he grew up his convictions soon became exactly the reverse of his parents', despite such deterrents as his uncle's threat to flog him for his precocious disputes against Calvinism. More cultivates his faculties of intuition and introversion as means of discovering the primal, divine spirit within—a concept of self-development which foreshadows the Romantics. An early spiritual crisis becomes an experience of Wordsworthian joy in a pastoral setting, quite unlike the harsh and terrifying crises of such men as Bunyan and George Fox. Though More's revelation is quieter and more private, he presents the scene with an art which may owe something to the 'tolle lege' episode of Augustine's *Confessions*:

> Et quod ad Dei Existentiam attinet, quanquam in dicto Agro lente obstipoque capite, pro meo more, incedens, lapillulosque summo pedis digito subinde propellens, versus istos Claudiani Musico quodam ac Melancholico murmure aliquando mecum repetere solebam vel potius mussitare,
>
> Saepe mihi dubiam traxit sententia mentem
> Curarent Superi terras, an nullus inesset

[16] p. 25. More is here attacking the Aristotelian theory that the human mind is at birth a *tabula rasa*; the theory was espoused by the Hobbesians, More's proximate target here.

'We are to take our Rise a little higher; and to premise some things which fell out in my Youth; if not also in my Childhood it self: To the End that it may more fully appear, that the Things which I have written, are not any borrowed, or far-fetch'd Opinions, owing unto Education, and the Reading of Books; but the proper Sentiments of my own Mind, drawn and derived from my most intimate Nature; and that every Humane Soul is no *abrasa tabula*, or mere Blank Sheet; but hath innate Sensations and Notions in it, both of good and evil, just and unjust, true and false; and those very strong and vivid.' (Ward, *Life of More* p. 5; see Bibliography I, under More).

Rector & incerto fluerent mortalia casu:
Integer tamen ille vegetusq; Divini Numinis sensus quem ipsa Natura
Animo me inseminaverat, facile omnibus hujusmodi levibus ac
Poeticis dubitationibus silentium imperavit. Immo vel in ipsa prima
Pueritia internus Divinae Presentiae sensus ita in mea mente viguit, ut
nullum Dictum, Factum, aut Cogitatum eum latere posse existima-
verim, nec ab aliis me natu majoribus aliter potui persuaderi. (p. vi)[17]

A second crisis in More's intellectual development comes after his
graduation from Cambridge, when he begins to doubt if his avid
pursuit of knowledge for its own sake is a worthy ambition. Pondering
an alternative ideal, 'the purging of the mind from all vices', he
plunges into the study of Ficino, Plotinus, and the other neo-Plato-
nists. Renewed joy and confidence are his reward, 'ita ut intra paucos
annos in laetissimum lucidissimumque Animae statum emerserim &
plane ineffabilem'[18] (p. viii); he enters upon a public career as poet
and philosopher, in which the story of his life is no longer to be
distinguished from that of his books.[19] But in his high valuation of

[17] And as to what concerns the Existence of GOD: Though in that Ground
mentioned, walking, as my Manner was, slowly, and with my Head on one
Side, and kicking now and then the Stones with my Feet, I was wont sometimes
with a sort of Musical and Melancholick Murmur to repeat, or rather humm to
my self, those Verses of Claudian;
> (Oft hath my anxious Mind divided stood;
> Whether the Gods did mind this lower World;
> Or whether no such Ruler (Wise and Good)
> We had; and all things here by Chance were hurld.)
Yet that exceeding hail and entire Sense of GOD, which Nature her self had
planted deeply in me, very easily silenced all such slight and Poetical Dubitations
as these. Yea even in my first Childhood, an inward Sense of the Divine Presence
was so strong upon my Mind; that I did then believe, there could no Deed,
Word, or Thought be hidden from him: Nor was I by any others that were
older than my self, to be otherwise persuaded. (Ward, pp. 7-8).

[18] Insomuch that within a few Years, I was got into a most Joyous and Lucid
State of Mind; and such plainly as is ineffable; (Ward, p. 15).

[19] More renounces the project of writing a full-scale autobiography; once he
has told enough to refute the *tabula rasa* theory, he is satisfied: 'Post susceptum
vero gradum ut innumera omittam, neque enim hic propriae vitae descriptionem
meditor, (quanquam id nonnulli ante me iique praeclari quidem viri fecerunt,
Cardanusque tam praecisam de Libris propriis rationem reddidit ut ne eos certe
omiserit quos felis urina corruperat) sed brevem tantum Introductionem ad
occasionem primi mei libri scribendi melius intelligendam; commode profecti
cecidit quod tantam studiorum frustrationem passus essem.' (p. vii.)

'But after taking my Degree, to pass over and omit abundance of things; I
designing not here the Draught of my own Life (though some, and those very
Famous Men too, have done that before me; and Cardan hath given so exact
an Account of his own Writings, that he hath not so much as omitted those that
were spoiled by the Urine of a Cat) but only a brief Introduction for the better
Understanding the Occasion of writing my First Book; It fell out truly very
Happily for me, that I suffer'd so great a Disappointment in my Studies.' (Ward,
pp. 11-12).

the spiritual powers which are latent in the child, and his corresponding rejection of infant depravity, he stands, with Vaughan and Traherne, among the most enlightened of his age.

Returning to the main stream of Anglican autobiography, we find once again that combination of piety and mundane ambition which seems typical of its practitioners. The autobiography and diary of Ralph Josselin have scant literary value, but fascinate by their revelation of his obsession with accumulating wealth—whether by adding more farmland to his holdings or screwing more tithes from his parishioners.[20] In a manner that Pepys has made familiar, he carefully calculates his net worth at the end of each year, interspersing pious ejaculations like a veritable Parson Trulliber:

> I am much in debt, but I have mony enough 84. 14. 0 owing unto mee to clear all my debts, and an 100 l. in my purse; this is the Lord's bounty; teach mee to serve thee with a glad and thankfull heart according to thy great goodnes; I found this yeare I saved some mony, and I hope have gaind acquaintance with and experience of God. (pp. 128-9)

Josselin was a Puritan at heart, though by judicious trimming (as we would expect) he managed to retain his cure after the Restoration. In two Anglican autobiographers of a later generation, Henry Wharton and William Taswell, we miss Josselin's anxious preoccupation with the state of his soul, though they share his concern for worldly success. Wharton's *Vita*, written between 1690 and 1695, illustrates the decline of the Anglican Church as a moral force in comparison with its condition a century earlier. Wharton was a young man of great ambition who chose the Church as the best outlet for his talents, and would doubtless have had a brilliant career if he had been less indiscreet. The precocious son of a Norfolk clergyman, he composed a Latin poem of twelve hundred lines for his thirteenth birthday, and followed it up with one of three thousand lines ,the next year. After recording these childhood achievements he gives a 'character' of himself in which he describes his fierce desire for praise, his eager scholarship, and his sexual proclivities; we learn that he does not pursue women, though his thoughts are lascivious, and is still a virgin as he writes (age twenty-three). He often gets drawn into sexual encounters, which he describes with the naïvety of a precocious scholar suffering from arrested emotional development. Like some clerical Joseph Andrews, he sometimes has to flee in order to save his virtue: 'Sub id circiter temporis a juvencula quadam virgine, formae

[20] *Diary*, ed. E. Hockliffe, Camden Soc, 3rd ser., XV. Josselin's title for the autobiographical introduction was 'A Thankfull Observacon Of Divine Providence & Goodness Towards Mee & A Summary View Of My Life: By Me Ralph Josselin.'

satis liberalis et illibitae hactenus famae, summis blanditiis ad
stumprum saepe invitatus, parum abfuit quin pudicitiae naufragium
fecerim.' (p. 109).[21]

Wharton's real vocation was scholarship rather than religion. He
was an assistant to Dr. Cave, Canon of Windsor, on his enormous
Historia Literaria, and later complained that Cave gave him in-
sufficient credit for his labours when the book was published. He
worked alone on the *Anglia Sacra* (1691), an extraordinary scholarly
achievement which was completed after the period covered in his
autobiography.[22]

The *Vita* is a private memoir, and it is all the more interesting
because of its intimacy and candour. The combination of extreme
precocity and disappointment in early manhood seems to have
arrested and blighted Wharton's emotional development, and to have
helped produce a character which can only be described as repellent:
conceited, over-reaching, priggish. The last sexual episode in the
work is typical: a beautiful young woman hints to Wharton that she
loves him, and he feels a reciprocal attraction; but he breaks off the
relationship because her dowry is not enough for him. He dies at
thirty with his ambitions unsatisfied, unmarried, worn out by excessive study. Religious feeling, as such, plays little part in the *Vita*; it is
concerned rather with such matters as the defence of pluralities or
with scholarly controversies. Yet it is a revealing record of the unhealthy condition of the Anglican Church as a whole, as well as of
Wharton himself.

William Taswell's *Commentaries* adds to the evidence of decay.[23]
He was the son of a rich merchant, but found his career at Oxford
balked when his father cut off his allowance:

> The misfortune too was, I was not old enough to go into orders, and
> incapable too of any employment which might render my circum-
> stances easy in life. And as I was always looked upon as a gentleman,
> I was ashamed to lay open the real exigency of my affairs; and, on the
> other hand, to be thought covetous and close-fisted because I with-
> drew myself from my acquaintance by an act of necessity only, I own

[21] 'At about that time a young virgin, quite attractive and of as yet unblemished
reputation, kept enticing me in the most shameless way to deflower her, and my
chastity came very close to being shipwrecked.'

[22] Wharton was a phenomenon of industry. 'Within the space of two years he
successfully completed an undertaking that might more properly have occupied
a committee for a generation.' David Douglas, *English Scholars, 1660-1730*,
2nd ed., p. 146.

[23] *Autobiography and Anecdotes by William Taswell, D.D.*, ed. G. P. Elliott, in
Camden Soc. *Miscellany*, II (1853). Taswell's title was *The Genealogy of a Family
in the West, and Commentaries upon his own Life*. The work was translated by
the Rev. Henry Taswell from the original Latin, now lost.

galled me extremely; therefore a sad melancholy seized me. I spent my time for whole weeks chiefly in walking about my room. I could not apply my mind to study. If I attempted to read any thing, my thoughts wandered elsewhere. (p. 16)

The Church was, as he suggests, the obvious career for a bookish younger son; and Taswell eventually took orders and had a fairly successful career, though he had hoped for preferment at Oxford. His autobiography is mainly *res gestae*, with a few passages of self-analysis; he shows little religious fervour, being much more concerned with his troubles in getting a position and scraping together enough money to live on. If Taswell's life was at all representative, it would seem that to take orders in the Anglican Church had by the end of the century become for many men a trade, as mundane as teaching or soldiering; in these circumstances, we should not be surprised at the absence of Anglican spiritual autobiography after the Restoration.[24]

What might account for the dearth of spiritual autobiographies by Anglicans? One consideration is that the great period of Anglican devotional writing ended before the Civil War; and in that period very few autobiographies of any kind were written in England. Secondly, the leading spirits of Anglicanism were highly educated and gentlemen; this combination of qualities usually ensured that their desires for creative self-expression found issue in more recognized and respectable literary genres than autobiography. Herbert's well-known summary of the theme of *The Temple* could be matched almost word-for-word with some of the statements of intention given by later, non-Anglican spiritual autobiographers; he called his poems 'a picture of the many spiritual Conflicts that have past betwixt God and my Soul, before I could subject mine to the will of Jesus my Master: in whose service I have now found perfect freedom'.[25] Herbert simply preferred the medium of lyrical poetry to the medium of prose spiritual autobiography—and who, after all, could criticize his choice? Autobiography had no pre-emptive claim on the attention of men gifted with literary genius and, in fact, relatively few major authors have been at ease, or successful, in the genre.

[24] It may be noted that Taswell gives interesting accounts of the plague of 1666 and the Great Fire of 1667—see pp. 9-14.

[25] Quoted in D. Bush, *English Literature in the Earlier Seventeenth Century, 1600-1660,* 1st ed., p. 136.

V
Presbyterian Autobiographers

BEFORE 1642, virtually all the leaders of the anti-episcopal movement were Presbyterians; but after that date many supporters of the Parliamentary cause began to split off into other, more radical groups.[1] In this chapter I will discuss the autobiographies written by the moderates, and in the next chapter those written by the radicals, the adherents of the so-called sects. Before beginning the discussion of Presbyterian works, however, it would be well to consider what the autobiographies of this and the following chapter have in common, and in what ways they differ from the Catholic and Anglican works already discussed.

Until now, few of the works analysed could be called spiritual autobiographies—records of the progress of a soul. Catholic autobiographers were mainly concerned with apologetics and with missionary activities; Anglicans were usually content to narrate the external events of their careers in the Church. Both Catholic and Anglican autobiographers conformed to the *res gestae* convention for the most part, even though their Churches offered them examples of more introverted and devotional approaches to religious writing. Among the autobiographers now to be discussed some, Presbyterians especially, stuck to a conservative and objective form; but many others obeyed the injunction of the Psalmist: 'Come and hear, all ye that fear God, and I will declare what he hath done for my soul'

[1] A brief note on these denominations may be useful. Presbyterians favoured a state church governed, not by bishops, but by a council of representatives from congregations, according to the Scots model. Independents (Congregationalists) wished each congregation to be free to choose its own form of worship; however, they soon dissociated themselves from those who they felt abused this liberty— the members of the radical sects. The Baptists, who overlapped to some extent with the Congregationalists, are best distinguished by their belief in baptism by total (adult) immersion rather than by sprinkling; they were divided in the seventeenth century into the Particular Baptists, who believed in strict predestination and election, and the more lenient General Baptists. Quakers denied the need for sacraments or formal liturgy, and relied on their inner light for guidance. They were persecuted mainly for their refusal to take oaths, bear arms, or reverence secular magistrates.

(Ps. lxvi, 16). These words epitomize the purpose of those seventeenth-century spiritual autobiographers who wrote for an audience of their partners in Christian fellowship, and they also define the writer's relation to his audience: the godly man recounts his experiences for the encouragement and edification of his fellow-seekers after holiness. In narrating his spiritual history, he adds two new dimensions to the basic mode of *res gestae*: first, spiritual experiences are no longer simple, objective events, but moments of intense emotional contact between God and the individual soul; second, the bond between the autobiographer and his reader (provided he seeks salvation) becomes vitally important—the reader's own eternal life may be at stake, and as he reads he becomes, potentially at least, a member of the communion of saints.

The importance of the interplay between writer and audience can be seen, early in the century, in the autobiographical tracts of Richard Kilby.[2] His first work, published anonymously in 1608, was *The Burthen of a loaden conscience: or the miserie of Sinne: Set forth by the confession of a miserable sinner*; in this confession of his many sins Kilby reinforced the drama of his spiritual conflicts by proclaiming that it still lay in the balance whether he was to be saved or damned. The note 'To the Printer' takes up this theme:

> ... I protest before God, that nothing be mitigated concerning me; by turning, *I am*, [sc. a sinner] into *I was*, etc. It is very needefull for a man to know what he is. I know none but my selfe, I iudge none but my selfe; I intreat others to giue me leave to iudge my selfe, because I feare the iudgement of God, and would perswade people to feare God, that they may escape his iudgement, and obtaine his mercies.

Here self-knowledge is not sought for its own sake (as in the private and gentlemanly lucubrations of Montaigne) but for the sake of the potential saints whom Kilby might be able to save. His text begins with an open appeal to them: 'All Christened people, men, women and children, I sinfull sinner, having by long, and wofull experience found the miseries of sinne, am desirous to confesse the same, that others may see and speedily turne away from it' (sig. A1r). Ten years later, Kilby was vouchsafed sufficient assurance of his salvation to publish a sequel to his first tract: *Hallelu-iah: Praise yee the Lord, For The Unburthening of a loaden Conscience: By his grace in Iesus Christ vouchsafed unto the worst sinner of all the whole world. Come, and heare all yee that feare God, and I will tell you what hee hath done for my soule*. Kilby's writings should remind us that religious introspection, though it doubtless sprang from a greater awareness of individual personality, was in its expression often governed by utilitarian and communal purposes.

[2] Minister of All-hallows, Derby; died 1617; *not* the Richard Kilby in *DNB*.

We may now confine our attention to the Presbyterian autobiographers; and since their works vary considerably in form, let us
first summarize some common characteristics of the eighteen works
to be discussed. Most of them (all but three) were written after 1660,
though six of the authors were born during the lifetime of Elizabeth
and ten before the death of James; Presbyterians usually wrote in old
age. Only one of them saw his autobiography published during his
lifetime (Henry Burton), and only two other autobiographies in this
group appeared during the seventeenth century, those of Gervase
Disney and Richard Baxter. Most were not published until they were
discovered and edited by eighteenth and nineteenth century antiquaries. In general, among religious autobiographers of the period,
only those who adhered to the sects wrote customarily for publication. Henry Burton's autobiography, an exception among Presbyterian works, was published in response to the popular enthusiasm
for its author when he was released from prison in 1640.[3] The typical
Presbyterian autobiography was not intended to circulate widely; it
might be drawn up for the good of the author's own soul, or for a
restricted audience of family, friends, or members of a congregation.
The average standard of literacy in these works was quite high, and
we find no incoherent rhapsodies like those often produced by authors
with more extreme religious views. Two Presbyterians explicitly noted
their indebtedness to Augustine's *Confessions*, and all were familiar
with more than just the Bible, the *unum necessarium* of the 'mechanick
preachers'. Many of these autobiographers had attended universities
and most were ordained ministers; those not in orders were substantial citizens and one, Sir William Waller, was a general. Six out of the
eighteen were Scots, and few could be considered Londoners—a
geographical dispersion that contrasts with the concentration of most
secular autobiographers in the capital. None of the eighteen were in
favour of radical social change, though, with one exception (Newcome), they were all anti-Royalist. But we need not pursue further the
attempt to establish common traits; the works themselves should
now be examined singly.

Autobiographers Born before 1600

We may begin with two autobiographies, Richard Norwood's
Journal[4] and Henry Burton's *Narration*, which illustrate in relatively

---

[3] *A Narration of the Life of Mr. Henry Burton* (1643). In 1641 had appeared
*The Christian Mans Triall: or, A True Relation of the first apprehension and
severall examinations of John Lilburne*; this autobiographical tract set a precedent
for Burton's work. For Burton's career see Haller, pp. 250 ff.
[4] *The Journal of Richard Norwood* (1959); this is the first publication.

pure form the private and public types of religious autobiography. The *Journal*, written in 1639, gives a fascinating and in some ways appalling view of the impact of Calvinism on a sensitive temperament already prone to hysteria. Since it is one of the first substantial spiritual autobiographies in English, Norwood's account of how he came to undertake the work is of particular interest:

CONFESSIONS

In the year of our Lord 1639, the 49th year of my age, a day which I had set apart to give unto the Lord by fasting and praying privately, upon some occasion (then) requiring it; amongst other things that day I endeavoured to call to mind the whole course of my life past, and how the Lord had dealt with me . . . I had also by me some catalogues, as of my sins so also of the mercies of God towards me through the whole course of my life, which I had made shortly after my conversion, and these were ever a great help to my memory in many things. (p. 3)

The influence of Augustine is evident, and will be discussed later; we note also the 'catalogues, as of my sins' which Norwood used as an *aide-mémoire*: these were probably similar in motivation to the 'experiences of the works of grace' or 'observations of God's providence' which many diligent soul-searchers compiled in order to keep themselves mindful of God's influence on their daily life. Norwood also placed at the head of his text a claim which he tried strenuously to substantiate: 'Jesus Christ came into the world to save sinners, of whom I am the chief. Richard Norwood.'

'I was born of Christian parents and under them educated till about fifteen years of age; in whom there was a severe disposition and carriage towards me suitable to that mass of sin and folly which was bound up in my heart, whereby it was moderated in some good measure' (p. 4). Though Norwood approved of his parents' strictness, the modern reader may be inclined to blame it for much of the guilt and emotional turmoil which their son suffered in later life. In his adolescence, sin overwhelmed him entirely: '[I] so grievously stained my life and lived so dissolutely that I even abhor the remembrance of those times' (p. 4). About one of these 'grievous stains' we wish he had told us more (even though it happened at Stony Stratford, not Stratford on Avon): 'At Stratford when I was near fifteen years of age, being drawn in by other young men of the town, I acted a woman's part in a stage-play. I was so much affected with that practice that had not the Lord prevented it I should have chosen it before any other course of life' (p. 6). Soon after this episode Norwood was apprenticed to a London fishmonger; but he left this employment to go to sea and to fight in the Dutch wars. He then travelled to Rome, having feigned conversion to Catholicism at Louvain in order to get a safe-conduct. On the way to Rome he fell in with a Papist sympathizer who half-convinced him of the truth of Catholicism; unfortunately, this flirtation with the Whore of Babylon had disastrous psychological effects: 'Notwithstanding though I seemed now to have more peace of conscience than before, yet about the same time, or presently after, before I parted company with that man, the Lord struck me with a grievous judgement, the marks and symptoms whereof I am like to bear to my grave, and even the thing itself in some measure' (p. 24). The divine judgement was 'the mare': religious hysteria in the form of terrifying nightmares. These dreams provide a textbook case of neurosis induced by an extreme sense of religious guilt:

> About the same time or presently after my entering into Italy I began first to be troubled with that nightly disease which we call the mare, which afterwards increased upon me very grievously that I was scarce any night free from it, and seldom it left me without nocturnal pollutions; besides, whilst it was upon me I had horrible dreams and visions. Oft-times I verily thought that I descended into Hell and there felt the pains of the damned, with many hideous things. Usually in my dreams methought I saw my father always grievously angry with me. This disease brought me very weak, and surely without the special power of God sustaining me I see not how life should have been continued. Besides having often a light burning in the room as is usual in those places, though I was not able to stir when the disease was upon me, yet I could usually remember where I was and who was in the room with me, and if they talked could understand what they said and could open my eyelids a little and see the light in the room. And sometimes I seemed to see a thing on my breast or belly like a hare or cat, etc.; whereupon I have sometimes taken a naked knife in my hand when I went to sleep, thinking therewith to strike at it, and it was God's mercy that I had not by this means slain myself. But after I had observed the danger whereinto the wily fiend was like to draw me, I left of that. When I departed out of Italy to go for England this disease began to abate, and afterwards more when I came into England. (pp. 26-7)

Norwood was about nineteen or twenty at this time, and much troubled with remorse for the habit of masturbation into which he had fallen; he refers to this problem throughout the *Journal*.[5] With such corroborative evidence, one may surmise that his nightmares were based on castration anxiety; the appearance in them of the 'grievously angry' father (after 'nocturnal pollutions') suggests that his father had probably threatened him with castration as punishment for infantile sex-play—the small furry animals in the dreams,

[5] Guilt caused by masturbation seems to have been fairly common among spiritual autobiographers, though they often only hinted obliquely at the problem; for an explicit reference, see the quotation from Trosse's autobiography on p. 71 below.

which he struck at with a knife, would represent the genitals.[6]

Norwood's sexual neurosis should not be dismissed as a mere historical curiosity. It has a wider significance, because he was not a weird or untypical figure; apart from the blatantly sexual nature of his hysteria, his spiritual life conformed closely to the usual Calvinist model. His fear of the angry, threatening father was a psychological counterpart to the Calvinist image of man cowering before a wrathful God. Freud has worked out in detail the analogy between neurosis and religion, suggesting, for example, that 'obsessional neurosis furnishes a tragi-comic travesty of a private religion', and 'the protestations of the pious that they know they are miserable sinners in their hearts correspond to the sense of guilt of the obsessional neurotic'.[7] In Norwood's case, his conviction that he was a 'miserable sinner' derived from sexual guilt; but the figure of the threatening father/Iahweh could terrorize the Calvinist for all kinds of other sins, real or imaginary.[8] The conscientious soul-searcher could easily work himself into a state of unbearable anxiety, which had as its root cause the arbitrariness and irrationality of God's choice of those whom he wished to favour or to afflict. The Calvinist's anxiety about election was analogous to that of a child trying to predict the actions and preferences of a capricious father; for him, above all, was it true that 'God is a father-substitute, or, more correctly, an exalted father, or yet again, a reproduction of the father as seen and met with in childhood.'[9]

We may now observe how Norwood, a representative enough Calvinist, came to terms both with God the Father and with his private neurosis. He returned to England from Rome, and made a voyage to the 'Sommer Islands' (Bermudas). On board ship he 'entered into a serious consideration of conversion and conforming myself to the will of God', and he decided that, in order to resolve his doubts, he 'would be regulated by Augustine'.[10] Many spiritual trials had yet to be endured, but at last he 'had an undoubted assurance of the remission of sins and sure reconciliation with God in Christ'

[6] Freud, *The Interpretation of Dreams*, p. 373 in *Basic Works*.

[7] 'Obsessive Acts and Religious Practices,' *Collected Papers*, II, 28, 31.

[8] Reinforcement of parental authority was part of Calvin's programme for Geneva; in the revision of the laws of 1543 it was made a capital crime for a child to strike his father. 'For they are monsters, and not men, who petulantly and contumeliously violate the paternal authority. Hence, the Lord orders all who rebel against their parents to be put to death.' *Institutes*, I, 345.

[9] Freud, 'A Neurosis of Demoniacal Possession in the Seventeenth Century', *Collected Papers*, IV, 449.

[10] Calvinists tended to favour Augustine over the other Fathers as a doctrinal guide, in part because his position on free will and determinism seemed reconcilable with the doctrine of election. In the *Institutes* there are as many citations to Augustine as to all other authors combined—though the *Confessions* are cited only once.

(p. 81). Guilt and terror gave way to a feeling of security and exaltation; while walking to visit a friend

> my heart was so abundantly replenished with heavenly joys in consideration and sure apprehension of the love and mercy of God towards me and of the continuance thereof forever, that I did not so much walk but rather went leaping all the way, though I did as it were something check and restrain myself from that action of leaping. . . . When I came thither someone was reading Augustine's *Confessions*, the place touching his conversion, etc., which ministered fresh matter of comfort and rejoicing. (p. 85)

This state of Godly intoxication, however, was followed by renewed attacks of Satan, even more corporeal and sexually disturbing than the earlier nightmares:

> sometimes he seemed to lean on my back or arms or shoulder, sometimes hanging on my cloak or gown. Sometimes it seemed in my feeling as if he had stricken me in sundry places, sometimes as it were handling my heart and working withal a wonderful hardness therein, accompanied with many strange passions, affections, lusts, and blasphemies. Also in bed sometimes pressing, sometimes creeping to and fro, sometimes ready to take away my breath, sometimes lifting up the bed, sometimes the pillow, sometimes pulling the clothes or striking on the bed or on the pillow. (p. 93)

Norwood gradually overcame these attacks; he was especially encouraged by a sermon, heard by chance, on Proverbs iii, 11-12: 'My sone, despise not thou the chastening of the Lord, neither faint when thou art rebuked of Him, for whom the Lord loveth he chasteneth, and scourgeth every son whome he receiveth.' The demons of Divine and parental disapproval finally departed. In the years after the period covered by the *Journal* Norwood prospered as one of the pioneers of Bermuda; he had a finger in many affairs, from a survey of the island to witch-trials, and was a respected and substantial citizen when he died in 1675.

External evidence suggests that Norwood had a more stable personality than one would expect from reading the *Journal*. In everyday life he was a successful colonist who was quite moderate in the outward practice of his religion. He took an intermediate position between Presbyterians and Independents during their quarrels over church discipline on the island; he also at one time urged the Bermuda Company to curb the ministers' excessive zeal for catechising (p. xlvii). Moreover, his nightmares and Satanic conflicts seem mild in comparison with some of the experiences described by autobiographers of more radical beliefs; it was not uncommon for these men to report having talked with God, seen visions of the future, or walked in the clouds. Presbyterian spiritual autobiographers were sober and restrained in their everyday life at least, even if internally they struggled with their tortured consciences and felt themselves suspended over hell fire. Norwood's guilt symptoms were perhaps more exaggerated and pathological than those of less imaginative men; but his spiritual development, measured against either Calvinist doctrine or the common experience of his fellow Presbyterians, was completely orthodox and followed a pattern which we shall encounter again many times in this and the following chapter.

Henry Burton's *Narration* was written and published under very different circumstances from Norwood's *Journal*. Norwood recorded, for his own edification, his struggles with a tortured conscience; Burton, on the other hand, was displaying himself to the public as a Puritan martyr who had been victimized by Laud's malevolence. The tone of self-accusation usually present in Calvinist autobiographies is missing in Burton's: it would have been out of place in a work of self-justification and propaganda. Burton's sub-title promises an account of his 'Sufferings, Supports, Comforts, and Deliverances'; the sufferings were inflicted by the villainous Laud, and the deliverance came by act of Parliament. The 'Preface to the Reader' explains why Burton chose to tell the story of his trials himself:

> Nor it it unusuall for men to set forth a description of their owne lives. Moses did so. David so. Paul so. And who fitter than a mans selfe, as being best acquainted with, and most privy to the many passages of his life. Nor had I undertaken this taske, but partly to satisfie the importunity of many godly friends, and partly to give a just account to Gods people of that divine support and comfort, which it pleased the Lord to uphold mee with, in all my tryalis. . . . For the rest, I am not ashamed to make my selfe herein a spectacle even to those that are without, this being but an anticipation, seeing we must all appeare before the Judgement Seat of Christ, that every one may receive the things done in his body, according to that he hath done, whether it be good or evill. (sig. A2v.)

Although Burton says he is 'not ashamed to make my selfe herein a spectacle', his statement is clearly defensive, with its careful citations of scriptural precedents and genteel yielding to 'the importunity of many godly friends'. This was not his usual tone, for he was a fiery and intemperate bishop-baiter; but to publish an autobiography while still alive was something unusual, and in his preface Burton reveals a fear that he might be accused of spiritual pride. On the other hand, however, he is not eager to give ammunition to his enemies by asserting that he is 'a child of wrath' or 'the chief of sinners'; Presbyterians, for the most part sober and respectable folk, usually confined such confessions to their private writings. It was left to the Baptists to make a special virtue of public self-abasement.

Burton tells his story in a relatively dry, factual style. He describes briefly his youth in Yorkshire, his studies at St. John's College, Cambridge, and his acquisition of an anti-episcopal bias while an undergraduate. He becomes a courtier, serving both Prince Henry (who died in 1612) and Prince Charles, and enters the ministry only when past thirty years old. When Charles accedes Burton presents him with a letter which warns against the Papist tendencies of Neale and Laud; for this he loses his place at court. He goes into opposition, beginning a period of twelve years as preacher and controversialist. For publishing 'seditious' books without authority he is condemned by the Court of Star Chamber, in 1637, to perpetual solitary confinement, two hours in the pillory, and loss of ears.[11] Burton describes in great detail his imprisonment at Lancaster on Guernsey; inevitably, he compares his life and sufferings to those of St. Paul (pp. 34-7). After three years he is released, by the intervention of Parliament, and makes a triumphal entry into London (Nov. 1640).

The *Narration*, though no masterpiece, recreates for us the political career of a Puritan zealot. It is also significant as an early example in Britain of an *ad hoc* autobiography: one motivated by its author's involvement in a major political issue, or by his desire to exploit some temporary notoriety. 'Testimonies' of this kind became increasingly numerous during the Commonwealth period, and imprisonment for religious dissent was often a stimulus to the autobiographical urge. Burton, an educated man and professional propagandist, was shrewd enough to see the political value of writing his own life as a contribution to Puritan martyrology; in the next twenty years many autobiographers were to take their cue from him.

We may now consider two men whose preaching and practice illustrate the relation between the Puritan habit of diary-keeping and the rise of autobiography.[12] John Beadle (d. 1667) exhorted the faithful to keep records of their spiritual experiences; Arthur Wilson (1595-1652) was one who hearkened to him and obeyed. Beadle expounded his message in *The Journal or Diary of a Thankful Christian* (1656), which is not a personal diary but a manual of religious conduct for Calvinists. It is, the title-page informs us, 'Presented in some Meditations upon Numb. 33, 2. "And Moses wrote their goings out, according to their Journeys, by the commandment of the Lord".' The Epistle Dedicatory extols the value of diary-keeping as an aid to the development of faith:

[11] Bastwick and Prynne suffered with him on the scaffold, June 14, 1637.
[12] On Puritan diary-keeping before the seventeenth century see *Two Elizabethan Puritan Diaries*, ed. M. M. Knappen; the diaries are those of Richard Rogers and Samuel Ward. For Ward's posthumous influence on the autobiographer Henry Newcombe, see p. 77 below.

> And what better means can be used for the advancement of faith in
> the growth and strength of it, then a rich treasure of experience; every
> experiment of Gods favour to us, being a good prop for our faith for
> the future. ... Now doubtless such as will be well stored with a
> treasure of experiments, had need keep a constant Diary by them of
> all Gods gracious dealings with them.

The Calvinist, lacking the constant reassurance which good works
or sacraments can provide, must rely on his inner experiences of
God's grace to maintain and strengthen his faith. A diary can be most
useful in helping to achieve peace of mind, as Beadle's publisher,
John Fuller, points out in his preface 'To the Reader'. Tradesmen,
merchants, lawyers, and physicians, Fuller notes, have their journals
and account books; housekeepers have books of daily expenses. 'A
Christian that would be exact hath more need, and may reap much
more good by such a Journall as this. We are all but Stewards, Factors
here, and must give a strict account in that great day to the high Lord
of all our wayes, and of all his wayes towards us' (sig. b2r). The diary
helps avoid the sin of unthankfulness, and to remember both good
and bad experiences:

> Nor only mercies and signall works of gracious providence, but
> judgements, great changes, overturnings, and the sins of the age are to
> be registred in this Christian Journall, as this Author well mixes the
> ingredients of this Diary. . . .
> There is a book of three leaves thou shouldest read dayly to make
> up this Diary; the black leaf of thy own and others sins with shame
> and sorrow; the white leaf of Gods goodnesse, mercies with joy and
> thankfulnesse; the red leaf of Gods judgments felt, feared, threatned,
> with fear and trembling. (sig. b4, r. & v.)

This is a fair summary of Beadle's detailed recommendations, which
fill nearly two hundred pages of text. Chapter II lists 'Nationall and
publick' matters to be noted in the diary, Chapter III 'what personall
and private passages of Providence those are which ought to be
recorded' (p. 48). These 'passages' fall into five classes:

> 1. Let every man keep a strict account of his effectuall calling, and
> of his age in Christ; and (if it may be) set down the time when, the
> place where, and the person by whom he was converted. (p. 48)
> 2. Take speciall notice of all divine assistance, and that either in the
> performance of the duties that are required of us, or in bearing those
> evills that are inflicted upon us. (p. 51)
> 3. Remember, and for that end put into your Journal all deliver-
> ances from dangers, vouchsafed to you or yours. And indeed, what is
> our whole life, but a continued deliverance? (p. 55)
> 4. All the instruments, all the men and means that God hath in pro-
> vidence at any time used for our good, must not be forgotten. (p. 58)

5. And finally, mark what returns, what answers God gives to your prayers, and set them down with a *Selah*, as most remarkable pledges of his love. (p. 62)

We see here the kinds of events that a Puritan diarist or auto-biographer would concern himself with. He might not be able to classify the incidents of his life quite as neatly as Beadle suggests; but spiritual autobiographers of all denominations seem to agree quite closely with Beadle's formula in their choice of subject-matter. In most cases, however, there is no direct influence visible, and we should not underestimate the degree to which Beadle's rules were merely a codification of the common practice of Puritan ministers in giving advice to introspective and conscientious believers.

The effect of Beadle's precepts can be documented in one instance. On July 21, 1644, Arthur Wilson (a minor historian, poetaster, and servant of noble Lords) heard Beadle preach at Leeze, in Essex:

His text was, Numbers xxxiii, 1. Theise are the journies of the children of Israel, &c, insisting upon this. That every Christian ought to keep a record of his owne actions & wayes, being full of dangers & hazards; that God might have the glorie. For this command was given to Moses, as in the second verse, by God himselfe; that there might be a remembrance to posteritie of the deliverances which God had & would worke for that people. And soe everie man, though of the meanest qualitie, may see the hand of the Divine Goodnes workinge for him in the many occurrences of his life. . . .

This made mee run backe to the beginning of my life, assisted by my memorie & some small notes; wherein I have given a true, though a mean deleniation, of eight & forty yeares progresse in the world.[13]

The autobiography which Wilson wrote at Beadle's prompting did not, however, conform to the usual Calvinist model. Wilson was no Zeal-of-the-Land-Busy when young, but a roaring-boy with 'a reputation of valour'. He also had ambitions of becoming a witty lover, ambitions scorned by the mature and censorious Presbyterian:

Yett, in the inter-mixture of time, I would steale to my booke. For I loved the sweetnes of philosophie & historie, I found it such an imbellishment to discourse. And I had a natural pride which raised mee to an affection to understand, as nere as I could, any thing which I had the least hint of. . . . And, though I knew my fortune would not permit me to be a lover, yett I was soe amorous as to expresse it foolishly in verse; & every beautiful object was a fit theme for my fancy: thinking then of no other heaven but a good face. (p. 463)

At this time Wilson served the Earl of Essex, under whom he fought in the Thirty Years' War. In 1630 his patron married and

[13] *Observations of God's Providence, in the tract of my life,* p. 475.

Wilson was discharged; he studied at Oxford for two years and thought of becoming a minister, but left to serve Robert Rich, Earl of Warwick. Though Wilson was still something of a swashbuckler (see p. 471), he gradually turned towards Puritanism, influenced by the growing militancy of the preachers in the mid-1630s and by the example of his master:

> Now preaching, the true glasse of the soule, discovered more unto mee than I had formerly seene; & good men, by how much they were eclipsed by the bishop's, did privately shine the brighter. And, since I came into this noble family, whether it were age & experience creeping upon mee, which showed me the uncertaintie & instabillity of humane things; or, by a clearer light, receyved from a powerfull ministrie; or, by the example of others, whose lives were fitt patternes to followe; or, by a divine spirit, operating upon all; I knowe not (for it breathes where it pleases) but I found in my selfe a greater affection to good duties. (p. 472)

Wilson travelled to Holland with Warwick in 1637 and served him as steward all through the Civil War; an uncharitable critic might suspect that a snobbish desire to imitate his master was the main cause of his conversion to Puritanism. Sincere or not, Wilson's autobiography lacks the spiritual fervour of either Norwood's or Burton's; it is essentially a record of secular affairs, rather cursorily moralized, and with much emphasis on lucky escapes from death with the aid of God's providence. Wilson came under the influence of Presbyterian preachers, but they do not seem to have inspired in him any very profound spiritual crisis. The main value of his work lies in its record of how a prescription for self-scrutiny could be passed from preacher to audience; though Wilson chose to interpret the prescription much more freely than a truly devout Presbyterian would have done.

For scrupulous conformity to a prescription, no better example could be found than the *Recollections* of Sir William Waller.[14] This work makes a relentlessly circumstantial comparison between Waller's life and that of St. Paul. Waller organizes his experiences under a series of texts from the Pauline scriptures: thus, 'In personall deliverances' describes his release from prison in 1662; 'In deaths oft' lists escapes from falling walls, diseases, and the hazards of war; 'In

---

[14] *Recollections Written by General Sir William Waller*, in *The Poetry of Anna Matilda* (1788). Anna Matilda, an eighteenth-century poetaster, mentions that she has made omissions from the ms. and has also excised some of the 'indelicate' terms from a section describing Waller's sicknesses. The British Museum copy is collated, in longhand, with another ms. in Wadham College, Oxford, 'Sir Wm. Waller's Experiences'.

Besides his spiritual autobiography, Waller wrote a *Vindication of the Character and Conduct of Sir William Waller* (1793), a defence of his actions as Parliamentary General in the Civil War.

journyings oft' equates Waller's escape from the Inquisition at Bologna with Paul's escapes on his apostolic journeys. We find here an extreme example of the Calvinist's tendency to weigh, classify, and compare all the events of his life in order to make it conform to a preconceived pattern. Waller even writes in a Biblical style. Clearly, the development of autobiography towards its modern form was not advanced by such laboured efforts to present one's life as a replica of the life of someone else, no matter how holy or admirable that other person's life might be. The work adds to the evidence that 'Renaissance individualism' will scarcely pass muster as an explanation of much Renaissance autobiography; for Waller—and he is far from alone in this—strives to make his life seem as similar as possible to that of an exemplar, rather than trying to assert the value or singularity of his individual personality.

A last member of this group of Presbyterians, Robert Blair, took Augustine, rather than Paul, as his model.[15] Blair's *Life*, written when he was seventy, was one of the earlier products of the autobiographical urge among Scottish Presbyterians. After a sinful youth, he was awakened to godliness and repentance by means of a book:

> These things [i.e. sins] I easily then digested, till the twenty-third year of my age, when, reading holy Augustine's Confessions, I observed how he in his old age laid to heart his childish faults—such as breaking into orchards and stealing of apples; not for any want, having abundance thereof in his father's house, but lest he should be inferior to his comrades. Though I was free from that temptation and sin, yet I was thereby set to work to ponder the paths of my youth: for sinful self-love is so strong, that though thy Word, O Lord, gives clear warning of the heart's deceitfulness above all things and desperate wickedness, yet we do not believe the same until we feel and find the same actually breaking out in our lives. (p. 6)

Blair was inspired to study Scripture and theology, having taken to heart Augustine's criticism of the education of youth in pagan literature. A few years later he began to keep a diary, 'having heard of the practice of some diligent Christians, who daily took brief notes of the condition of their souls, marking both what failings and escapes they were overtaken with, as also what speed they came and progress they made in the ways of God' (p. 31). The autobiography ends with Blair's departure for America in 1636, in search of 'the liberty of the ministry'; he later returned and became minister of St. Andrews. His narrative deals mainly with external events, though all are made to serve a moral purpose; its main importance lies in the variety of the influences which led to its being written: the *Confessions*, diary-keeping, participation in clerical controversies, and the desire to leave

[15] *The Life of Mr. Robert Blair*, ed. T. McCrie. Written 1663.

67

a memoir for the use of his family and friends all played a part.

Of the same generation and calling as Blair was John Livingstone; his *Life*, a sober and largely historical narrative, need not detain us.[16]

Autobiographers Born after 1600

In this group, more numerous than their predecessors, I have found it convenient to discuss ministers and laymen separately.

(a) *Ministers*. Of eight autobiographies in this group, most incline rather to the chronicle-style of Burton's *Narration* than to Norwood's more searching examination of conscience. Three works, however, are mainly subjective in form: Oliver Heywood's *Autobiography*, George Trosse's *Life*, and Thomas Halyburton's *Memoirs*.[17]

Heywood prefaced his 'Relation of the most considerable passages of my life' with a long examination of the state of his soul; he considered this task a duty for all devout ministers:

> Since the god of the spirits of al flesh hath breathed into me the breath of life and made me a living soul, since he hath put into my soul that godlike reflecting faculty of conscience, since also he hath so frequently called upon me to descent into mine oune hart, to commune therewith, to search and try my wayes, to examine my selfe, to proue my worke, I desire as the lord wil helpe me to deal freely, plainly & ingeniously with my selfe in so weighty & necessary a business as this is that concernes the weal or woe of my immortal soul to al eternity. (p. 133)

The chief purpose of Heywood's self-examination is to find what grounds he has for numbering himself among the elect:

> tis my desire to search & see what obedience & grounds of hope I haue to beleeue & be persuaded that my soul is built upon the rock of ages, that I am within the bond of the covenant ... wch I doe to this end that I may giue diligence to make my calling, and election sure, not in itself, but to my selfe, that I may see whether I haue that wedding garment. (p. 134)

After a 'graceles, christles, & thereby hopeles & helples' childhood Heywood first experienced the joys and reassurance of grace, and so intensely that only the language of eroticism seemed adequate to describe it: 'After the lord jesus had been standing at the door of my

[16] *A Brief Historical Relation of the Life of John Livingstone*. Written c. 1670.

[17] *The Rev. Oliver Heywood, B.A. 1630-1702; his Autobiography, Diaries, Anecdote and Event Books*, ed. J. Horsfall Turner, 3 vols.; the autobiography is in vol. 1, pp. 133-202. *The Life Of the Reverend Mr. Geo. Trosse, Late Minister of the Gospel In The City of Exon ... Written by Himself. Memoirs of the Rev. Thomas Halyburton*. Written 1700.

hart & knocking, at last he put his finger in at the hole of the doore, and by his spirit removed the great barre of my unwillingnes & unbeleefe, and he sweetly moved my hart to close with him.'[18] This intuition of a mystical, sexual union with Christ was the obverse of his struggle to remain chaste by restraining his 'darling and dalilah lusts . . . original lusts, natural concupiscence, this is the spring, head, and root of al my corruptions' (p. 144). His scruples even extended to the conjugal bed: 'I am often jealous lest my conjugal loue should degenerate into or be mixed too much with carnal and sensual delight.'[19] We cannot now tell, however, whether he was a monster of lust or merely inordinately scrupulous in sexual matters; the latter alternative is far more likely.

After the introductory review of the state of his soul, Heywood begins his chronological 'Relation . . . of my life'. The four reasons he gives for composing this narrative are typical of Calvinist spiritual autobiographers: to clear his conscience of past misdeeds; 'to inferre a good caution from the by-past for the remaining part of my life'; 'to review by-past providences as a motiue to thankfulness'; 'to compare my past and present state and obserue my proficiency in christianity, to see whether I be better this year than the last' (p. 151). From this justification of his project he turns again to speak, even more vehemently, of the wickedness of 'this poore miserable creature', young Oliver Heywood. Self-denunciations of this kind are so common in spiritual autobiographies of the period that Heywood's version may serve to represent a whole class of similar statements:

> But tho my parents were godly yet my birth and my nativity was in sin, and so was my conception, for they were instruments to bring me into the world not as saints but as man and woman . . . in wch respect my father was an Amorite and mother an Hittite (ezek. 16, 3) thereby I am by nature a child of wrath, a limb of satan, exposed to shame and ruine despoiled of gods image, having satans superscription, and guilt with propensity to sin, and contrareity to good incorpurated in my primitiue constitution; and that too too fruitful root begun to sprout in infancy, I cannot remember the time or age, state or place wherein I was free from sin or perpetating thereof. . . . I remember how proud I was of any little coveted excellency, how fond I was of trifles, how backward to good exercises, how forward to sinful practices, how tractable to follow bad examples . . . the time was when with children in playing I vented my selfe in many barbarous ways, yea undoubted

[18] p. 136. Cf. Song of Solomon, v, 4, 5.
[19] p. 147. Distrust of uxoriousness was not characteristic solely of medieval Catholicism—'Marriage contracted in the Lord ought to exhibit measure and modesty—not run to the extreme of wantonness. This excess Ambrose censured gravely, but not undeservedly, when he described the man who shows no modesty or comeliness in conjugal intercourse, as committing adultery with his wife.' *Institutes*, II, viii, 44.

oathes . . . so foolish was I and ignorant even as a beast before god, and since our first parents aspired to be as gods we all became as beasts that perish,—when I was a child I spake as a child, yea rather like a devil incarnate, oh the desperate wickednes of my deceitful hart. (pp. 153-4)

Heywood proceeds to expatiate on his special weakness, a 'natura constitution exceedingly inclined to lust'; however, he absolves God of blame for creating him thus, 'my owne corrupt hart is the principal cause, it was an unadvised act in Origen to dismember himself, to avoid fornication' (p. 154).

Heywood's childhood was of such signal depravity that after it almost any other experience would be an anti-climax; and the story of his studies at Trinity College, Cambridge, of his ministry in Lancashire and his ejection from it by the Act of Conformity (1662) is much less spirited than the earlier part of his autobiography. This falling-off in intensity from youth to maturity is a common feature of spiritual autobiographies. The crisis of religious belief and anxiety over election usually comes between the ages of ten to twenty-five, after which the soul endures less torment and uncertainty; the excitement of the early crisis cannot be maintained indefinitely, external events gradually take on more importance, the presence of both God and the Devil makes itself felt less vividly. In Heywood's autobiography, his incoherent style and lack of a sense of structure contribute to the relapse into tediousness which occurs as soon as his passion is somewhat abated. The main value of his work lies in the opportunity it gives us to observe directly, and in detail, how the mind of a Presbyterian zealot deals with his religious obsessions; but a relatively short glimpse would be enough for most readers.

The *Life* of George Trosse was first published with his funeral sermon, for which he had chosen the text himself: 'This is a faithful saying, and worthy of all acceptation, that Christ Jesus came into the world to save sinners, of whom I am chief.'[20] J.H., the preacher, notes that Trosse made this choice because 'in a very great measure St. Paul's Case was his' (*Sermon*, p. 7). These claims prepare us for another tiresome litany of self-accusation; but Trosse was both a better writer and a man of wider experience than the usual Calvinist breast-beater. He drew on ample resources of emotionalism and bizarre incident to further the avowed purpose of his narrative: 'For the terrifying of Presumptuous and Secure Sinners, for the encouraging and perswading of such as are sensible, and humble, to make a Return to GOD thro' CHRIST' (sig. a2). Trosse had been in youth 'a violent enemy to Puritans', eager for travel and luxury. At the age

---

[20] I Tim. i, 15. This detail comes from the author of *The Sermon preach'd at his Funeral*, which is bound with the *Life* but has separate pagination.

of fifteen he was able to make a voyage to Brittany, where he arrived 'a profane Atheist, a rooted Enemy to the Power and Profession of real Godliness' (p. 5). From then on he progressed steadily in wickedness; his narrative is distinguished for the gusto and rhetorical art devouted to recording his sinful career. Drunkenness and lechery are the predominant vices in his self-indictment (though he claims to have broken all ten commandments), and we find further evidence of the role of masturbation in creating anxiety and fear of hell among scrupulous young men: 'a lewd Fellow-Servant led me to practise a Sin, which too many Young Men are guilty of, and look upon it as harmless; tho' GOD struck Onan dead in the Place for it' (p. 19). Trosse's abominations brought on a spiritual crisis, in which strange voices gave him orders and tempted him to 'Curse God and die' (p. 50). Serious and recurrent attacks of lunacy tormented him until, at about twenty-six, he regained full sanity and went to study at Oxford for seven years. For the rest of his life he was a nonconformist minister in Exeter. The general course of Trosse's spiritual development scarcely differs from that of dozens of other Calvinist autobiographers; yet we feel that he gives us more of his essential self than they, and that his descent into madness was a response to an authentic and personal horror of sin.

With the *Memoirs* of Thomas Halyburton (b. 1674) we return to a more standardized anguish. Halyburton was a Scot who for the last two years of his life was Professor of Divinity at St. Andrews. His memoirs cover the first twenty-six years of his life; he summarizes their content as the 'rise, progress, interruptions, revivals, and issues of the Lord's strivings with me' (p. xiv). Since the only noteworthy feature of the memoirs is their increased soberness when measured against earlier Presbyterian autobiographies, a paragraph on the same theme as one by Heywood (quoted above, p. 69) should give sufficient idea of the direction in which spiritual autobiography was evolving:

> I came into this world, not only under the guilt of that offence, whereby many, nay, 'all were made sinners', and on account of which 'judgement passed upon all men to condemnation'; but, moreover, I brought with me a nature wholly corrupted, a heart 'wholly set in me to do evil'. Of this the testimony of God in his word satisfies me. And in this I am strongly confirmed by undoubted experience, which fully convinces me, that from the morning of my days, while under the advantage of Gospell light, the inspection of godly parents, and not yet corrupted by custom, the imaginations of my heart, and the tenor of my life, were 'evil, only evil, and that continually'. (p. 19)

Halyburton may convince himself that he was a depraved child; but he scarcely convinces us.

F   71

To complete this group of ministers, six men remain to be considered, though the last three may be dismissed in a footnote: Richard Baxter, Adam Martindale, Henry Newcome, John Shawe, Elias Pledger, and James Fraser of Brea.[21]

Baxter's autobiography occupies a middle ground between Anglican *res gestae* and the more self-analytical works of such militant Presbyterians as Heywood. It was written between 1665 and 1685 in three parts, of which the first, having in it more of his life and less of his times, is the most unified and interesting. His approach throughout is mainly historical: he tells the story of his life in a style typical of the *res gestae* tradition, and links his career to the major events of contemporary history. But he adds to the first part a penetrating self-analysis which traces his intellectual development, and the changes in his habits, since youth. This analysis is sober and objective; it stands outside the confessional tradition, and is much more akin to Mill's autobiography than to Augustine's. Baxter rejects outright the kind of emotional soul-searching indulged in by such men as Norwood or Heywood:

> And for any more particular account of heart-occurrences, and God's operations on me, I think it somewhat unsavoury to recite them, seeing God's dealings are much what the same with all his servants in the main, and the points wherein he varieth are usually so small that I think not such fit to be repeated. Nor have I anything extraordinary to glory in which is not common to the rest of my brethren, who have the same spirit and are servants of the same Lord. (p. 103)

Just as he dissociated himself from the radicals of the Parliamentary cause on doctrinal questions, so Baxter held himself aloof from their practice of proclaiming their dealings with God to the world at large.

Baxter uses a sandwich-construction for the first part of his autobiography. The personal analysis is concentrated at the beginning,

---

[21] Baxter, *Narrative of the most memorable passages of his Life and Times* in *Reliquiae Baxterianae* (1696); I have quoted from the more readily available abridged edition by J. M. Lloyd Thomas, *The Autobiography of Richard Baxter*.

Shawe's *Memoirs* were written for the son of his old age, 'a few words that may give you some knowledge of me, and of the lineage whence you are descended . . . and also some directions for the better ordering your life and affairs thro' your pilgrimage here below' (pp. 121-2). What follows is an entirely tedious chronicle of personal and historical events.

The only interest of Pledger's conversion-narrative (still in manuscript) comes at the beginning, where we can look over his shoulder and see him hesitating between use of an impersonal third-person narrative and the direct 'I': 'Elias Pledger was born in that fatal year 1665 in ye month of July in ye parish of little Baddon in ye County of Essex. I ['he' scratched out in ms.] was born of godly parents; my father being a minister of the presbiterian perswasion. . . .'

Fraser's *Memoirs* are unimportant; for a summary of them see D. Hendrichs, *Geschichte der englischen Autobiographie von Chaucer bis Milton*, p. 29.

and in a concluding section which contrasts his views at fifty with those of his 'unriper times'. The first analysis, of his youth, is in confessional form, complete with a list of sins from apple-stealing to 'love of romances, fables and old tales' (p. 5); the later analysis deals with his mature convictions in a more tolerant, though still humble, mood. Between these two personal sections Baxter gives a rather dry narration of the chief events of his life from 1633, when he was eighteen, to 1660. He stresses the effect on his life of the Civil War, and often goes out of his way to discuss the war in a general rather than a personal context; we remember that he called his work a narrative of his life and *times*. This concern with historical events is accompanied (as is common in seventeenth-century autobiographies) by a tendency to slip into chronicle style, with a correspondingly superficial treatment of his personal motives and feelings. His description of his mother's death suggests how horrible her last illness must have been to her sickly and highly-strung son; yet he leaves almost everything to our imagination: 'When I came home from London I found my mother in extremity of pain, and spent that winter in the hearing of her heart-piercing groans (shut up in the great snow which many that went abroad did perish in) till on May the 10th she died' (p. 14). The death of Cromwell, by contrast, moves Baxter to write a long character of him, and survey of his career; the disproportion in Baxter's accounts of the two deaths is typical of the historical, rather than personal, emphasis in the middle section of part one. Contemporary history becomes an even more dominant concern in parts two and three; for the student of autobiography, therefore, the analytical passages of part one deserve most attention.

The theme of the opening section of part one is the state of Baxter's soul in youth; of the conclusion, 'the alterations of my soul, since my younger years' (p. 128). He treats his intellectual development as part of this soul-history, since his studies were mainly in divinity. When young he was an eager student of logic and metaphysics, but he later wearied of the finer points of controversial theology, and favoured a more devotional kind of Christianity. This shift of interest is hinted at in the opening section, and explained fully in the conclusion. Here is the first account of his student days:

> And these [logic and metaphysics] had my labour and delight, which occasioned me (perhaps too soon) to plunge myself very early into the study of controversies, and to read all the Schoolmen I could get; for next practical divinity, no books so suited with my disposition as Aquinas, Scotus, Durandus, Ockam and their disciples; because I thought they narrowly searched after truth and brought things out of the darkness of confusion; for I could never from my first studies endure confusion. (pp. 9-10)

At this point Baxter qualifies his love of the Scholastics only mildly and incidentally, so that he communicates vividly to the reader his youthful enthusiasm for theological niceties. In autobiographies such as Heywood's, by contrast, one gets no sense of how the author really enjoyed his childish occupations because they are so rigidly condemned by the censorious adult Calvinist. Baxter, more open-minded, states his mature judgement without suppressing or unfairly distorting his earlier views:

> In my youth I was quickly past my fundamentals and was running up into a multitude of controversies, and greatly delighted with metaphysical and scholastic writings. . . . But the elder I grew the smaller stress I laid upon these controversies and curiosities (though still my intellect abhorreth confusion), as finding far greater uncertainties in them than I at first discerned and finding less usefulness comparatively, even where there is the greatest certainty. And now it is the fundamental doctrines of the Catechism which I highliest value and daily think of, and find most useful to myself and others. . . . And as I can speak and write of them over and over again, so I had rather read or hear of them than of any of the school niceties which once so much pleased me. (p. 108)

Baxter's confession of his childhood sins, like his discussion of his taste for the Schoolmen, is stated early in the autobiography and returned to later, with a rather different emphasis. The first mention is stern and censorious:

> But though my conscience would trouble me when I sinned, yet divers sins I was addicted to, and oft committed against my conscience; which for the warning of others I will confess here to my shame.
> 1. I was much addicted, when I feared correction, to lie, that I might scape.
> 2. I was much addicted to the excessive gluttonous eating of apples and pears; which I think laid the foundation of that imbecility and flatulency of my stomach which caused the bodily calamities of my life.
> 3. To this end, and to concur with naughty boys that gloried in evil, I have oft gone into other men's orchards and stolen their fruit, when I had enough at home. (p. 5)

The list continues with five other minor transgressions. In the later version, Baxter takes a more mature view of his faults, and stresses sins of omission rather than sins of commission:

> In my younger years my trouble for sin was most about my actual failings in thought, word or action (except hardness of heart, of which more anon); but now I am much more troubled for inward defects and omission or want of the vital duties or graces in the soul. . . . Hereto-

fore I placed much of my religion in tenderness of heart, and grieving for sin, and penitential tears; and less of it in the love of God, and studying his love and goodness, and in his joyful praises, than now I do. (p. 112)

Here again, both youth and age are treated in terms of their particular concerns, and we are shown the development and change of Baxter's convictions as he grows older; he does not deny the evil of his childhood sins, but neither does he care to wallow in them forty years after the event, as many other autobiographers do.

Baxter concludes his self-analysis with an exposition of his motives for writing his autobiography. He begins with an apologia: 'and having transcribed thus much of a life which God hath read, and conscience hath read and must further read, I humbly lament it, and beg pardon of it, as sinful and too unequal and unprofitable. And I warn the reader to amend that in his own which he findeth to have been amiss in mine' (p. 129). He apologizes for both past and future: he makes no radical distinctions between particular periods of his life (unlike most 'twice-born' spiritual autobiographers), but considers himself always a struggling and fallible Christian. The chief value of the autobiography, he states, is its advertisement of God's glory: 'But what I have recorded hath been especially to perform my vows and declare his praise to all generations, who hath filled up my days with his unvaluable favours, and bound me to bless his name for ever' (p. 129). He was also moved by the desire to tell the truth about himself, and the hope 'that young Christians may be warned by the mistakes and failings of my unriper times, to learn in patience . . . and to reverence ripe experienced age' (p. 129).

The great lesson which Baxter felt he had learned by hard experience was the need for charity and forbearingness in doctrinal disputes; he applied the lesson partly by preaching concord to all who would listen, and partly by setting himself above the battle except when basic principles were at stake. The style and form of his autobiography reflect the balance and moderation of his thought, which strove for inclusiveness and for the widest possible sympathy; he was a righteous man, but wholly without fanaticism. Probably the chief merit of his work is the deep understanding of the processes of intellectual and spiritual development which it reveals; Baxter had a better sense of how his mind had evolved than all but a very few British autobiographers of his time, and he shows a quite unusual subtlety in analysing the experiences which led him to his final position of charity and ecumenical tolerance. Moreover, in maturity he achieved a humaneness and integrity in his style of thought which were shared, in a violent age, by only a small minority of enlightened men. His own words may best sum up his virtues:

And therefore I am less for a disputing way than ever, believing that it tempteth men to bend their wits, to defend their errors and oppose the truth, and hindereth usually their information. And the servant of the Lord must not strive, but be gentle to all men, etc. Therefore I am most in judgement for a learning or a teaching way of converse. In all companies I will be glad either to hear those speak that can teach me, or to be heard of those that have need to learn. (pp. 131-2)

The *Life of Adam Martindale* introduces a much less attractive personality than Baxter's.[22] Martindale was the type of minister who found it hard to distinguish between his own convictions and the operation of God's special providence. An elder sister of his, for example, went away to London against her parents' will, and on her return caught a fatal case of smallpox; even for a Lancashire Calvinist Martindale's comments seem unduly sanctimonious:

Whereas my mother who, not withstanding her beautie, was very humble, lay with a cleare and seemingly smiling countenance after she was dead, as if she had beene still alive; my sister that was too proud of hers became extremely ugly before she died, her face being sadly discoloured, and so swelled that scarce any forme of a visage was discernible. (p. 18)

He was probably not the most popular boy at school, either, which was 'almost two miles from my father's house, a great way for a little fat short legged lad (as I was) to travell twice a day; yet I went it cheerfully (provided I might get out soone enough to be there betimes), such was my innate love to learning; nor was that any great thankes to me, it came so easily' (p. 11). Incidentally, his lack of censoriousness towards his childhood behaviour is unusual for a Presbyterian.

Martindale uses the *res gestae* form, and works through his life soberly and systematically; each chapter ends with 'observations upon some passages in the foregoing chapter', a collection of trite and moralistic proverbs which he considers relevant to the events of the chapter. He is not much given to expressions of zeal: we hear of few 'soul-occurrences', and relatively little about his awakening to 'the desperatenesse and damnablenesse of a naturall estate' (p. 36). His change from the profession of school-teacher to that of minister seems to have been motivated as much by practical as by spiritual reasons (pp. 55-60). Lacking the imprint of either literary talent or a strong character, the *Life* has only a residual value as social history.

Henry Newcome, the last of this group of ministers, was both a Presbyterian and a staunch royalist; his autobiography reflects this

---

[22] Ed. Rev. Richard Parkinson, in *Remains Historical and Literary*, Chetham Soc., vol. IV.

duality by drawing on both the Anglican tradition of *res gestae* and the Puritan habit of diary-keeping.[23] As befits a Cambridge graduate and parson's son, he begins his autobiography by citing some learned and respectable precedents for such an enterprise:

> Junius, that eminent divine, hath left his own life writ by himself, which he thus begins: 'Miserationes Domini narrabo quum rationes narrabo miserae vitae meae; ut glorificetur Dominus in me qui fecit me. De me dicam, Domine, coram te; ac potius de te dicam, Domine, agente in me; et enuntiabo veritatem quam singulari gubernatione tua voluisti explicatam in me pro misericordia infinita tua . . .' And reverend and eminent Bishop Hall hath left some choice memorials of his own life, of which he says, 'What I have done is worthy of nothing but silence and forgetfulness, but what God hath done for me is worthy of everlasting and thankful memory. . . .' And having had some account of things all along from my younger years, and having now a vacancy from my public employment, I thought it might not be amiss to contract and methodize some of those accounts into this entire narrative, which I design especially to the use of my children after me. (pp. 1-2)

The 'accounts' referred to here are the entries in Newcome's diary, which he had begun to keep at Cambridge when he was nineteen. In his systematic way, he records also the circumstances under which he began the diary:

> In the year 1646, when I had been two years at Cambridge, upon some working on my soul, (in that way that then, in the ignorance and heat of youthfulness, I was capable of) I was induced to begin a diary. It was chiefly begun upon the occasion of hearing that Dr. Ward, (the late Master of Sydney, and Margaret professor in Cambridge) had left a diary of his life in his study, from his being sixteen years of age. I thought it was a very brave thing to have such a thing left from so early a time of his life, and so set upon it. It is in my hands; and how strangely I took pains to set down my sins every day, and usually still the same, I have oft reflected upon. (p. 14)

Newcome's work provides us with useful evidence of how the various traditions of religious autobiography and diary-keeping were actually becoming known to, and beginning to influence, the pious intellectuals of the universities. Unfortunately, after rather few pages of his autobiography Newcome relapses into diary form and goes on to write a completely unimaginative and tedious chronicle of his pastoral affairs. But his work does show that by about the middle of the seventeenth century a rudimentary autobiographical tradition was beginning to be established in Britain.

[23] *The Autobiography of Henry Newcome, M.A.*, ed. R. Parkinson, in *Remains Historical and Literary*, Chetham Soc., vol. XXVI.

(b) *Presbyterian Laymen.* Four autobiographers conclude this chapter: Walter Pringle (b. 1625), Joseph Lister (b. 1627), Gervase Disney (b. 1641), and George Brysson.[24] They made no major contributions to autobiographical tradition, and only Disney's life was published before the nineteenth century; but they do show that there was some scope for lay autobiography within the Presbyterian church, in contrast to the dearth of religious autobiographies by Catholic and Anglican laymen.

Pringle's *Memoirs,* in which he both confesses his own sins and exhorts others to avoid them, were entitled by him 'Some few of the free mercies of God to me, who am most unworthy, and my will to my children; left to them under mine own hand' (p. 1). Like Martindale, he alternates factual and moralizing passages; but whereas Martindale provides some ten parts of fact to one of moralizing, with Pringle the ratio is reversed. His fondness for lengthy exegesis of his deeds may be in part due to the circumstance that his audience is one which needs to be carefully instructed, viz., his own children:

> Since my God gave me children, it hath been much upon my mind to record, for their use, the wonderful goodness of God to me; which I have delayed to do for some years. . . . However, I will labour as the Lord (without whom I can do no good) shall give it me, to stir up and exhort my children to flee from the wrath which is coming upon a lost world, and to lay hold on the offered salvation. (p. 1)

Both religious and secular autobiographers of the seventeenth century seem to display an unusually strong interest in their ancestors and their posterity, even in an age when the family was a more dominant social unit than it is now. Religious autobiographers, however, tend to pass briefly over their family origins and to concentrate on the instruction of their children, with Calvinist autobiographers placing particular emphasis on the inculcation of godly habits in the younger generation.

Pringle's spiritual development recapitulates, without great originality or stylistic grace, the Pauline–Calvinist archetype. He fails to convince us that we should take his wickedness at his own valuation: 'In the year 1639, I was at Leith school: then did youthful lusts and corruptions begin to prevail over me, being stronger in me than the grace of God. . . . I confess that for ten years together, I was the chief of sinners' (p. 6). We scarcely believe that he was the 'chief of sinners' when there were so many other rival claimants to the title, including John Bunyan, Richard Norwood, Oliver Cromwell, and Sarah

---

[24] *The Memoirs of Walter Pringle,* ed. Walter Wood. *The Autobiography of Joseph Lister,* ed. T. Wright. *Some Remarkable Passages in the Holy Life and Death of Gervase Disney. Memoirs of Mr. William Veitch and George Brysson,* ed. T. McCrie. Pringle and Brysson were Scots.

Wight—who achieved that bad eminence at the age of twelve.[25] The precise dating and explicit motivation of Pringle's *Memoirs* give them some significance for documenting the evolution of Presbyterian (and also of Scottish) autobiography; but intrinsically they are dull and uninspired.

In the autobiographies of Joseph Lister and Gervase Disney we observe English Calvinism in the process of losing its fire and evolving into the milder faith of Defoe and Richardson. Lister, who wrote his autobiography in extreme old age,[26] had been brought up in a fanatically Puritan and anti-Royalist home, under a mother who was a severe disciplinarian. Of course, his evil ways deserved stern correction, even at the age of nine: 'O how near was I to death at this time! and had I died then, surely I had gone down to the pit' (p. 4). He finally convinced himself, however, that he was not marked for eternal torment: 'at last God was pleased to step in with light, and love, and clear satisfaction' (p. 29). Having successfully weathered this spiritual crisis, Lister went off to London to make his fortune, but after three years he returned to his native Yorkshire and became a farmer. He married, had two sons who became Nonconformist ministers, and prospered in his worldly affairs. The quotations above may suggest that Lister was another conventionally excessive breast-beater; this would be inaccurate, for in most of his autobiography he is drier and more practical than men like Heywood and Pringle. We can observe the eighteenth-century outlook creeping in as we mark the transition from the ranting Puritanism of Lister's parents to his own preoccupation with good husbandry in the later part of his life.

Gervase Disney was of a similar stamp to Lister. His *Life*, which was published in 1692 (a year after his death), mingles Calvinist spiritual rhetoric with descriptions of worldly prosperity. In the sub-title, conventional rhetoric previals:

> Some Passages most remarkable in the whole Course of my Life, collected, taken, and methodised, by my own Hand, out of my Diary (for the most part); though I have not omitted other Things, as they have occur'd to Memory.
>
> In which I have discovered my darke Side, in the Days of my Unregeneracy; as also my brighter Side, after it pleas'd the Lord to touch my Heart with a Sense of Sin, to awaken my Conscience, to shew me my undone and lost Condition by Nature, and my need of a Saviour. (sig. Br.)

At the beginning of the work Disney stresses again the warfare between God and the Devil for his soul:

---

[25] See Tindall, *John Bunyan*, p. 37.
[26] He was eighty-one, and died soon after (1709).

> I have endeavoured as Impartially to view my dark Side, as Bright;
> and both for these Reasons: By the former, I discover the miserable
> Corruption of my wretched Nature, the Wiles and Subtilties of a busy
> Devil, who goes about like a roaring Lion, seeking whom he may
> devour. By the latter, I would discover the wonderful Free Grace of
> God to me, who was one of the worst and greatest of Sinners, in
> bringing me from under Satan's Slavery and Dominion. (p. 11)

However, this high-pitched statement of purpose gives way to a
plodding account of Disney's parents and siblings. We then pass on
to his youth, which is marked by the usual sins: he is an idle
apprentice who steals from the till and frequents pot-houses and
brothels (though he preserves his chastity none the less). Sermons
begin the 'Works of Grace' in his soul, though it is not until his
marriage, at the age of thirty, that he settles down on the land to
practice a devout Nonconformism and enjoy a steadily increasing
income. In narrating these events, Disney displays no extraordinary
zeal. His spiritual development follows the usual course of sin and
regeneration, but he intersperses the account with discussions of more
worldly topics—clearly, he was not obsessed with religion to the
exclusion of the things that are Caesar's. Whatever his own self-
valuation, we find it hard to believe that Disney was either a great
saint or a great sinner; rather, he exemplifies the increased practicality
and soberness of the post-Civil War generations of British Nonconformists, the heirs of a once-militant Puritanism. Like Pringle,
Disney left his autobiography as a legacy of good advice to his family:
the prudent husbandman transmitted to posterity not just his
financial capital, but his spiritual also.

George Brysson practised a similar economy with his experiences
of the work of grace:

> Being now of a good old age, and near to eternity, I thought it my
> duty to leave some remarks of God's providence towards me, in the
> course of my pilgrimage, which I think may be useful to my children,
> and other Christian friends who may have occasion to read the same,
> to let them know how kind the Lord hath been to me in my pilgrimage
> state here. (p. 267)

Brysson was a servant by profession, and also a frequenter of con-
venticles after 1674, when they were forbidden. His account of his
religious experiences is undistinguished; the most interesting section
of his memoirs tells of his service with the Duke of Argyle's expedition
of 1685, and subsequent flight in the heather. After his escape from
the redcoats Brysson married, had nine children, and lived well into
the new century—a typically quiet and productive end for our last
Presbyterian autobiographer.

VI

The Autobiographers of the Sects

MOST OF the sectarian autobiographers were Baptists or Quakers, though a few Ranters, Muggletonians, and other eccentrics have bequeathed us the stories of their careers (which were usually lively ones). Though particular sects developed rigid autobiographical conventions, we find a wide range of works overall, extending from the half-insane rhapsody of Joseph Salmon to the restrained and literate reminiscences of the rich merchant William Kiffin.

Above all, the sectaries were prolific writers of every kind of controversy and testimony, autobiography included. The great outburst of autobiographies among them from about 1648 on formed part of an extraordinary welling-up of popular expression, a nation-wide extension and democratization of spiritual fellowship. This extension of the market for spiritual experience was made possible by the breakdown of government control of the press after 1642; even the poorest citizens were able to get their works into print.[1] Men like Bunyan could now, through print, communicate with tens of thousands of men where they had formerly been limited by the carrying-power of their own voices. In some degree, the increase of autobiographies by 'mechanick preachers' meant only that personal statements of religious experience which had before been delivered orally to a congregation could now, with the aid of technology, be disseminated among a large and dispersed reading public. However, a new impetus must also have been at work, for the majority of our present group of autobiographers belonged to sects which were either weak or non-existent before 1642; during and after the Civil War these sects engaged in vigorous propagandizing and seized on cheap printing as an effective means of spreading their beliefs. Autobiography had a direct and truthful quality which could be relied on to make a strong appeal to the unconverted.

[1] The twenty thousand Thomason Tracts (1641-60) bear witness to the enormous increase in pamphleteering associated with the Civil War and its aftermath. The Licensing Act of 1643 attempted to censor and control the press, but it was easily evaded.

Sectarian autobiography reached a point of transition in 1660. In the decades before this date uninhibited zealots such as Salmon, Arise Evans, and Richard Coppin wrote, and immediately published, their autobiographies; the genre of 'enthusiast' autobiography was established in these years. After 1660 some sects dwindled and died, and all were harassed by the government. Their members produced autobiographies less frequently (except for the Quakers), and it became more common for them to be published only after their authors' deaths. The sectaries also became considerably less militant and eccentric than they had been under the Commonwealth. A wide gap had once divided the Presbyterians from the mass of enthusiast, socially radical sectaries; but towards the end of the century this distinction became blurred, partly because the Clarendon Code (1661-65) placed all nonconformists in the same predicament, and partly because the lunatic or anarchist fringe of the sects was no longer a significant force. To clarify broad trends in sectarian autobiography, this chapter will first discuss the genre to 1660, and then for the period 1661-1700; finally the Quakers, a distinct and largely autonomous group, will be discussed separately.

Sectarian Autobiography to 1660

The execution of Charles I in January 1649 marked the beginning of a period of broadly-diffused religious excitement which was even more intense than that of previous years. This excitement was too powerful and too undisciplined to be fully contained within the institutional limits of Presbyterianism. Innumerable zealots took to the streets and market-places; there they mounted their tubs, each proclaiming his own revelation and doctrine. The more literate among them called on the printers to aid the dissemination of the spiritual experiences which had been granted them. A vast pamphlet literature thus came into existence between 1649 and 1660, most of it more or less directly personal in tone—though coherent autobiographies were relatively few.

Probably the first true autobiography to be published by an 'enthusiast' preacher was Arise Evans's *An Eccho to the Voice from Heaven*, which appeared in 1652. Evans was in his forties when his autobiography was written, and he had been advertising himself as a prophet since 1633, without much success. In 1652 he had first published *A Voice from Heaven*, to which certain critics had objected: 'what grounds have ye to open the Scripture thus? and what Calling had you to declare such things unto the World?'[2] Evans replied to this attack on his credentials with *An Eccho*; invoking St. Paul's self-

[2] *An Eccho*, 'To the Reader', seventh objection.

defence in Acts xxii and xxvii, he proclaimed his intention to match Paul's apologia with his own 'Narration of the Life, Calling, and Visions of Arise Evans'. However, the opening of the 'Narration' suggests that Evans may have identified with an even more exalted model than Paul:

> And because these Lines may go over all the earth, I am a Man that is a Brittain by Nation, born in a part of it, now called Wales, at the County of Merionith, in the Parish of Llangluin, a mile from the Bearmouth: being Arise the son of Evan the son of Arise the son of Owen the son of Arise the son of Evan the son of David the son of Arise the son of Griffith the son of the Red Lion the son of the Ren. (pp. 1-2)

Evans was a precocious child, 'and because I was so young and so active in learning, all concluded that God had designed me for some great work' (p. 2). He soon came to share this faith in his messianic powers, and his faith was strengthened when, at the age of fourteen, he prayed so fervently that 'I was lifted above the earth and carried up a space in the clouds as I went on my way' (p. 8). He became a successful tailor in London, but after a few years lost his wealth and passed through a spiritual crisis. God appeared to him in a dream and told him to go to his book, which he opened at Ephes. v, 14: 'Awake thou that sleepest, and arise from the dead, and Christ shall give thee light' (pp. 12-13). Evans took this revelation as a sign that he should become a preacher and expositor of scripture. One of his first acts in this new capacity was to write to Charles I to warn of the danger to his kingdom from Puritans and Papists; when the letter was not answered, he went to the court at Greenwich to expound his visions:

> and when I came into the Hall among the guard, I asked where the King was, and they looked upon me, seeing me, having my Bible under my arm, said, what will you do with the King, I told them that I had a message from God unto him, then they laughed, saying, when did God speak unto you? (p. 25)

Needless to say, this second approach was no more successful than the letter had been. Evans then went out into the countryside to spread his message, but on his return his family had him shut up as a lunatic. After three days they relented and let him go; but the Anabaptists, against whom he had preached, managed to get him put away for three years in Bridewell (1635-38). The rest of his autobiography is mainly an exposition of his dreams, visions, and prophecies.

Despite his checkered career and strange ideas, Evans' autobiography does not read like the work of a lunatic. His style is usually clear, and his opinions on matters unrelated to his obsessions are reasonable. He was a visionary rather than an out-and-out madman;

his kind of megalomaniac temperament can be met with quite frequently among sectaries, whether autobiographers or not. In fact, it
would scarcely be an exaggeration to say that the proliferation of
autobiographical pamphlets between 1650 and 1660 can be attributed
to the endemic megalomania of itinerant preachers and prophets. A
typical case of this aberration can be seen in the Ranter Joseph
Salmon, a preacher with a certain gift for sublime utterance, who
'arose and (as it were) shooke of my night dresses, and appeared to
my selfe, like the sunn, dawning out its refulgent splendor, from
behind the darke canopies of the earth'.[3] Salmon's *Heights in Depths*,
from which this episode is taken, is a rather incoherent spiritual autobiography, similar in content to his fellow-Ranter James Bauthumley's *The Light and Dark Side of God* (1650). Abiezer Coppe and
George Foster wrote personal testaments (though not full autobiographies) which are even more extraordinary. Coppe was a Ranter
and Leveller, whose *Fiery Flying Roll* (1649) and *A Second Fiery
Flying Roule* (1649) were burnt by the hangman; they are eloquent
ravings, mixed with some acute social criticism.[4] George Foster's call
to action was *The Sounding of the Last Trumpet* (1650), in which he
described his apocalyptic visions and conversations with God. He
was clearly mad. Later autobiographies by the sectaries were pitched
somewhat lower than the unbridled effusions of 1649-52.

Richard Coppin's *Truth's Testimony* (1655) has already been quoted
(p. 33 above) in illustration of the exemplary, sermonizing tone which
many sectaries adopted in their autobiographies. The work is mainly
a controversial tract, containing 'The Authors Call and Conversion
to the truth, his practice in it, his publishing of it, and his several
Tryals for the same' (sub-title). He went from the Church of England
to Presbyterianism, then Anabaptism, and finally to his own religion
of untrammelled personal inspiration and prophesying—a spiritual
progress which was repeated, though with more verve and imagination, by Lawrence Clarkson (orClaxton).

Clarkson's life epitomizes the experience of a whole generation of
seekers after true religion. He tells his story in *The Lost Sheep Found*
(1660), sub-titled 'The Prodigal returned to his Fathers house, after
many a sad and weary journey through many Religious Countreys. . . .
As all along every Church or Dispensation may read in his Travels,
their Portion after this Life. Written by Laur. Claxton the onely true
converted Messenger of Christ Jesus, Creator of Heaven and Earth.'
As a fifteen-year-old boy (1630) in Preston, Clarkson, who had been
brought up in the Church of England, began going to hear Puritan

---

[3] *Heights in Depths and Depths in Heights* (1651), p. 9; quoted in Tindall, p. 28.
[4] Coppe later recanted, and published *Copps Return to the Wayes of Truth . . .
and the Wings of the Fiery Flying Roll Clipt* (1651).

preachers 'who when they came, would thunder against Superstition, and sharply reprove Sin, and prophaning the Lords-day; which to hear, tears would run down my cheeks for joy' (p. 4). He turned Presbyterian and moved to London; but the campaign against the Scots (1639) brought disturbing consequences—'this I observed, that as the Presbyterians got power, so their pride and cruelty increased against such as was contrary to them, so that | Thirdly I left them, and travelled to the Church of the Independents; for this I observed as wars increased, so variety of Judgements increased' (p. 8). He was soon dissatisfied with the Independents in turn, and became an itinerant Antinomian preacher. Before long, Anabaptism proved more attractive and Clarkson was dipped in the moat of the Tower of London; however, he and his new wife were arrested for baptizing adults indiscriminately (pp. 12-13). At his arraignment, where he encountered the accusations of immorality commonly laid to the charge of Dippers, he defended himself with some skill:

> Then said Sir John Rowse, we are informed you dipped six Sisters one night naked. [Clarkson] That is nothing to me what you are informed, for I never did such a thing; [Judge] Nay further, it is reported, that which of them you liked best, you lay with her in the water? [Clarkson] Surely your experience teacheth you the contrary, that nature hath small desire to copulation in water, at which they laughed; But, said I, you have more cause to weep for the unclean thoughts of your heart.[5]

Despite his forensic talents, Clarkson was sent to jail with his wife. On his release he saw 'the vanity of the Baptists' and entered 'the society of those people called Seekers, who worshipped God onely by prayer and preaching' (p. 19). He became a travelling evangelist again, seeking in each town members of his sect to give him food and lodging. At Canterbury 'there was some six of this way, amongst whom was a maid of pretty knowledge, who with my Doctrine was affected, and I affected to lye with her, so that night prevailed, and satisfied my lust, afterwards the mayd was highly in love with me' (p. 22). Before long, Clarkson began to incorporate sexual encounters of this kind into his religious practice, using Titus i, 15, 'Unto the pure all things are pure' as a justification:

> Now observe at this time my judgement was this, that there was no man could be free'd from sin, till he had acted that so called sin, as no sin, this a certain time had been burning within me, yet durst not reveal it to any, in that I thought none was able to receive it, and a great desire I had to make trial, whether I should be troubled or satisfied therein. (p. 25)

[5] p. 15. For a scurrilous but amusing anecdote similar to this see *Mercurius Fumigosus* (1654), no. 5, p. 40. British Museum press-mark E. 745 (11).

To 'make trial' Clarkson joined the conspiratorial society of the Ranters, who were related, at least in doctrine, to the earlier Adamites or 'Brethren of the Free Spirit'.[6] They called their sect 'My One Flesh', and received gladly Clarkson's preaching that 'till you can lie with all women as one woman, and not judge it sin, you can do nothing but sin . . . and Sarah Kullin being then present, did invite me to make trial of what I had expressed, so as I take it, after we parted, she invited me to Mr. Wats in Rood-Lane, where was one or two more like her self, and as I take it, lay with me that night' (pp. 25-6). Clarkson became both popular and notorious, especially after he published his views in *A Single Eye* (1650); 'so that men and women came from many parts to see my face, and hear my know-ledge in these things, being restless till they were made free, as then we called it. Now I being as they said, *Captain of the Rant*, I had most of the principle women came to my lodging for knowledge, which then was called The Head-quarters' (p. 26). The scandal rose so high that he had to retire to the country, where he guided himself by the precept of Ecclesiastes: 'eat, drink and be merry'. He took up with one Mrs. Star, practicing his religion in ways somewhat contrary to popular notions of Puritan behaviour:

> Mrs. Star and I went up and down the countries as man and wife, spending our time in feasting and drinking, so that Tavernes I called the house of God; and the Drawers, Messengers; and Sack, Divinity; reading in Solomons writings it must be so, In that it made glad the heart of God . . . we had several meetings of great company, and that some, no mean ones neither, where then, and at that time, they improved their liberty, where Doctor Pagets maid stripped her self naked, and skipped among them, but being in a Cooks shop, there was no hunger, so that I kept my self to Mrs. Star, pleading the lawfulness of our doings as aforesaid, concluding with Solomon all was vanity. (pp. 28-9)

Unfortunately for Clarkson, Parliament had issued a warrant for his arrest; though after catching him they sentenced him only to a month's imprisonment followed by banishment, and the second part of the sentence was not carried out. On his release he set out again on his travels, this time practicing 'Astrology, physick and magick'.

---

[6] The main Adamite ritual was usually held in a cellar; the brethren stripped naked as they entered, in an attempt to recreate the paradisal state of Adam and Eve before the Fall. It has been suggested that Hieronymus Bosch's 'The Garden of Earthly Delights' was inspired by his membership in the sect; see William Fraenger, *The Millennium of Hieronymus Bosch* (1952). On the Ranters, see further R. Barclay, *The Inner Life of the Religious Societies of the Commonwealth* (1876), Chapter xvii; also Norman Cohn, *The Pursuit of the Millennium*, second edition, appendix.

Although he performed some minor conjurations with the aid of a witch he was soon disillusioned with warlockery, after having

> several times attempted to raise the devil, that so I might see what he was, but all in vain, so that I judged all was a lie, and that there was no devil at all, nor indeed no God but onely nature, for when I have perused the Scriptures I have found so much contradiction as then I conceived, that I had no faith in it at all, no more then a history . . . I neither believed that Adam was the first Creature, but that there was a Creation before him, which world I thought was eternal . . . I really believed no Moses, Prophets, Christ, or Apostles, nor no resurrection at all: for I understood that which was life in man, went into that infinite Bulk and Bigness, so called God, as a drop into the Ocean, and the body rotted in the grave, and for ever so to remain. (pp. 32-3)

Even though it was written after recantation, this may well be the first overt confession of atheism to be printed in English; and it is significant that Clarkson should have been brought to this point through his disillusion with necromancy—as Luther had already observed, 'No Devil, no God'. Clarkson went on preaching, none the less, 'not minding any thing after death, but as aforesaid, as also that great cheat of Astrology and Physick I practised' (p. 33). His last resting-place was a return to Faith instead of reason; he became a Muggletonian, that is, a believer in Lodowick Muggleton and John Reeve as the two 'witnesses' mentioned in Revelation xi. The second half of Clarkson's autobiography merely expounds his Muggletonian 'commission' at wearisome length.

Clarkson was markedly superior in intellect to the majority of poor, distracted religious fanatics who, at that time, followed similar careers. He was a witty and cunning flounter of the law, a sensitive observer of social trends, and, one must assume, a persuasive orator. His prose style is ingratiating in a pert way, though it is rambling and ungrammatical. The amazing variety of his religious beliefs provides the central interest of his autobiography, and also poses a nice problem of motivation. Was Clarkson an extraordinarily acute critic who unerringly sought out the weak point of each religious doctrine until he drove himself to atheism, or was he merely a fickle, over-excited grasper at every new fashion in belief? He himself explained his search by saying that he 'laboured for perfect cure and peace in my soul' (p. 3); but elsewhere he represented his progress as a series of vain efforts by the reasoning faculty to grasp at certainty, ending with the realization that certainty could only be provided by faith. His relapse from a disillusioned atheism into the rank absurdity of Muggletonianism indicates that even a man with Clarkson's critical ability and force of personality could not live without God. Englishmen of the seventeenth century were not yet ready to inhabit *that* 'heart of darkness'; but Clarkson was one of the first explorers of its margins. He has yet to receive his due as a significant figure in the history of ideas during the years 1642-60.

Sectarian Autobiography after 1660

We encounter here a work which has long been accepted as one of the great English autobiographies: Bunyan's *Grace Abounding to the Chief of Sinners* (1666).[7] The book was probably based on the account of his spiritual experiences which Bunyan would have been required to submit before being admitted to communion with the Bedford Baptists.[8] His entry into this group took place in 1655; during the eleven following years he undoubtedly pondered much on his spiritual development, and he probably revised and enlarged his written accounts of his soul-history. By the time *Grace Abounding* appeared in book form it was no longer primarily a credential of godliness, but had now become a spiritual handbook and personal apologia designed for the edification of fellow-Christians. Bunyan offered his own experience as a model which could help less diligent or systematic self-scrutinizers:

> My dear children, call to mind the former days, 'and the years of ancient times: remember also your songs in the night; and commune with your own heart' (Ps. lxxvii, 5-12). Yea, look diligently, and leave no corner therein unsearched, for there is treasure hid, even the treasure of your first and second experience of the grace of God toward you. Remember, I say, the word that first laid hold upon you; remember your terrors of conscience, and fear of death and hell; remember also your tears and prayers to God; yea, how you sighed under every hedge for mercy. (p. 5)

Bunyan's exhortations here have much in common with those of John Beadle in *The Journal or Diary of a Thankful Christian*.[9] The most striking, and in a way disturbing feature of such precepts for self-examination is their confident assumption that the spiritual experiences of the elect will always conform to a single basic pattern. Bunyan's recommendations to his readers are almost commands: 'remember ... how you sighed under every hedge for mercy'. Not only does he prescribe a particular, self-condemnatory attitude towards the past; he also puts forward a model of spiritual development which his flock are expected to fulfil in their own lives. The

[7] I have quoted from the modernized edition of G. B. Harrison (1928); the work is divided into numbered paragraphs, which I have cited to facilitate reference to other editions.
[8] See Roger Sharrock, *John Bunyan*, p. 35.
[9] See p. 63 above.

danger here was that men of diverse experience would, yielding to the influence of such preachers as Bunyan, attempt to force their life-histories into a Procrustean pattern. The doctrine of childhood depravity already imposed a stringent check on originality and spontaneity; it led Calvinist autobiographers to compete with each other in confessions of precocious wickedness, with the result that their histories blur together in the reader's mind, and individual reminiscences can scarcely be distinguished from each other. 'I had but few equals, especially considering my years, which were tender, being few, both for cursing, swearing, lying, and blaspheming the holy name of God'—these are Bunyan's words, but they could come equally well from a hundred or a thousand of his contemporaries. Though *Grace Abounding* is the most powerful English work of its kind in the seventeenth century, we should none the less recognize that Bunyan's influence, both by practice and by precept, worked mainly to blunt the autobiographical sensibilities of his less gifted fellows.

W. Y. Tindall has performed a useful service to Bunyan criticism by demonstrating the conventional nature of the structure, and spiritual experiences, of *Grace Abounding*.[10] Ministerial auto-biographies were commonly divided into three parts, describing the authors' conversion, calling, and ministry; Bunyan more or less followed this scheme, though he combined the second and third parts into a sketchy 'Brief Account of the Author's Call to the Work of the Ministry' (par. 265-317), and added to this 'A Brief Account of the Author's Imprisonment' (par. 318-39). But *Grace Abounding* is mainly a conversion-narrative, a record of Bunyan's spiritual trials up to the time that 'my former darkness and atheism fled away, and the blessed things of heaven were set within my view' (par. 262). His struggle was the more intense in that other people, and indeed external events of any kind, played very small roles in it; the young Bunyan was clearly a rather self-centred and lonely religious thinker—his various spiritual advisers always disappointed him, and he left them to return to his obsessive poring over the Bible.

The account of Bunyan's early youth is the best-known part of *Grace Abounding*, perhaps because to the average reader it seems so unusual a childhood, darkened by Bunyan's gloomy and chronic preoccupation with his many sins . . .

> the which . . . did so offend the Lord, that even in my childhood he did scare and affright me with fearful dreams, and did terrify me with dreadful visions; for often, after I had spent this and the other day in sin, I have in my bed been greatly afflicted, while asleep, with the apprehensions of devils and wicked spirits, who still, as I then

[10] *John Bunyan*, Chapter 2.

thought, laboured to draw me away with them, of which I could never
be rid. . . .

These things, I say, when I was but a child but nine or ten years old,
did so distress my soul, that when in the midst of my many sports and
childish vanities, amidst my vain companions, I was often much cast
down and afflicted in my mind therewith, yet could I not let go of my
sins. (pars. 5, 7)

However, such passages do not rise much above the general level of
contemporary confessional writing; moreover, it should be clear by
now that the experiences which Bunyan describes are entirely conventional. *Grace Abounding* was one of his earlier works, and as it
progressed his writing improved—though this improvement has been
obscured by the modern reader's tendency to lose patience with self-
accusatory narratives. The later sections of *Grace Abounding*, which
describe how Bunyan, in early manhood, wrestled with temptations
to renounce his faith in God, have not been given their due. These
later temptations spring from problems of scriptural interpretation;
in describing them, Bunyan lapses now and then into a spontaneous,
exalted Old Testament rhetoric which is strangely impressive:

Now I blessed the condition of the dog and toad, and counted the
estate of everything that God had made far better than this dreadful
state of mine, and such as my companions was; yea, gladly would I
have been in the condition of dog or horse, for I knew they had no soul
to perish under the everlasting weights of hell for sin, as mine was like
to do. Nay, and though I saw this, felt this, and was broken to pieces
with it, yet that which added to my sorrow was, that I could not find
that with all my soul I did desire deliverance. (par. 104)

In youth, Bunyan had mainly physical temptations to contend
with; in maturity, the threat came from the darker sins of blasphemy
and despair. The lustful doctrines of the Ranters were an early danger
to his salvation:

These would also talk with me of their ways, and condemn me as
legal and dark; pretending that they only had attained to perfection
that could do what they would, and not sin. Oh! these temptations
were suitable to my flesh, I being but a young man, and my nature in
its prime; but God, who had, as I hope, designed me for better things,
kept me in the fear of his name, and did not suffer me to accept of such
principles. (par. 45)

We can guess how a way of life like Lawrence Clarkson's might have
allured a young man of strong passions; but at that stage Bunyan was
still able to stand firm against temptation:

I had one religious intimate companion all this while, and that was
the poor man that I spoke of before; but about this time he also

turned a most devilish Ranter, and gave himself up to all manner of filthiness, especially uncleanness; he would also deny that there was a God, angel, or spirit. . . . When I laboured to rebuke his wickedness, he would laugh the more, and pretend that he had gone through all religions, and could never light on the right till now. He told me also, that in a little time I should see all professors turn to the ways of the Ranters. Wherefore, abominating those cursed principles, I left his company forthwith, and became to him as great a stranger, as I had been before a familiar. (par. 44)

It was not until later in life that Bunyan began his agonized struggles with two great problems of belief: whether his faith was strong enough to ensure his inclusion among the elect, and whether the Christian religion itself was true. The abject misery described in par. 104 (quoted above) was inspired by his awareness that 'everyone doth think his own religion rightest, both Jews and Moors, and Pagans! and how if all our faith, and Christ, and Scriptures, should be but a think-so too?' (par. 97). Bunyan was able eventually to dispel such doubts, and even to feel sure of his place among the elect (par. 128). But this was only the prelude to greater struggles, in which the devil himself took an active part. For an entire year Bunyan suffered from a hysterical compulsion 'to sell and part with this most blessed Christ, to exchange him for the things of this life, for anything' (par. 133). He claims to have felt as if he were 'tortured upon a rack for whole days together' (par. 136). Finally, the psychic tension generated by his over-active conscience became intolerable and he broke down entirely:

one morning, as I did lie in my bed, I was, as at other times, most fiercely assaulted with this temptation, to sell and part with Christ; the wicked suggestion still running in my mind, Sell him, sell him, sell him, sell him, sell him, as fast as a man could speak; against which also, in my mind, as at other times, I answered, No, no, not for thousands, thousands, thousands, at least twenty times together. But at last, after much striving, even until I was almost out of breath, I felt this thought pass through my heart, Let him go, if he will! and I thought also, that I felt my heart freely consent thereto. Oh, the diligence of Satan! Oh, the desperateness of man's heart!

140. Now was the battle won, and down fell I, as a bird that is shot from the top of a tree, into great guilt, and fearful despair. Thus getting out of my bed, I went moping into the field;

Two full years of 'an expectation of damnation' followed this yielding, before he was able to believe that the blood of Christ could redeem even so great a sinner as himself. He returns to the fold; but, after such trials as he has described, the story of his ministry comes as an anticlimax.

The interpretation and evaluation of *Grace Abounding* are made more difficult by the work's avowedly didactic purpose. A man like Oliver Heywood might write the story of his spiritual torments for his own instruction; but Bunyan, a more militant and outward-looking evangelist than Heywood, wished above all to show the conscience-stricken faithful that no sin was too great to be redeemed by Christ. Bunyan drove home the lesson by presenting himself as Judas reincarnate, a man who sold Christ 'for the things of this life, for anything'. This smacks a little too much of the pulpit—the unchari-table might say, of the tub. While Bunyan is establishing his claim to be 'the chief of sinners' we know already that 'grace abounding' will inevitably save him, and that his place will be assured in the latter-day glory: 'as I was sitting by the fire, I suddenly felt this word to sound in my heart, I must go to Jesus; at this my former darkness and atheism fled away, and the blessed things of heaven were set within my view' (par. 262). Bunyan had a spontaneous, almost instinctive eagerness to use this experience for the edification of fellow-Christians: 'Then with joy I told my wife, O now I know, I know! But that night was a good night to me, I never had but few better; I longed for the company of some of God's people that I might have imparted unto them what God had showed me' (par. 263). But despite Bunyan's apparent artlessness, when every incident of a man's life is made to serve a didactic, evangelical purpose one inevitably fears that the forces of distortion and self-deception may also be at work. It is hard indeed to find a seventeenth-century Calvinist spiritual autobiography which does not end with the author indicating that *he*, at least, has been granted direct assurance from God of his election.[11] This predictable happy ending to the Calvinist's narrative of the sins and temptations of his youth often makes the entire work seem factitious. Bunyan's success in *Grace Abounding* lies mainly in the skill he uses to persuade us that the outcome of his struggles really was doubtful.

Vavasour Powell's autobiography is in a much milder vein than *Grace Abounding*.[12] Powell's spiritual crisis was a relatively straight-forward affair: until the age of twenty he was 'very active in the pursuit of the pleasures and vanities of this wicked world' (p. 2); he then confessed his sins and became an itinerant Baptist preacher. His last spiritual doubts were resolved when, on his sickbed, God pre-

[11] One may quote in this context the title of chapter IX, book II, in Downame's *The Christian Warfare* (1634): 'That wee may bee assured of our election proued by diuers Arguments.'
[12] *The Life and Death of Mr. Vavasor Powell*, in T. Jackson, *Library of Christian Biography*, vol. 12.

sented to him the text 'he that believeth on the Son hath everlasting life' (p. 16). He became a chaplain in the Parliamentary army, was wounded at Anglesey, and had some success in healing women by prayer. His *Life* has quiet charm, but does not aspire to the intensity of *Grace Abounding*; it is pithy and gentle, a successful work on a minor scale. The conclusion epitomizes Powell's self-effacing and catholic temperament:

> These few things, of many which I have observed in myself, concerning the Lord's gracious and wonderful dealing with me. I have set down, not as boasting or seeking praise to myself, but to keep a memorial of the Lord's benefits; and to stir up others, into whose hands these few notes may come, to have confidence in the power and goodness of God, who is the Saviour of all men, but especially of them that believe in him. (p. 23)

Powell's inclusive concept of Christianity was not shared by the famous Lodowick Muggleton, co-founder of Muggletonianism. *The Acts of the Witnesses of the Spirit* (1699),[13] published a year after its author's death, documents his claim to be one of the two witnesses of the spirit mentioned in Revelation xi, and to be the equal of Moses and Christ. Only quotation can do justice to Muggleton's talent for mixing the portentous and the trivial; we may begin with his infancy:

> 7. And I Lodwick Muggleton, was Born in Bishopsgate-Street, near the Earl of Devonshire's House, at the corner house call'd Walnuttree-Yard.
> 8. My Father's Name was John Muggleton, he was a Smith by Trade, that is a Farrier, or Horse-Doctor, he was in great Respect with the Post-Master, in King James's Time; he had three Children by my Mother, two Sons and one Daughter, I was the youngest, and my Mother lov'd me.
> 9. But after my Mother Died, I being but young, my Father took another Wife; so I being young, was expos'd to live with Strangers in the Country. (p. 6)

This early sorrow of adoption may have contributed to Muggleton's later derangement; but he managed to live an outwardly respectable life until he was 'about Forty Years Old, and in the Year 1650'. He had for a few years before this been somewhat dissatisfied with both Presbyterians and Independents; in 1650 he was caught up in the general religious excitement, which was then reaching its peak. Self-proclaimed prophets and prophetesses abounded; two men, who said they were more than prophets, drew Muggleton's particular attention:

---

[13] *The Acts* was written *c.* 1680-88; quotations are from the corrected page-for-page reprint of 1764.

3. John Tannye, he declared himself to be the Lord's High-Priest, and that he was to act over the Law of Moses again; therefore he Circumcised himself according to the Law. . . .

5. And as for John Robins, he declared himself to be God Almighty; and that he was the Judge of the Quick, and of the Dead; and that he was that first Adam that was in that innocent State; and that his Body had been Dead this Five Thousand, Six Hundred and odd Years, and now he was risen again from the Dead; and that he was that Adam Melchisedeck that met Abraham in the Way, and received Tythes of him. (p. 20)

Robins also said that he had raised Cain, Judas, and others from the dead, a claim which Muggleton investigated personally: 'I saw all those that was said to be raised by John Robins, and they owned themselves to be the very same Persons that had been Dead for so long time' (p. 21). Apparently chagrined by Robins' success, Muggleton fell into a state of deep depression and spiritual crisis. His self-confidence in his divine mission did not revive until a year later, when his friend John Reeve received a message from above 'and said unto me, that God had given him a Commission, and that he had given Lodowick Mugleton to be his Mouth: And said, at the same time was brought to his Mind that saying, that Aaron was given to be Moses's Mouth' (p. 41). The two of them began their 'Commission' by routing Tannye and Robins in verbal battle, and continued by touring London disputing with other sectaries, and damning to hell all who would not believe that Reeve and Muggleton were the two witnesses of the spirit. In 1653 they were arrested for blasphemy and brought before the Lord Mayor—who did not cow them in the least:

30. Then said the Lord Mayor unto John Reeve, what it was that God spake unto you?

31. John related the Words God spake unto him three Mornings together; the same Words that are written in that Book in your Hand.

1. The Lord Mayor answered John Reeve, and said, He did believe it was the Devil that spake to him.

2. Then to this I answered and said, Sir, you have sinned against the Holy Ghost, and will be Damn'd. (p. 70)

This exchange cost Muggleton and Reeve six months in Bridewell, and their troubles multiplied afterwards; Reeve died four years later, and Muggleton met with more and more opposition on his missionary journeys. He embroiled himself in many quarrels with the Quakers; an especially lively one was with William Penn (pp. 125-30). In 1677 he was again arraigned for blasphemy and sentenced by Judge Jefferies to six months imprisonment and three spells in the pillory, which he endured with unshaken conviction:

16. I was maul'd by the People, some cast Dirt, and Mud out of the Kennel at me, others rotten Eggs, and Turnips, and others Cast Stones at me, some Stones weighed a Pound; and out of the Windows at the Exchange, they cast down Fire Brands . . . at my Head, which if they had lighted upon me, would have done the Work, as they desired.

17. I was bruised and battered, and my innocent Blood was shed, tho' not unto Death, for God's Cause. (pp. 168-9)

Muggleton's story ends as he looks forward to the Last Judgment, when he and John Reeve will sit on thrones and 'judge all those wicked despisers and persecutors of us when we were upon Earth, with the same Judgment in the Resurrection, as we did here on Earth' (p. 179). While awaiting this final vindication he leaves his autobiography 'as a Legacy for the Age to come upon Record, that the unbelieving World may be convinced when I am turned to dust, as my Father Adam is' (p. 178). *The Acts of the Witnesses of the Spirit* thus survives as the bible of Muggletonianism; conceived as the sacred text of a (now extinct) religion, it was, at least, the most ambitious British autobiography of its time.

During the last quarter of the seventeenth century the auto-biographies written by sectaries reveal a definite flagging of spiritual energy, a diminution parallel to the declining fortunes of the sects themselves. *The Life and Death of Mr. Hanserd Knollys* (1692) traces the career of a prominent Baptist preacher and millenarian; it is conventional and uninspired both in style and content.[14] Francis Bampfield's autobiography has already been mentioned (p. 30) for its remarkably detailed attempt to present its author's life as a repetition of St. Paul's.[15] The result is a literary curiosity, though only the specialist need be curious of it. William Kiffin's *Life* tells the story of a rich and rather self-satisfied Baptist who turned from preaching to trade.[16] Kiffin wrote the work in thanksgiving for the 'eminent providence I observed from the Lord towards me' (p. 2), and as an edifying record for his children. The form is *res gestae* rather than spiritual autobiography; there is much emphasis on the author's troubles as a dissenter, though he was clearly less militant and more businesslike than most sectaries.

We may end this discussion of the non-Quaker sects by considering a book in which Baptist spiritual autobiography has hardened into a strict, almost stylized convention. Charles Doe's *A Collection of Experience of the Work of Grace* (1700) shows how the pattern of Bunyan's *Grace Abounding* could be adapted for use by almost any

---

[14] For Knollys' career see Haller, pp. 270-72 and Tindall, pp. 123-5.

[15] *A Name, an After-one; or a Name, New One In the Latter-Day-Glory* (1681).

[16] *Remarkable Passages in the Life of William Kiffin*, ed. W. Orme.

other Baptist autobiographer.[17] Doe published his own autobiography, and added to it those of Will Davenport and an anonymous eighteen-year-old apprentice. The purpose of the compendium
was to convince its readers that the most ordinary Londoners could
find enlightenment and salvation through faith; as the title-page put
it, the book was published

> Not to Applaud the Persons, but for the Comfort of Saints, both
> the New-born in Christ and the Beclouded-Believer, may here see that
> it hath been with the Souls of other saints as with theirs; And also it
> being Matter of Fact, may convince the Unregenerate that there is
> indeed such a thing as the working of the Spirit of God upon the
> Soul. . . .
>
> Printed for Cha. Doe, a Comb-maker.

Will Davenport, the first autobiographer, tells how the bad influence of a fellow-apprentice overcame his strict Church of England
upbringing, with the result that he 'immediately arrived at that degree
of Wickedness, for Swearing, Lying, Sabbath-breaking, and all
manner of filthy and frothy Discourse, that I think few of my Age
exceeded me' (p. 1). He is frightened out of this evil way of life by a
sermon, and lives more decently for three years. At the end of this
time the way to a higher plane of religious experience is opened by a
meditation, probably not of his own invention: 'one day, as I was
walking by my self, and considering of my Estate, me thoughts I saw
my self hang over a bottomless Pit by a small Cobweb, and every
blast of Wind did so shake me, that I was amazed I was not dropt
long before' (p. 3). Now that such thoughts occupy his mind he is
obviously a dissenter in spirit, and soon he leaves the Established
Church for the Congregationalists. The occasion of his autobiography, however, is his decision to switch from the Congregation-
alist to the Baptist belief, and the conclusion of his narrative is a
formal statement of his change of allegiance:

> And these are a few of the Reasons that makes me desire to be
> admitted into Communion with you, though very unworthy as to my
> self, but the Grace of God is sufficient for all that truly rely upon it;
> and so I humbly trust it shall be for me an unworthy Shrub, William
> Davenport.
>
> He was Baptized (or Dipt) and admitted a member. (p. 8)

This brief and stilted recital may suggest the kind of testimony that
would have been required of Bunyan when he joined the Bedford
Baptists in 1655. The next autobiography in the collection, by the

---

[17] Doe was the publisher of Bunyan's collected works (1692), and also his
first biographer. On confessions as a requirement for church membership, see
G. F. Nuttall, *Visible Saints*, pp. 110-13.

young apprentice, repeats the familiar story, and makes a familiar claim—he is terrified into repentance by reading Bunyan's *The Groans of the Damn'd,* and summarizes his history thus: 'these were the Dealings of God with my Soul, blessed be the Lord Jesus Christ, who hath Saved me, the chiefest of Sinners' (p. 28).

Doe's own autobiography is somewhat atypical, in that it deals mainly with his spiritual experiences *after* he saw the light and became a Baptist. In addition to some anecdotes about Bunyan, we hear of Doe's many perplexities concerning Election and Fore-appointment:

> I was Travelling to a Fair, and about the middle of a Field, 35 Miles off of London, I saw a kind of a Bug crauling across my Path, and immediately there started into my mind, did God, do you think, from before the Foundation of the World decree or Fore-appoint that this little creeping Creature and I should meet in this place at this time, or that I should come from London to meet this thus? And the Case is the same of every little thing I meet with or see now, and so of every body else, and of every thing, and at all times. (p. 53)

This kind of precise calculation of the moral implications of chance events is in keeping with Doe's businesslike approach to the conduct of his temporal affairs. His mentality has much in common with that of another dissenter of his generation, Daniel Defoe—

> If God has made all these things, He guides and governs them all, and all things that concern them; for the Power that could make all things must certainly have power to guide and direct them.
> If so, nothing can happen in the great circuit of His works, either without His knowledge or appointment.[18]

Here Robinson Crusoe, with his tranquil affirmation of an orderly universe, takes a rather similar view of God's foreknowledge to that expressed in the previous quotation. Both Defoe and Doe seem much more concerned with the finger of God in the events of everyday life, and less obsessed with gloom and damnation, than the Civil War generation of sectaries. The holy fire of dissent dies down in the years around 1700, before flaring up again with Wesley in the mid-eighteenth century; this waning of spiritual intensity is faithfully reflected in the autobiographies of successive generations of sectaries in the seventeenth century.

Quaker Autobiography

The Quakers were prolific autobiographers, and I have not aimed at an exhaustive treatment of their works; the attempt would in any case

[18] *Robinson Crusoe* (Nelson ed., n.d.), p. 91.

be otiose, since Luella M. Wright's *The Literary Life of the Early Friends 1650-1725* has already covered this subject in full detail. I will therefore discuss only a few of the more important Quaker auto-biographical writings, especially those which have some relation to other types of contemporary autobiography.

It is a common misconception that all Quaker autobiographies follow a stereotyped pattern; in fact, two very distinct auto-biographical modes were used, and a few miscellaneous works cannot readily be assigned to either category. The first mode includes the early Quaker tracts, which began to appear in 1654. These are usually brief, subjective testimonies of faith, cast in the form of conversion narratives or confessions. They were published during their authors' lifetimes and were similar, in their evangelical purpose, to the proselytizing tracts of other sects. The second mode of Quaker auto-biography includes the numerous journals, mainly objective in style, of which George Fox's *Journal* is the best known. These works began to appear from 1690 on as posthumous tributes to the life-work of a later, and more staid, generation of Friends.[19] Journal-writers were generally faithful to a standard pattern established by the first practitioners of the genre (Caton, Fox, Burnyeat, and others), and this conventionality was frequently accentuated by the pious literary executors who arranged the journals for publication. A third group of miscellaneous Quaker lives includes works by men whose interests extended beyond Quakerism, or who used a non-Quaker auto-biographical convention. Henry Lampe, for example, led an eventful and cosmopolitan life before he became a Quaker, and he described these early adventures openly and without apology in his *Curriculum Vitae*. The *Adventures by Sea* of Edward Coxere (a convert to Quakerism) is even more secular in emphasis; it is therefore discussed in Chapter VIII with other travel autobiographies.

Richard Farnsworth's *The Heart Opened by Christ* (1654) may well be the first Quaker autobiographical work. This short tract opens with its author's spiritual awakening: 'About the 16 year of age of my natural life, the Lord did begin to work under a cloud, and let me see the vanity that I lived in.' Farnsworth describes his progressive dis-illusionment with Anglican ritual, and completes the tract with a long controversial attack on Anglican doctrine. Two features of this other-wise undistinguished work deserve comment: first, we find in it no trace of the 'Journal of the Life of X' convention which later became

---

[19] Several of these journal-writers were, of course, among the founders of the sect; but by the time of their old age they had shed the intense, sometimes insane religious excitement displayed in the tracts written by newly-converted Quakers in the 1650s.

standard; second, Farnsworth's autobiographical urge apparently derived from his having crossed swords with the 'priests' of the Church of England, with a concomitant eagerness to proclaim his new Quaker convictions. Thus the earliest Quaker autobiographies, like those by adherents of other sects, seem to have been part of the general impulse to give testimony of personal belief and to contribute to theological controversies. It was not until some forty years after Farnsworth's tract that the emphasis in Quaker autobiography shifted from apologetics to the history of the Society, as recorded in journals of the travels and sufferings of its founders.

By 1656 Quaker autobiographical tracts had become quite formalized; a glance at three of them issued in that year will indicate the nature of the genre. George Rofe, writing from jail in Suffolk, includes in his *The Righteousness of God to Man* 'a true Declaration how I lived before I knew the truth, how I came to know the truth, and overcame deceit' (pp. 14-18)—a fair summary of the contents of many similar Quaker testimonies. Francis Howgill develops the characteristic Quaker imagery of the inner light shining against the darkness of unregeneracy: 'for the simples sake, (who have erred for lack of true knowledge, as I did in times past) I shall declare unto you a little in short of my travells in Aegypts-Land, where darknesse is so thick, that if yee wait but diligently to see your selves, you will feele it also'.[20] William Ames, in *A Declaration of the Witness of God Manifested in me from my Youth*, is more succinctly autobiographical than Rofe or Howgill. He traces his spiritual development from carnal depravity as a child, and hypocrisy as a church elder, to the time when he hears of the light of Christ and sees the wickedness of his ways. Ames's account of the central Quaker doctrine of personal autonomy may suggest why this sect so diligently fostered self-analysis and was so prolific of autobiographies:

> I came to witness through the Light, and I had no more need to be taught of Men, or to look without me for a teacher. For this shewed me what was good, and what the Lord required of me. And when I looked out, and went from it, this would reprove me, and let me see wherein I had offended, and this would rise up in Judgement against the offender. (p. 14)

To complete his quite typical case-history, he describes how he has achieved salvation and peace of spirit through reliance on God's Light (pp. 15-16). Trust in the Light, however, could be intoxicating to less sturdy souls, and some of the earlier Quakers were given to hysterical denunciations of unbelievers, public nudity, and similar anti-social acts. One finds this illustrated in William Bayly's spiritual

[20] *The Inheritance of Jacob Discovered*, p. 5.

autobiography, which degenerates into incoherent rantings; he and Richard Hubberthorn serve to remind us that the lunatic fringe of early Quakerism was almost as mad as the most extreme Prophetic and Messianic sects.[21]

The first autobiography to be published in the form which was to typify more than a hundred years of subsequent Quaker hagiography was that of William Caton. His *Journal* appeared in 1689, twenty-four years after his death; the delay was caused by fear of the licensing laws. In this work we can already recognize the standard pattern of the Quaker journal: the rather perfunctory account of Caton's conversion is outweighed by a long enumeration of his ministerial labours. John Burnyeat's *Journal*, published two years after Caton's, has the same structure; Wright lists twenty-four other journals of this kind published by 1726.[22] Some authors, such as Benjamin Bangs, give detailed and lively accounts of their 'convince-ments'; but more often the initial conversion is disposed of in a few barren phrases,[23] and the journal-writer then begins a relentless succession of *res gestae*. Innumerable prayer-meetings in England, Ireland, Holland, and North America are recorded, with the author's religious musings at each and his travels from one to the next. For members of a sect devoted to the 'inner light' and holding a strongly personal concept of religion, the Quaker journal-writers seem strangely preoccupied with the externals of their faith; they concentrate on their persecutions and proselytizing as if the experience of the inner light were something ineffable, or to be taken for granted. There is a striking contrast between the intense spiritual fervour of the early Quaker tracts and the pedestrian, repetitive piling-up of routine activities in the journals. Because of this repetitiveness, we will discuss only two journals which distinguish themselves from the mass—those of Thomas Ellwood and George Fox.

Thomas Ellwood has survived in scholarly footnotes by virtue of his friendship with Milton; but his autobiography is also worth knowing for the liveliness and flexibility which make it stand out from the general run of Quaker journals.[24] Instead of the usual censoriousness, for example, Ellwood displays both insight and humour in recounting his childish pranks:

[21] Bayly, *A Short Relation or Testimony of the Workings of the Light of Christ in me, from my Childhood;* Hubberthorn, *A True Testimony of Obedience to the Heavenly Call.*

[22] *Literary Life*, pp. 161-2.

[23] See, for example, *A Journal of the Life ... of William Edmundson*, 2nd edition, pp. 8-9.

[24] *The History of the Life of Thomas Ellwood*, ed. C. G. Crump. The first edition appeared in 1714, one year after Ellwood's death.

being a little busy boy, full of spirit, of a working head and active
hand, I could not easily conform myself to the grave and sober rules,
and, as I then thought, severe orders of the school; but was often
playing one waggish prank or other among my fellow-scholars, which
subjected me to correction, so that I have come under the discipline of
the rod twice in a forenoon; which yet brake no bones. (p. 3)

Ellwood's light touch, as compared with most Quaker autobiographers, reflects his more worldly and cultivated upbringing: his
father was a landowner and J.P., with acquaintances among the lesser
nobility. When Ellwood and his father went to visit the Isaac
Peningtons, who had just become Quakers, they were dismayed by
the atmosphere of sober piety which they encountered at their host's
establishment: 'so great a change, from a free, debonair, and courtly
sort of behaviour, which we formerly had found them in, to so strict a
gravity as they now received us with did not a little amuse us, and
disappoint our expectation of such a pleasant visit as we used to have,
and had now promised ourselves' (p. 9). Ellwood was none the less
impressed by the Peningtons' seriousness, and he began to frequent
Quaker meetings in spite of his father's opposition. He soon became
a convinced Quaker, and embarked on a long and intense psychological battle with his father, who kept him prisoner at home and beat
him for refusing to take off his hat.[25] Regardless of maltreatment,
Ellwood persevered in his faith, eating with the servants to avoid his
father's anger. Three years later, in 1662, he was arrested in the
repression following the revolt of the Fifth-Monarchy Men; he later
was imprisoned in Bridewell and Newgate under horrible conditions
(pp. 94-116).

Ellwood's conversations with Milton concerning 'Paradise Lost'
and 'Paradise Found' are too well-known to need re-telling here;
they may be found on pp. 144-5 of his *History*. After this point the
autobiography falls off in interest: long accounts of dead controversies intrude, interspersed with more, and worse, poems. Ellwood
unfortunately had little sense of autobiographical structure or 'plot'.
His main talent is for observation and anecdote, and he has a special
gift for thumb-nail character-sketches—his is one of the few Quaker
autobiographies which are populated by real people. Moreover,
without deviating from the basically objective mode of the Quaker
Journal, Ellwood succeeds in communicating (though indirectly) a
faithful and sensitive portrait of his own temperament. His auto-

---

[25] Confined for the winter, Ellwood began to write poetry; his verses on
various occasions are scattered throughout the *History*. His first poem, con-
veniently brief, may serve as a sample of his talent: 'The winter tree | Resembles
me, | Whose sap lies in its root: | The spring draws nigh; | As it, so I | Shall
bud, I hope, and shoot' (p. 41).

biography, like that of Arthur Wilson (see p. 65 above), shows that a man of courtly education and tastes could achieve a certain freshness of style and theme even when he was writing under the influence of a narrow denominational convention of autobiographical writing.

George Fox's *Journal*, which was the chief model for later Quaker lives after its publication in 1694, reveals clearly the differences between the Quaker journals and other sectarian autobiographies. The contrast can best be seen by setting Fox beside Bunyan's *Grace Abounding*. Bunyan, we note, writes mainly of his spiritual crisis and conversion, appending only a rather sketchy account of his ministry; Fox, however, disposes of his early period of religious uncertainty in a few pages which serve as prologue to the long and circumstantial description of his missionary life. Secondly, where Bunyan presents his spiritual crisis as a struggle with his own weakness and despair, Fox is oppressed mainly by a terrible sense of the *world's* evil—the denial of Christ's teaching by sinful humanity. As R. M. Jones observes in the preface to his edition of the journal,[26] Fox has little sense of his own depravity; rather the contrary, in fact: 'when I came to eleven years of age, I knew pureness and righteousness; for while I was a child I was taught how to walk to be kept pure' (p. 1). However, his childhood was not illumined by Traherne's visionary delight or transcendental innocence:

> In my very young years I had a gravity and stayedness of mind and spirit not usual in children, insomuch that, when I saw old men carry themselves lightly and wantonly towards each other, I have had a dislike thereof risen in my heart, and have said within myself, 'If ever I come to be a man, surely I should not do so nor be so wanton'. (p. 1)

This note of priggish self-esteem continues to appear from time to time in Fox's narrative. His spiritual development takes the form of a search, not for personal purity and freedom from sin, but rather for a religion uncorrupted by the vanities of *others*, especially hireling priests. After periods of great distress he achieves personal transformation through a mystical revelation of the external, cosmic struggle between darkness and light:

> I saw also that there was an ocean of darkness and death, but an infinite ocean of light and love, which flowed over the ocean of darkness. And in that also I saw the infinite love of God; and I had great openings . . . a great work of the Lord fell upon me, to the admiration of many, who thought I had been dead, and many came to see me, for about fourteen days' time. For I was very much altered in countenance and person as if my body had been new moulded or

---

[26] *George Fox, An Autobiography.* Note that I do not quote from this edition, but from *The Journal of George Fox*, ed. John L. Nickalls.

changed. . . . My sorrows and troubles began to wear off and tears of joy dropped from me, so that I could have wept night and day with tears of joy to the Lord, in humility and brokenness of heart. And I saw into that which was without end, and things which cannot be uttered, and of the greatness and infiniteness of the love of God, which cannot be expressed by words. (pp. 19-21)

Fox's illuminations derived from his insights into the nature of God's all-embracing love, as opposed to Bunyan's Calvinist vision of his own election and separation from the sinful mass of humanity. Fox's vision is certainly the nobler of the two, but one tends to lose sight of its worth in the subsequent long recitals of journeys and imprisonments; whereas Bunyan, with his powerful style and intense single-mindedness, sustains the narrative of *Grace Abounding* at a higher pitch of religious excitement.

After his vision of the 'infinite ocean of light and love,' Fox sets out on his missionary journeys, and his narrative becomes very uneven. An account of random voyages and sufferings tends to lapse into shapelessness unless the author exercises strict control over his material. Fox, however, is insensitive to literary form; his organizing principle is simply to recount events in the order they happened, and he has a particular weakness for long reports of religious disputes in which he feels that he confounded his opponent. Though eloquent and moving passages are scattered here and there, especially when Fox describes the persecutions to which he was subjected, the bulk of the journal is taken up by the routine events of Quaker missionary life. He does pass through another spiritual crisis in 1670, during which he is severely depressed, with psychosomatic deafness and blindness (pp. 569-76); but the vision of the New Jerusalem which comes to him at this time is described without much exaltation, and the episode seems rather a simple vicissitude in his life than a complete rebirth. Perhaps Fox (like many other Quaker autobiographers) had too little inner conflict, was too invincibly self-righteous, to write a great spiritual autobiography. Moreover, he was attempting in his journal to write the history of his sect as well as his personal history, and such a double purpose might have confounded more subtle literary craftsmen than he. We cannot accuse Fox of being the slave of convention, for, when he wrote, the standard form of the Quaker journal had not yet been established; but his own journal, by its overbearing influence on subsequent works, contributed to the premature fossilization of the genre. Quaker journals which were not published immediately after their authors' deaths are often more vivid and individual than those which were rushed into print by pious literary executors; these editors almost certainly revised the journals before publication in order to make them more 'correct' and edifying.[27] Even without this posthumous revision, there seems little doubt that the Quaker autobiographers would have written better if they had not had such authoritative models to imitate. In this case at least, widespread publication was a definite handicap to the free and vigorous development of autobiography.[28]

[27] See L. M. Wright, p. 163.

[28] Among the miscellaneous Quaker lives referred to at the beginning of this section, that of Henry Lampe, *Curriculum Vitae*, is the most interesting. Lampe was the son of a prosperous merchant at Königsberg, in Prussia; he had a picaresque career as alchemist, mercenary, tutor, apothecary, and military doctor before he finally became a Quaker and settled at Ulverstone. His autobiography is an entertaining record of the vagaries of a young man of small fortune and remarkable gullibility; conversion to Quakerism apparently did not induce him to make any radical revaluation of his previous secular career.

Secular Autobiography

VII

Introduction to Secular Autobiography

DESPITE THE barriers erected by rival, isolationist denominations,
and the reluctance of many British religious autobiographers to
publish their works, it is clear that by the end of the seventeenth
century a native tradition (or traditions) of religious autobiography
had been established. Secular autobiography, however, lacked a
central, unifying concern with divine providence and salvation; we
find instead a bewildering multiplicity of themes and literary forms,
with each autobiographer groping for a means of self-expression
suited to his particular needs. In the seventeenth century it was
relatively easy to write about one's relationship with God: the pulpit
offered a supply of commonly-accepted images and suggested an
appropriate tone, while a long tradition of devotional literature—
descending from the Old Testament, and becoming directly imitable
with the Pauline epistles and Augustine's *Confessions*—made spiritual
self-analysis respectable and showed even the most ignorant 'mechan-
icks' how to go about it. But for one mainly preoccupied with secular
life the situation was different. Englishmen were still uncertain of the
meaning and value of life in the everyday world of getting and
spending, and the philosophical justification of 'life for its own sake'
had not yet been clearly formulated and defended against clerical
opposition. Though we may find it both easy and convenient to
divide seventeenth-century autobiographies into 'religious' or 'secular'
according to whether the author focuses on his religious development
or on his worldly life, this distinction was by no means clear to many
autobiographers at the time. Sir Robert Sibbald's *Memoirs* deal
mainly with secular concerns, yet he begins with a quotation from
Psalms which succinctly defines the purpose of spiritual autobiography as a genre: 'Come and hear, all ye that fear God, and I will
declare what he hath done for my soul'.[1] Even in Rousseau we still

---

[1] *Memoirs*, p. 49; the quotation is from Psalms 66, xvi.

find the language of spiritual autobiography, though his emphasis has shifted from the Divine to the human: 'Let the last trump sound when it will, I shall come forward with this work in my hand, to present myself before my Sovereign Judge, and proclaim aloud: "Here is what I have done".'[2] None the less there were many seventeenth-century autobiographers who, as one would expect, gave their strongest commitment to their worldly careers; though this commitment was not inconsistent with a reluctance to abandon conventional pieties. Clergy and laity seem to have accepted a tacit division of labour, with priests, ministers, and clergy holding a virtual monopoly on religious autobiography, and laymen usually renouncing any claim to spiritual authority. The term 'secular autobiography' therefore seems to me both useful and necessary, though it should not be taken as more than an indication of the main emphasis of works included in this category.

Before autobiography established itself as a widely-practised genre the usual means of literary self-revelation was lyrical poetry, of which the language, structure, and forms could not readily be adapted to convey the story of a man's entire life, with its variations of emotional intensity and its wide range of experience. But the greater flexibility of narrative prose as an autobiographical medium also involved new difficulties. In Britain, very few secular autobiographies were published before the middle years of the eighteenth century, so that in the two preceding centuries each man who set out to tell what he had experienced had to find his own literary form and choose his own emphasis. Moreover, all kinds of social inhibitions hindered autobiographers from expressing themselves freely and directly; again and again these authors, by their inarticulateness or apologetic attitudes, reveal an inability to come to terms with their own selfhood. Fundamental to the autobiographical urge is a sense of one's importance as an individual; in the twentieth century this is usually taken for granted, but in the seventeenth it was neither taken for granted— except in so far as men claimed significance because they lived under God's providence—nor supported by a general theory of democratic individualism as it is today. The seventeenth-century autobiographer tends to claim individual significance by virtue of some specific quality or accomplishment, or because he has been a witness to the affairs of the great; hence the variety of motivation and subject-matter in his works.

An example may help to clarify my antithesis between a *general* sense of importance today and a *specific* one then: Richard Boyle, later Lord Cork, arrived at Dublin in 1588 with £27 and his clothes;

---

[2] *Confessions*, p. 16.

by buying land cheaply during the civil turmoil of the last years of the century he became enormously rich and the greatest landowner of his age. With such a record of accumulation to his credit, his auto-biography was inspired, quite understandably, by his sense of divine aid in the achievement: 'And it pleased the Almighty by his divine providence to take me, I may say justly, as it were, by the hand, and lead me into Ireland.'[3] Boyle seems a little bewildered by his Midas touch, but he feels an obligation to commemorate his good fortune, if only to ensure that his descendants should know how it came to him. That he attributes his success to divine aid rather than to his own shrewdness and ruthless greed may seem hypocritical; but the psycho-logical mechanism responsible for his self-deception is a familiar one, and a man is unlikely to be honest in his autobiography if that virtue is lacking in his everyday life.

Other seventeenth-century secular autobiographers felt themselves to be distinguished by extensive travels, by having taken part in important events (especially those of the Civil War, Commonwealth, and Restoration), by having discovered new scientific facts or held high offices, or by achievements of many other kinds. As a group, these men ranked higher on the social scale than spiritual auto-biographers. This is not surprising; religious writers, as we have seen, derived their sense of importance from their dealings with God, and after 1640 it was men of the artisan or lower-middle classes who tended to have the fewest inhibitions about publishing accounts of their spiritual experiences. But in secular affairs it was the gentry or aristocracy who were both more assertive in their daily affairs and more likely to have the experiences of travel, military command, or political office which helped to arouse the autobiographical urge. Once the urge was present, the literary models which might help in expressing it were rather few. They will be briefly discussed in the next section.

Models, Classical and Continental. Very few autobiographical writings of ancient Greece have survived. In Latin literature we have numerous passages of incidental self-revelation but no real auto-biographies in the sense defined in Chapter I of this book. Unfortu-nately many autobiographies written in Imperial times—including works by Augustus himself, Tiberius, Claudius, Hadrian, and Septimus Severus—have been lost, except for a few random quota-tions; these works seem to have been mainly records of *res gestae* and

---

[3] *True Remembrances*, p. 4. The name of God is often on Boyle's lips, but since his autobiography is almost entirely about the means by which he became rich and respected I have included it in the secular works. He was, of course, thoroughly unscrupulous and immoral.

some may have used third-person narration.[4] The Imperial aristocracy recognized a duty to venerate the great men of the past,
especially their own ancestors, and to commemorate their deeds;
Tacitus' formulation of this duty became a *locus classicus*:

> To hand down to posterity the work and ways of famous men was
> our fathers' custom: our age has not yet abandoned it even now,
> indifferent though it be to its own children, whenever, at least, some
> great and notable virtue has dominated and overpowered the vice
> common alike to small states and great—misapprehension of integrity
> and jealousy. But in our fathers' times, just as the doing of deeds
> worth recording was natural and more obvious, so also there was
> inducement then to the brightest spirits to publish such records of
> virtue. Partisanship was not the motive, or ambition; a good conscience
> was its own reward; nay, many men even counted it not presumption,
> but self-respect, to narrate their own lives.[5]

The disappearance of so many Roman autobiographies, however,
indicates that such works were held in low esteem—the Emperor
Hadrian even published his *Vita* under the name of a freedman.[6] One
great work in the mode of *res gestae* did survive, Caesar's *Commentaries on the Gallic Wars*; this cold and impersonal monument to
militarism was not the best of models for Renaissance autobiographers. None the less it was widely imitated. Aeneas Sylvius,
later Pope Pius II, wrote his *Commentaries* (*c.* 1464) in Latin and
followed Caesar's form closely. In France there were the *Commentaires* (1559) of Martin du Bellay, and in England the *Commentaries* (1602) of Sir Francis Vere, which describe his campaigns in
the Spanish Netherlands.[7] In all these works the use of third-person
narration reduces the autobiographical interest by casting external
events into strong relief and so hindering the direct communication
of the writer's states of mind. Matthew Robinson, writing in the
1670s, relied on Suetonius rather than Caesar as a model; the result is
no more than a literary curiosity (see p. 154 below).

The Renaissance man who was striving to understand his individual
nature and his relationship to the external world found more inspiration in those classical authors who stood at the opposite pole from
Caesar's terseness and impersonality: in Plutarch's *Moralia* (one of
Montaigne's favourite books), in Seneca's *Epistulae Morales*, and in

---

[4] See G. Misch, *A History of Autobiography in Antiquity*, I, 208-309. My
discussion of classical models is indebted throughout to this work. Ovid's *Tristia*
IV, x, is a brief autobiography; see p. 160 below for a reference to it by a later
autobiographer, the Duchess of Newcastle.

[5] *Agricola*, opening sentences, tr. M. Hutton (Loeb ed.); quoted in Misch,
pp. 210-11.

[6] Misch, p. 242.

[7] Vere's work was not published until 1657, forty-eight years after his death.

the *Meditations* of Marcus Aurelius. Many of the better-educated and more introspective British secular autobiographers had a taste for the Stoics—Sir Robert Sibbald modelled his philosophy of life on Seneca and Epictetus, while Sir John Bramston justified his autobiography with a Senecan maxim.[8] But the fact remains that no ancient Greek or Latin works have survived which truly conform to the genre of subjective autobiography; so that although we may notice classical influences on many Renaissance autobiographers, cases of direct imitation can be found only among the followers of Caesar and Suetonius. Renaissance historians and autobiographers inherited from antiquity, and pursued with enthusiasm, the idea that noble deeds, even one's own should be commemorated. But secular autobiography, when conceived of as something more intimate and structured than mere *res gestae*, is a post-medieval invention and not part of the classical heritage.

In modern Europe, autobiographers began to write earlier on the Continent than in England. Family chronicles of an objective type were being written in Florence as early as the thirteenth century and Petrarch, in the following century, inaugurated subjective autobiography in Italy.[9] He was followed by Aeneas Sylvius, Cellini and Girolamo Cardano, the two latter writing in the second half of the sixteenth century. But none of these works was translated into English before the eighteenth century, and Cellini was not published at all until 1728.[10] Educated Englishmen could of course read such autobiographies as had been published in Latin and perhaps Italian; but few autobiographers seem to have done so except for Herbert of Cherbury, Richard Baxter, and Henry More, who show some knowledge of Cardano's *De Vita Propria Liber*. Sir Thomas Hoby, of all people, might be expected to have been influenced by the stirrings of the autobiographical urge in Italy; yet his *Booke of the Travaile and Lief of me Thomas Hoby* (*c.* 1565) is an almost completely objective narration of his travels, with no exploration of his inner life. Another prominent Italian traveller, John Milton, revealed much about his personal life in various passages of his works, but there is no particular reason why we should ascribe his autobiographical impulse to his Italian journeys.

French influence was more direct and visible than Italian but, with

[8] See below, Chapter IX.
[9] I refer to the *Lettera ai Posteri* (written in Latin, 1351); some scholars might consider Dante's *La Vita Nuova* (*c.* 1292) the first subjective autobiography by an Italian.
[10] The first translation of Cellini's autobiography into English, by Thomas Nugent, appeared in 1771; Cardano was not translated until 1930.

the possible exception of Montaigne, not very fruitful. The dominant autobiographical form in sixteenth and seventeenth century France was the memoir, usually of military or political affairs; the *Commentaires* of the soldier Blaise de Monluc and De Thou's *Mémoires* are two of the best-known examples. Monluc, though he eschewed third-person narration, acknowledged his debt to Caesar; he created a masterpiece of military autobiography, but none of the numerous British military memoirists of the seventeenth century rivalled his achievement. De Thou's *Mémoires* belong to political history rather than autobiography; Bishop Burnet, when writing in imitation of De Thou, filled his *History of his Own Time* with facts, dates, and observations yet told nothing, except by implication, about what he himself felt when participating in these events.[11] The literary interest of the *Autobiography* of Sir Simonds d'Ewes is similarly reduced by the author's overriding concern with the contemporary history in which he was involved. Clarendon's *Autobiography* is more subjective than Burnet's *History*, but uses third-person narration and concentrates on politics rather than on Clarendon's personal life.

The influence of Montaigne on seventeenth-century British autobiographers must have been subtle and indefinite, if indeed it existed at all; I do not recall a single reference to him in the autobiographies of this period I have read. On the other hand, British writers were aware of the high degree of sophistication and popularity achieved by French seventeenth-century memoirs; but this success was not of a kind designed to help autobiography develop a greater inwardness and subjectivity. The dominance of neo-classicism in seventeenth-century France discouraged the indulgence of waywardness or personal peculiarities in literature; to the modern view, these are precisely the qualities that an autobiographer needs to cultivate.

Motives for Writing. Anna R. Burr, in her study of autobiography, constructed a table of the reasons for which men wrote their autobiographies. She found four main categories of motivation: 'self-study and science'; 'use of children or descendants'; 'religious witness'; 'for amusement, or to recall the past'.[12] The fatal defect of this kind of classification is that it does not reveal the actual reasons for writing autobiographies, but only the professed ones, or perhaps the most superficial. Why, for example, should English aristocrats write autobiographies 'for the use of their children or descendants'

[11] Burnet's *Autobiography*, already discussed in Chapter IV, was originally intended to form an appendix to his *History* but was suppressed by his executors. Its emphasis on Burnet's personal career contrasts with the deliberate self-effacement of the *History*.

[12] *The Autobiography*, Appendix A.

with some frequency during the seventeenth century, but not at all during the fourteenth century? Herbert of Cherbury, a typical representative of this class, says at the beginning of his *Autobiography* that he writes for the particular instruction of his descendants because (he implies) they will share his own 'natural inclinations and humours' and presumably will be faced with similar problems—'for which reason,' he says, 'I have thought fit to relate to my posterity those passages of my life, which I conceive may best declare me, and be most useful to them.'[13] From the narrative which follows, however, one suspects that Herbert's naïve egotism, together with his love of reminiscing about past triumphs, are the real spurs to his enterprise; he is eager for posterity to know about the compliment paid his good looks by Queen Elizabeth ('It is pity he was married so young'), about his many duels and his other adventures.

The lesson of Herbert's autobiography can be repeated, with variations, for many others. To discover why secular autobiography became a popular genre in the Renaissance one must do more than simply classify the authors' explicit motives for writing. These stated motives are usually half-truths, attempts to make the writing of an autobiography look respectable or to fit it into some accepted tradition. An additional reason why we should discount professed motives for writing is that so many autobiographers seem apologetic, even devious, about their undertakings; in seventeenth-century Britain no autobiographer dared begin in such an unabashedly self-centred way as Rousseau did:

> I have resolved on an enterprise which has no precedent, and which, once complete, will have no imitator. My purpose is to display to my kind a portrait in every way true to nature, and the man I shall portray will be myself. Simply myself. I know my own heart and understand my fellow man. But I am made unlike any one that I have ever met; I will even venture to say that I am like no one in the whole world. I may be no better, but at least I am different. Whether Nature did well or ill in breaking the mould in which she formed me, is a question which can only be resolved after reading of my book. (*Confessions*, p. 16)

Rousseau's grandiloquence may be contrasted with William Lilly's humble and matter-of-fact address to the man who asked him to write an autobiography, Elias Ashmole: 'Worthy sir, I take much delight to recount unto you, even all and every circumstance of my life, whether good, moderate, or evil; Deo gloria.'[14] The underlying motives of Lilly and Rousseau in describing their lives may have been

---

[13] *Autobiography*, ed. Sidney Lee, pp. 1-2.
[14] *History of his Life and Times* (1774), p. 8.

quite similar; but in the hundred years between these two statements the dramatic posture of the autobiographer *vis-à-vis* his audience had changed. Unlike Rousseau, the typical Renaissance autobiographer was more concerned with actual deeds than with the exploration and glorification of individuality in its own right. Benvenuto Cellini, though in his own way as great an egotist as Rousseau, gives a reason for writing his autobiography which merely re-phrases Tacitus (see p. 110 above): 'No matter what sort he is, everyone who has to his credit what are or really seem great achievements, if he cares for truth and goodness, ought to write the story of his own life in his own hand.[15] Instead of a direct claim to individual importance, Cellini made a subtler claim to his readers, cast in the form of an incomplete (and imperfect) syllogism: 'Men who have done great deeds should write autobiographies; I am writing an autobiography; ergo . . .'

The 'opening gambits' of Rousseau and Cellini help to illustrate a principle to be kept in mind whenever the question of the autobiographer's motivation arises: an autobiography, since it is almost invariably written to be read by someone else, cannot be a piece of pure and disinterested self-expression. Rather, it is a 'performance' staged by the autobiographer for the benefit of his audience. Erving Goffman, in *The Presentation of Self in Everyday Life* (p. 242), states the implications of this confrontation thus: 'When an individual appears before others, he knowingly and unwittingly projects a definition of the situation, of which a conception of himself is an important part.' Although autobiography, unlike everyday life, does not allow direct audience-participation, the autobiographer can use various devices to manipulate his audience's response. In literary jargon he 'adopts a persona', if only by selecting from his life-experiences a limited number for presentation to the audience— though he is more likely to draw on the full resources of arrangement, emphasis, or even lying.

The modern autobiographer, aided by familiarity with other auto-biographies, can choose among a variety of roles or, more precisely, strategies of self-presentation. He may attempt to disarm criticism by claiming, like Rousseau, that he will reveal himself utterly and without shame or fear; Frank Harris's *My Life and Loves* and the autobiographical novels of Henry Miller exemplify this strategy, in which sexual confessions are used to establish the author's good faith and willingness to hold back nothing, however discreditable. At the opposite extreme are many autobiographies by generals (e.g. Guderian, Montgomery) which concede nothing and attempt to show how more and greater victories could have been won if only the author's advice had been followed. Examples need not be multiplied;

[15] *Autobiography*, p. 15.

clearly, the modern autobiographer can draw on a tradition which gives him a wide choice among accepted conventions of self-presentation. The Renaissance autobiographer, however, faced a more difficult and confusing task, for he had to organize his 'performance' without much help from literary tradition, unless he was using a particular religious convention. St. Teresa, writing a narrative of spiritual awakening, could use the precedent of Augustine's *Confessions* as a guide to presenting her experience in a way which she could be fairly sure would be acceptable and edifying to her audience. But the secular autobiographer had to find his own way; and in a time of such rapid changes in habits of thought he would find it hard enough to arrive at internal equilibrium and self-knowledge without the burden of having to explain himself to the outside world in addition. We should remember, also, that except in religious thought the techniques and the language itself of self-analysis were still in a rudimentary state. The difficulty of undertaking to describe oneself was eloquently stated by Montaigne:

> My history must be fitted to the present. I may soone change, not only fortune, but intention. It is a counter-roule of divers and variable accidents, and irresolute imaginations, and sometimes contrary: whether it be that my selfe am other, or that I apprehend subjects, by other circumstances and considerations. Howsoever, I may perhaps gaine-say my selfe, but truth (as Demades said) I never gaine-say: Were my mind setled, I would not essay, but resolve my selfe. It is still a Prentise and a probationer.[16]

Montaigne was of course an unusually sensitive and Protean individual; but for that very reason he epitomizes the age's widespread concern with pinning-down a personal identity which had become more elusive than it had ever been before.

The Renaissance secular autobiographer had both to justify or rationalize his project, and to find the means by which he could carry out his aim, i.e. find a form and a language for self-expression. In the next two chapters, covering the objective and subjective modes in secular autobiography, we will see how, and to what extent, British autobiographers solved these problems.

[16] *Essays*, III, p. 23.

VIII
Secular Autobiography: the
Objective Mode

Travel and Military Memoirs

IN THIS chapter I will discuss some travel, military, and political memoirs which illustrate the *res gestae* convention in more or less pure form—though one should bear in mind that nearly all seventeenth-century secular autobiographies are more objective and closer to *res gestae* than their modern equivalents. By their very existence these specialized memoirs testified to a widespread, and largely novel urge for self-commemoration among Englishmen of that time; but they were an innovation of limited value. Autobiography could progress as a genre only to the extent that it did more than simply record external life-events; the mainly factual memoirs surveyed in this chapter indicate the imaginative rigidity of the *res gestae* convention, though they occasionally suggest ways in which more personal and psychologically interesting forms could develop.[1]

Sir Thomas Hoby's *A Booke of the Travaile and Lief of Me* may serve as well as any to exemplify the limitations of travel-memoirs. His book has a great deal to say about his travels, and virtually nothing about his personal life; it consists of a series of descriptions of European towns and of his journeys from one to the other. Hoby omits all reference to his parentage and childhood, and begins the narrative with an account of his studies, at age seventeen, under Martin Bucer. This reticence about his private life continues; for example, Hoby mentions his marriage but says nothing about his wife's personality or his feelings towards her. In his work, as in most travel-memoirs, the topography overshadows the personality of the traveller. We need not linger over the host of seventeenth-century travel memoirs; Fynes Moryson's *An Itinerary* (1617) and Captain

---

[1] For the development of autobiography in the eighteenth and nineteenth centuries see W. Shumaker, *English Autobiography*, and John N. Morris, *Versions of the Self*.

116

John Smith's *True Travels* (1630) are popular and representative works. The genre was a more or less static one; the *Memoirs* (c. 1678) of Sir George Courthop show that, more than a hundred years after Hoby wrote, an autobiography could concern itself with travel still to the exclusion of almost all other interests, and be written in the same unreflective way.

An exception to the rule of unrelieved impersonality in travel memoirs occurs in Edward Coxere's *Adventures by Sea*, the journal of an ordinary seaman of lower-class origin and scant education.[2] Many other seventeenth-century sailors kept journals, but Coxere was more observant and more sensitive than usual, and he also had some skill in organizing his experiences into autobiographical form. His work is a curious hybrid of adventure-tale and spiritual autobiography, for about halfway through his narrative he meets some Quakers and is converted to their belief. The Quaker tradition of spiritual auto-biography was one of the most flourishing but also one of the most restrictive of the century; Coxere, however, does not conform at all to the classic Quaker pattern. The earlier part of his *Adventures* is a forthright narrative of his voyages, enlivened by a dry, mildly cynical wit and a keen eye for nature. His prose, despite its haphazard grammar, is easy and vivid:

> Nearest the land was low sand land, in some places a little hillish. The most live creatures which we saw on the shore was crabs; they had holes and burrowed in the ground like rabbits from the water. There was also in the sand fine shells so curious for colours as if a painter had been at work on them, of which we got abundance (p. 22)

Coxere, unlike most contemporary travel-writers, does not hesitate to tell how he felt during the crises and difficulties that afflicted him. His account of his capture by a Turkish warship in 1657, shortly after he was married, displays this quality:

> We, not being able to hold the dispute with him any longer, was forced to yield to those unreasonable barbarians, to whom we became their slaves, a heart-breaking sorrow. Considering my condition, knowing what I had before worked for I was deprived of, and what little I had was mostly with me, so that I knew I had not wherewithal to release myself, so that I knew not but that I might a ended my days a slave under the hands of merciless men; then the consideration of my poor wife at home, who had such an exercise with my troubles before, and now big with the second child, and this falling the heaviest blow at last: the reader may judge something how it might be with me at that time. (p. 81)

[2] Coxere wrote *c*. 1690; his work was first published in 1946, ed. E. H. W. Meyerstein.

The self-revelation here is not extraordinarily eloquent or profound, but it is a considerable step forward from the barren impersonality or conventional sentiments which one usually meets in similar episodes in earlier travel books.

After his conversion by the Quakers, Coxere's religion became more important to him than even his livelihood (Quaker sailors were almost unemployable because of their refusal to fight if the ship was attacked). But the *Adventures* does not turn into a spiritual auto-biography; nor does Coxere, after his conversion, revise his account of earlier events so as to bring out their religious significance. His conversion is recorded in its due place, but only as one vicissitude among many in his life, and his narrative is organized around his successive voyages rather than according to the stages of his spiritual development. It is possible, however, that Coxere might never have written down his *Adventures* were it not for his contact with the Quaker tradition; moreover, had it not been for the introspection fostered in him by Quakerism he might have produced no more than a routine voyage-journal.[3]

Military memoirs of the sixteenth and seventeenth centuries tend to share the deficiencies of travel memoirs; we need discuss only two examples, one typically dry and the other somewhat unorthodox and lively. Thomas, Lord Fairfax's *Short Memorials* may serve to repre-sent its conventional brethren. Its two parts correspond to the twin obsessions of retired military gentlemen: reminiscence and self-vindication. The first part, 'A Short Memorial of the Northern Actions in which I was engaged', claims a religious inspiration: 'In Gratitude to God for his many Mercies and Deliverances, and not to deprive my self of the Comfort of the Remembrance, I shall set down, as they come into my mind, those things wherein I have found the wonderful Assistance of God to me in the Time of the War in the North' (pp. 1-2). The account of Fairfax's campaigns which follows is clear, practical, and rather impersonal; it sticks closely to the immediate details of battles and sieges, ignoring entirely the religious and social issues about which the war was fought. The second part, 'Short Memorials of Some things to be cleared during my Command in the Army', was written after Fairfax had been forced into retire-ment by the more radical faction in the army. The purpose of this section of his memoirs is pure self-defence: 'By the Grace and Assistance of God, I shall truly set down the Grounds of my Actions during this unhappy War, and especially of those Actions which

[3] For an illuminating discussion of an engaging group of more or less auto-biographical travel-narratives see G. A. Starr, 'Escape from Barbary: A Seven-teenth-Century Genre,' *Huntingdon Library Quarterly* XXIX (1965), pp. 35-52.

seem'd to the World most questionable' (p. 93). Fairfax's mood is sad and disillusioned, yet the code of the British officer seems to inhibit him from expressing whole-heartedly his disappointment at his abortive military career. One gets a better understanding of what seventeenth-century warfare was really like by reading the memoirs of lower-ranking soldiers, such as Thomas Raymond or Sydnam Poyntz. Great captains are rarely so frank about their reasons for joining the army as Poyntz is in his blunt assertion that 'To bee bound an apprentice that life I deemed little better than a dogs life and base'.[4] Poyntz was an avaricious and disloyal mercenary in the Thirty Years War; his autobiography is thoroughly untrustworthy as historical evidence, and crude in style. Yet when he is toying with a concubine in the privy of a Turkish harem, or has the third horse in one day shot under him, his prose always seems worthy of the occasion:

> My last horse that was shot had almost killed mee for beeing shot in the guts, as I thinke, hee mounted on a suddaine such a height, yea I thinke on my conscience two yeards, and suddaine fell to the ground upon his bum, and with his suddaine fall thrust my bum a foot into the ground and fell upon mee and there lay groveling upon mee, that hee put mee out of my senses. (p. 127)

After this bloody encounter Poyntz, with £2,000 of accumulated wages and plunder, sets off for home, where he had left his German wife in charge. What he finds there is described with a poignant spareness of diction:

> mee thought a private life after these wandring wearisome marches did relish sweetly in my thoughts and so after a long march I came nere home, where I heare the true tryall of fortunes mutability, which was that my Wife was killed and my child, my house and my goods all pillaged: My Tenants and Neighbours all served in the same sauce, the whole Village beeing burned; nether horse, Cowe, sheep nor Corne left to feed a Mouse, This when I came home I found too true some poore people got into the ruines living with roots: this went nere mee. (pp. 127-8)

Some other military memoirs, more conventional than Poyntz's, may be listed briefly. Robert Monro's *Expedition with the Worthy Scotch Regiment* (1637) gives another view of the Thirty Years War. Memoirists of the Civil War and after include Sir James Turner, Bulstrode Whitelocke, John Hodgson, James Lord Audley, Andrew Melvill, and John Sheffield, Duke of Buckingham. James II wrote, in French, an account of his campaigns in 1652-60. In general, these works are more important to the historian than to the literary student.

---

[4] *The Relation of Sydnam Poyntz, 1624-36*, p. 45.

Finally, Thomas Raymond's *Life*, while not by a professional soldier, has some of the most amusing and vivid descriptions of seventeenth-century warfare to be found in any contemporary memoirs (see below, pp. 137-9).

Political Memoirs

Seventeenth-century political memoirs include one masterpiece of its kind, Clarendon's *An Account of the Life of Lord Clarendon*,[5] but the average is more fairly represented by the *Autobiography* of Sir Simonds d'Ewes or the *Memoirs* of Sir John Reresby. D'Ewes' work is a chronicle of political events and court-anecdotes, written for the benefit of his family and posterity. His self-importance apparently prevented him from giving any extended account of his intimate affairs, and his work is consequently one of the dullest of early auto-biographies. Reresby's *Memoirs* are more entertaining, but their interest is much greater in the earlier part of his life, before he became an active politician and M.P.; in the political part of his book he is no more imaginative than d'Ewes. The *Memoirs* as a whole are considered in Chapter IX.

Clarendon's autobiography, like most political memoirs, is not rich in personal revelation. The nature of his trade inclines the politician to curb his spontaneity and to guard his emotional life from out-siders; Clarendon conforms to this tendency by narrating his life in the third person, thus interposing a curtain of formality and im-personality between himself and his audience. As a result his auto-biography, the longest and most serious written in English until then (1668-72), impresses us as the testament of a great historian, states-man, and observer of men, yet fails to satisfy our curiosity about the inner nature of the man who wrote it. The book's fame rests on the 'characters' of Clarendon's friends and enemies which it contains; these brief and brilliant sketches of their subjects are in the tradition of the contemporary character-books. Yet this tradition was a dangerous one for the autobiographer to work in, because of its emphasis on wit and aphoristic generalizations at the expense of searching psychological analysis of the individual subject. Of a man like Sidney Godolphin, who could easily be brought to life on the page by caricaturing his peculiarities and neuroses, Clarendon wrote inimitably (p. 24). But his character of himself, though elegant and apparently candid, somehow fails to differentiate itself from his characters of others. It begins thus:

[5] Both a folio and an octavo edition were published in the same year, 1759; my page-references are to the folio.

He had without Doubt, great Infirmities; which by a providential Mercy were seasonably restrained from growing into Vices, at least into any that were habitual. He had Ambition enough to keep him from being satisfied with his own Condition, and to raise his Spirit to great Designs of raising himself; but not to transport him to endeavour it by any crooked, and indirect Means. He was never suspected to flatter the greatest Men; or in the least Degree to dissemble his own Opinions, or Thoughts, how ingrateful soever it often proved, and even an affected Defect in, and Contempt of these two useful Qualities cost him dear afterwards. He indulged his Palate very much, and took even some Delight in eating and drinking well; but without any Approach to Luxury; and, in Truth, rather discoursed like an Epicure, than was one. (p. 35)

Of this one can only say that it is not Clarendon's fault that the romantic revolution has come between him and us. He was attempting to write a history of himself comparable in weightiness and elevation of style to Cicero or Tacitus; but nowadays any such attempt is bound to be condemned from the start as assuming a radically dishonest pose—no one, we like to think, can reveal the truth about himself in such stately and symmetrical antitheses. If he wishes to convince us of the depth of his feelings, he must use the language of Wordsworth rather than, say, of Dr. Johnson in *Rasselas*. The modern prejudice in favour of the confessional type of autobiography is overwhelming, despite the fact that many of the most successful English autobiographies—those of Gibbon, Mill, and Newman, for example—are more concerned with the authors' intellectual development than with their emotional lives. Moreover, an autobiographer does not necessarily come closer to the 'truth' about himself merely by confessing to acts or feelings of which other men are usually ashamed.

To evaluate Clarendon's work fairly, then, we must take him upon his own terms. He wrote his autobiography in exile, banished from England by the envy of Parliament and the ingratitude of Charles II, and he was determined to vindicate himself to posterity. The truth about the political events in which he took part was of more importance to him than self-exploration. All he asked of his readers was a willingness to believe that when he described himself in the words below he spoke no more than simple truth:

That which supported, and rendered him generally acceptable, was his Generosity (for He had too much a Contempt of Money) and the Opinion Men had of the Goodness, and Justice of his Nature which was transcendent in him, in a wonderful Tenderness, and Delight in obliging. His Integrity was ever without Blemish; and believed to be above Temptation. (p. 35)

121

IX

Secular Autobiography: the
Individualists

TRAVEL, MILITARY, and political memoirs have an easily recognizable purpose and can be evaluated for the distinctive merits we seek in them. The autobiographies to be considered in this chapter, however, present much greater problems to the critic—in part because their authors were often themselves uncertain as to what they were trying to do and how they should go about it. For the political or military memoirist, the choice of an autobiographical role was relatively simple: he would present himself as a public figure, brave and shrewd in battle or wise and loyal in the council room, ever seeking the public good. To this central self-conception he would add some details of his private life and inclinations; often, he would demonstrate his good faith by confessing certain venial and socially-acceptable faults which proved him to be a man like other men. In the autobiographies now to be discussed, however, this kind of convention is either less rigidly applied or ignored altogether. There were many reasons why some autobiographers enjoyed a greater freedom in self-definition, though, as I have already indicated (in Chapter II), I think the increased social mobility of seventeenth-century Britain was especially important. A high proportion of the present group of secular autobiographers seem either to have changed their social position, or to have been particularly sensitive to contradictions and incongruities in it.

These autobiographers were mostly of higher than average social rank, for reasons which seem obvious enough: illiteracy was widespread among working-class Englishmen, and even if one of them was able to write an autobiography the chances of his manuscript being preserved were quite small. The exceptions to this rule occur among the swarm of lower-class religious zealots who emerged during and after the Civil War, and among workers who were able to acquire a more sophisticated outlook, such as the seamen Coxere and Edward Barlow.

The Courtiers: Robert Cary, Herbert of Cherbury, Sir Kenelm Digby

The autobiographers Robert Cary, Earl of Monmouth (b. 1560), Edward Lord Herbert of Cherbury (b. 1583), and Sir Kenelm Digby (b. 1603) represent three rapidly-evolving generations of the English aristocracy. Their narratives of courtly adventure illustrate a variety of approaches to self-portraiture among early secular writers, and show how a more subjective point of view emerged in successive generations. Cary's *Memoirs*, though they give us a clear idea of the author's temperament, are mainly historical in the tradition of *res gestae*. Herbert of Cherbury's *Autobiography* is a blend of historical events and personal trivia. Digby's *Loose Fantasies* is a sentimentalized autobiography of youth in which facts are freely distorted, real people are concealed behind romantic pseudonyms, and the author focuses on emotional development rather than on external events. Cary still accepts, implicitly, the notion that a man's identity is best revealed by his deeds, especially those which link him most closely to the external forms and rituals of civilization.[1] With Digby, however, reality has become completely stylized and subordinated to his attempt at maintaining a particular role and convention of self-presentation—where Cary sees his life as history, Digby sees his as drama.[2]

Cary's *Memoirs* are remembered for the descriptions of his meetings with Queen Elizabeth, especially the interview of 1602 when she was mortally sick. But they have a more general value as a picture of the adventurous, extrovert life led by a typical younger son of the Elizabethan nobility. From the beginning of his career, Cary was an attractive young man whose eye was firmly fixed on the main chance. He was brave, resourceful, stoical in misfortune, crafty and determined when the opportunity for advancement presented itself. His great chance came when Elizabeth fell sick for the last time:

> Shee tooke mee by the hand, and wrung it hard, and said, 'No, Robin, I am not well,' and then discoursed with mee of her indisposition, and that her heart had been sad and heavy for ten or twelve dayes, and in her discourse she fetched not so few as forty or fifty great sighes. I was grieved at the first to see her in this plight; for in all my lifetime

[1] Such as, for example, announcing to James I his accession to the throne of England, or enforcing rough and ready justice in the Scottish border settlements.

[2] My argument here is based solely on the generational gap; none of these three men saw each other's works, and Herbert of Cherbury's autobiography was written some twenty years after the other two—which were written at almost the same time, in the late 1620s.

before I never knew her fetch a sigh, but when the Queene of Scottes
was beheaded. (pp. 136-7)

Cary's grief was undoubtedly sincere; none the less, after a short and
one-sided consultation with his conscience he wrote to James VI,
informing him of the Queen's illness and promising that he would be
the first to arrive at Edinburgh with news of the Queen's death when
it should finally come. Thanks to a cunning escape from the Council's
guards, and to amazing horsemanship, Cary was as good as his word.
He rode from London to Edinburgh in two and a half days:

> Very early on Saturday I tooke horse for Edenborough, and came to
> Norham about twelve at noone, so that I might well have been with
> the King at supper time: but I gott a great fall by the way, and my
> horse with one of his heels gave mee a great blow on the head that
> made mee shed much blood. It made mee so weake that I was forced
> to ride a soft pace after, so that the King was newly gone to bed by the
> time that I knocked at the gate. I was quickly lett in, and carried up to
> the King's chamber. I kneeled by him, and saluted him by his title of
> England, Scotland, France and Ireland. (pp. 150-51)

The anger of the Council at this coup was so great that Cary was
forced out of the position of gentleman of the bedchamber which he
had begged of the King, and he was in bad favour until 1610 when he
gained a place in the entourage of Prince Henry. From then on he
thrived, becoming Earl of Monmouth in 1626.

If we are to believe the prayer with which they begin, Cary's
Memoirs were written as a spiritual exercise: 'O Lord my God . . .
give mee of thy grace to call to minde in some measure thy great and
manifold blessings, that thou hast blessed mee withall; though my
weaknesse be such, and my memory so short, as I have no abilities to
expresse them as I ought to do, yet Lord bee pleased to accept of this
sacrifice of praise and thanksgiving' (p. 1). But Cary's religion is the
rough piety of the man of action; he takes his faith for granted, and
does not attempt to write a spiritual autobiography. There is no
development of his religious views, no soul-searching inquiry into his
past sins. The connection between religion and action in Cary's mind
is illustrated by a passage describing his delight in upholding the law
in the violent, semi-feudal world of the Scots Marches:

> Thus after I had passed my best time in court, and got little, I betooke
> myself to the country, after I was past one and thirty years old, where I
> lived with great content: for wee had a stirring world, and few days
> passed over my head but I was on horseback, either to prevent
> mischiefe, or to take malefactours, and to bring the border in better
> quiet than it had been in times past. God blessed mee in all my

actions, and I cannot remember that I undertooke anything in the time that I was there but it tooke good effect.[3]

The invocation of God at the beginning of what turns out to be an overwhelmingly secular narrative with an occasional pious comment may seem inappropriate to the modern reader; yet the practice is common among seventeenth-century autobiographers. Cary's opening prayer gives us a significant clue to the mood in which he undertook his *Memoirs*—humble, a little confused about how to proceed, eager to point out God's mercies in the many vicissitudes of his life, above all, self-consciously aware that he had an important business on hand. His sober invocation is very typical of the seriousness with which most seventeenth-century autobiographers look back on their past deeds; though equally typical is the way in which his natural ebullience and vivid apprehension of the flavour of particular encounters, stratagems, and skirmishes transcend the announced moral framework of his narrative. The *Memoirs* reveal a temperament in which the sensuous excitement of stirring events and of self-assertion in action overwhelms, and somehow puts in a reduced perspective, his attempt to see his life as a whole and *sub specie aeternitatis*. In this he is a true Elizabethan adventurer, but also a microcosm in which we can see the dialectical struggle (typical of the age) between the attitude that sees everything as an exemplum figuring forth a moral truth, and the attitude that sees reality directly in its sensuous immediacy.

In the *Autobiography*[4] of Herbert of Cherbury we find a further decline in the degree to which religion controls the author's response to experience. At the start, he professes an intention to examine his conscience, in the tradition of spiritual autobiography: 'so as my age is now past threescore, it will be fit to recollect my former actions, and examine what had been done well or ill, to the intent I may both reform that which was amiss, and so make my peace with God, as also comfort myself in those things which, through God's great grace and favour, have been done according to the rules of conscience, virtue and honour' (p. 2). But he is entirely without the spirit of self-abasement characteristic of such spiritual autobiographers as Bunyan; Herbert is always the soul of honour, the cynosure of all eyes and the defender of the oppressed. The closest he comes to remorse of conscience is in his typically self-indulgent confession of certain fleshly sins:

[3] In his preference of the backwoods to the Court Cary went against the trend of aristocratic fashion at the time, which suggests that even in his own generation he should be considered a bit archaic in his tastes. For the attraction of London and the Court, see Stone, *Crisis of the Aristocracy*, Chapter VIII.

[4] Ed. Sidney Lee (1892).

my quartan ague ... when it quitted me, left me in a more perfect health than I formerly enjoyed, and indeed disposed me to some follies which I afterwards repented, and do still repent of; but as my wife refused to come over, and my temptations were great, I hope the faults I committed are the more pardonable. Howsoever I can say truly, that, whether in France or England, I was never in a bawdy-house, nor used my pleasures intemperately, and much less did accompany them with that dissimulation and falsehood which is commonly found in men addicted to love women. (pp. 208-9)

Despite his respect for the outward forms of religion, Herbert foreshadows the eighteenth century in his beliefs and in the relatively slight influence of doctrine on his actions.[5] The substantial motives which shape his autobiography are, first, his desire to instruct his descendants and, second, the often ludicrous egotism which leads him to assume that the smallest details of his adventures will interest posterity. This latter trait makes him more akin to Cellini or Cardano than to the usually self-effacing British autobiographer of the time.

Herbert begins his autobiography by proclaiming his intention both to instruct others and draw up his spiritual accounts, then launches into an account of the antiquity and greatness of his family tree; he continues with an extended digression on the proper education of a Renaissance gentleman. The account of his own life is little more than two-thirds of the work (which is, however, incomplete) and consists of a series of anecdotes about his duels and other courtly exploits. Herbert was made a Knight of the Bath shortly after James's accession, an honour which seems to have gone to his head. He took his oath of knighthood with utter seriousness, and in later life stuck to it faithfully in spite of ridicule:

There is another custom likewise, that the knights the first day wear the gown of some religious order, and the night following to be bathed; after which they take an oath never to sit in place where injustice should be done, but they shall right it to the uttermost of their power; and particularly ladies and gentlewomen that shall be wronged in their honour, if they demand assistance, and many other points, not unlike the romances of knight errantry. (p. 84)

He could never resist a challenge, and would often invent grounds for a duel when none really existed. At the siege of Juliers in 1610 he was

[5] Herbert's *De Religione Gentilium* (Amsterdam, 1663) has been called the charter of the Deists; it attempts to prove that all religions recognize the same five main articles. Aubrey's anecdote, if true, neatly sums up Herbert's faith: 'James Usher, Lord Primate of Ireland, was sent for by him, when in his death-bed, and he would have received the sacrament. He sayd indifferently of it that "if there was good in any-thing 'twas in that," or "if it did no good 'twould doe no hurt". The Primate refused it, for which many blamed him. He then turned his head to the other side and expired very serenely.' (*Lives*, p. 135).

almost killed when one Colonel Balagny challenged Herbert to accompany him on a two-man charge against the massed enemy artillery (pp. 114-15). When Herbert wished to continue the trial of manhood, however, he met with a ribald rebuff:

> [I said] I heard he had a fair mistress, and that the scarf he wore was her gift, and that I would maintain I had a worthier mistress than he, and that I would do as much for her sake as he, or any else durst do for his. Balagny hereupon looking merrily upon me, said, 'If we shall try who is the abler man to serve his mistress, let both of us get two wenches, and he that doth his business best, let him be the braver man'; and that, for his part, he had no mind to fight on that quarrel. I, looking hereupon somewhat disdainfully on him, said he spoke more like a paillard than a cavalier; to which he answering nothing, I rid my ways. (pp. 122-3)

Most critics of the work have complained of Herbert's continual ruffling, his lack of self-criticism, and his dwelling on episodes which make him look foolish while slighting his more substantial achievements in scholarship and philosophy. Yet it is unfair to say, as Patrick Cruttwell does, that 'What emerges is a naïve and ineffectual braggart'.[6] In his autobiography, Herbert is attempting to bring to life an intrinsically noble ideal, that of the Renaissance gentleman. He fails, and the blame can be laid partly on his own weaknesses; but the unresponsiveness of the society in which he lived must also be taken into account. The ideals of magnificence and knightly honour were accessible to a Sir Philip Sidney in a way they could not be to Herbert, who in the prime of his life found himself in the England of James I and the Duke of Buckingham. Herbert's real failure was his inability to realize that times had changed; it is a curious paradox that this man, who in his philosophical ideas was a century ahead of his time, should in his life have guided himself by the antiquated notions of a chivalry that he attempted vainly to revive. The triumphs of knightly courtesy and courage that he relates somehow fail to ring true—we feel that often he was not a hero but merely a nuisance, and there is a note of senility in his obsessive repetition of past successes.

An autobiography is not necessarily vitiated by gross and insensitive egotism, as Cellini's example proves, but with Herbert boastfulness is complemented by the suppression of the more contemplative part of his nature. To exaggerate one's exploits is a temptation to which most autobiographers yield in some degree, and without doing much harm to the literary merit of their works; but to restrict one's account to the relatively narrow segment of experience in which one feels most successful almost guarantees that the integrity of the autobiography will be fatally compromised. None the less, Herbert's

[6] *The Shakespearean Moment*, p. 179.

addition of a modicum of psychological analysis to the skeleton of *res gestae* marks an important advance in British secular auto-biography; any attempt to delve deeper in search of the springs of action was to the good.

Sir Kenelm Digby's *Loose Fantasies* is the first British auto-biography which describes its author's 'sentimental education'.[7] We may surmise that Digby himself felt his project to be unusual, and perhaps somewhat embarrassing—why else would he give his charac-ters pseudonyms, and leave instructions for the manuscript to be burnt in the event of his death? A codicil describes the circumstances under which he composed his 'fantasies'; it deserves note as one of the first documents in English to give a detailed, first-hand account of the genesis of a literary work.[8]

Leaving behind his wife Venetia and two infant sons, Digby had sailed for the Mediterranean in December 1627 on a privateering expedition financed and commanded by himself. After a successful battle against French and Venetian ships the following June, his ships were scattered by a storm and he put in at the island of Milo to refit. He was received by the governor of the island and, being in a pensive mood, 'I soon perceived that my courteous host was much troubled at my retirement, and omitted nothing that might avail to divert me from it; and among other things, made me a liberal offer to interest me in the good graces of several of the most noted beauties of that place, who in all ages have been known to be no niggards of their favours' (p. 323). To avoid the appearance of churlishness in refusing his host's offer, Digby pretended to have some serious business on hand; in fact, he decided to 'set down in writing my wandering fantasies as they presented themselves to me' (p. 325). He was only twenty-five at the time, so it is not surprising that his autobiographical fantasies took the form of a romanticized version of his courtship of the notorious Venetia Stanley.

Digby had an axe to grind in telling the story of his relations with Venetia; for she was as renowned for her loose morals as for her beauty—if Aubrey is to be believed, she was 'much enclining to a Bona Roba (near altogether)'.[9] She was also three years older than Digby, and had engaged in several well-publicized liaisons before she married him. His reaction to the mockery aroused by his marriage was to extol their love as an example of the highest contentment to

---

[7] *Private Memoirs of Sir Kenelm Digby* (1827). The anonymous editor (Sir Nicholas Harris Nicholas) 'castrated' the title as well as the body of the work.

[8] I exclude such essentially conventional accounts as the openings of Chaucer's dream-visions, or the first sonnet of Sidney's *Astrophel and Stella*.

[9] *Lives*, p. 101.

which man could aspire; he would hold up for admiration 'the perfect friendship and noble love of two generous persons, that seemed to be born in this age by ordinance of heaven to teach the world anew what it hath long forgotten, the mystery of loving with honour and constancy, between a man and a woman' (p. 6). Although Digby was ostensibly not writing for publication, he wrote as if for an invisible audience of detractors, with the vehemence and over-emphasis typical of works of controversy. Thus, he gave himself the name of 'Theagenes', the hero and paragon of constant love in Heliodorus's *Aethiopica*;[10] while Venetia became 'Stelliana', a name suggesting beauty and chastity in its owner.

The *Loose Fantasies* begins with an elaborate statement of the theme of purity and constancy, exemplified by the idyllic friendship of Theagenes and Stelliana as small children:

> [they] the very first time that ever they had sight of one another, grew so fond of each other's company, that all that saw them said assuredly that something above their tender capacity breathed this sweet affection into their hearts. They would mingle serious kisses among their innocent sports: and whereas other children of like age did delight in fond plays and light toys, these two would spend the day in looking upon each other's face, and in accompanying these looks with gentle sighs, which seemed to portend that much sorrow was laid up for their more understanding years. (pp. 16-17)

These later 'sorrows' take the form of innumerable obstacles to the smooth course of their love, some of which seem to the unprejudiced reader to be of their own making. Stelliana has to fight off the attentions of the nobleman Ursatius (the Earl of Dorset), who goes so far as to kidnap her and carry her off to a lonely country house; she escapes with her virtue intact, only to become compromised by her intimacy with Mardontius, a young nobleman living nearby who shelters and protects her. Finally she agrees to marry Mardontius, but is discarded when he falls in love with 'a new rural beauty' (p. 110) and releases Stelliana from her troth. Meanwhile Theagenes, the supposed ideal lover, is also behaving in somewhat questionable fashion. He is often absent on trips to 'Athens' (Paris) and 'Alexandria' (Madrid). In Athens he barely escapes the clutches of a nymphomaniac Queen of Attica (Marie de Medici), and in Alexandria he makes a local beauty fall in love with him for a bet. He is also nearly murdered by a gang of ruffians hired by an admirer of yet another maiden. A true Renaissance youth, Theagenes spends much of his time pondering such eternal problems as free will and determinism; his search for wisdom is aided by a 'Brachman of India' whom he meets on the road (pp. 119 ff). These were pursuits in which Stelliana,

---

[10] Which Digby presumably read in William Underdowne's translation (1587).

perhaps, could not well accompany Theagenes; for, says Aubrey of Venetia, 'when her head was opened there was found but little braine' (*Lives*, p. 101).

In the last third of the *Fantasies*, after the lovers have finally married, Digby's concern to defend the propriety of his union becomes almost obsessive. He proclaims that 'the love of a virtuous soul dwelling in a fair and perfect body, is the noblest and worthiest action that a man is master of' (p. 239). But he is not sufficiently firm in this conviction to remain at home and devote himself to Stelliana. His detractors have been busy; in response, despite Stelliana's complaints at his plans to leave her, he undertakes to perform 'some generous action that might give testimony to the world how his affections had nothing impaired the nobleness of his mind, nor abated the edge of his active and vigorous spirits' (p. 301). This 'generous action' was the privateering voyage to the Mediterranean in the course of which his memoirs were written.

The *Fantasies* presents one of the most complete and detailed accounts of the progress of a love-affair which had been written in English up to that time. But Digby's approach is still quite different from the striving for verisimilitude of the eighteenth-century novelist. In addition to the use of pseudonyms, and of a style much closer to *Euphues* than to *Pamela*, Digby tries to endow the lovers' emotions with a constancy, purity, and ideal significance which they do not seem to have had in actual fact and which no normal pair of lovers could hope to achieve. Theagenes and Stelliana are presented as 'types of that trinity and unity living in eternity' (p. 9), and as the only perfect lovers who have ever lived. The romantic notion of heightening the intensity of self-portrayal by telling the whole truth about oneself, including follies and weaknesses, has no place here; instead, Digby strives for intensity by removing the 'lower' elements of the story and attempting to make the lovers seem like mythological heroes and heroines. In this formulation of the lovers' role, as in many other respects, Digby reveals himself as a true Renaissance Platonist.

His work both expresses the Renaissance literary ideal of sexual love, and suggests why the ideal was losing its power. The *Arcadia* and the *Loose Fantasies* include similar incidents, in which the lover finds his way secretly into his mistress's bedroom. Sidney describes the encounter between Pyrocles and Philoclea thus:

> for the king at his parting had left the chamber open, and she at that time lay, as the heate of the countrie did well suffer, upon the top of her bed, hauing her beauties eclipsed with nothing but with a faire smocke, wrought all in flames of ash-colour silke and gold, lying so upon her right side, that the left thigh downe to the foot, yeelded her

delightfull proportion to the full view, which was seene by the help of a rich lampe, which thorow the curtaines a litle drawne cast forth a light upon her, as the Moone doth when it shines into a thinne wood. . . .[11]

Here is how Theagenes views Stelliana, in similar circumstances:

For as she rolled herself about, the clothes that were sunk down to the other side, left that part of the bed where she now lay wholly uncovered; and her smock was so twisted about her fair body, that all her legs and the best part of her thighs were naked, which lay so one over the other, that they made a deep shadow where the never satisfied eye of Theagenes wished for the greatest light. . . . Her belly was covered with her smock, which it raised up with a gentle swelling, and expressed the perfect figure of it through the folds of that discourteous veil, which yet was too weak a let for Theagenes's exalted fantasy, who, not satisfied with the external appearing beauties, did by profound contemplation dive into and represent unto himself the fairer hidden parts.[12]

In the second passage, written some forty years after the first, the heroine has, despite the formal language of erotic romance, become an all too fleshly creature. She 'rolls herself about' and lies with her smock twisted about her body. The effect of this injection of realism into the Renaissance erotic convention is almost pornographic; Theagenes' honest desire is in fact coarsened by being expressed in this kind of prissy Arcadian diction. The language of the *Loose Fantasies* is the medium of a sixteenth-century Platonic idealism whose day has passed; it is a language which cannot describe the real, sublunary world without revealing a radical incompatibility between form and content. We have already marked the anachronism of Herbert of Cherbury's attempt to present himself as a seventeenth-century knight of the Round Table; Digby's attempt to apotheosize his love for Venetia was similarly compromised from the start, partly by her notorious wantonness, but more by his inability to reconcile the flesh and blood Venetia, whom we glimpse from time to time, with the pastoral heroine Stelliana.

The value of the *Loose Fantasies* does not lie in its hopelessly creaking pastoral machinery, its immature philosophizing, or its unconvincing deification of Stelliana; we should look, rather, to Digby's attempt to explore with some degree of subtlety the difficulties and misunderstandings in his courtship of Venetia—the temptations to which she was subjected, the rival attractions for him

[11] *The Countesse of Pembrokes Arcadia* (1598), p. 369.
[12] This quotation is taken from a passage 'castrated' from the 1827 edition. I quote from an appendix containing the expurgated passages in E. W. Bligh, *Sir Kenelm Digby and his Venetia* (1932), p. 294. It seems almost certain that Digby was imitating the passage just quoted from the *Arcadia*.

of fame or wealth to be gained by diplomacy or war in distant places. These were immediate problems for the lovers, and direct treatment of them made the pastoral framework irrelevant. In the *Loose Fantasies* the familiar conventions of sixteenth-century romance are becoming threadbare, while the themes and conventions of the sentimental novel can be vaguely discerned in the background; though they will not be fully and consciously realized until the eighteenth century.[13]

In the three aristocratic autobiographers of this section we find definite contributions to the development of autobiography as a genre—yet, to no obvious or promising end. From the extroverted, historical narrative of Cary we move to the flamboyant self-dramatization of Herbert and the intermingling of fantasy with reality in Digby; there is an appearance of progress; but Herbert's work, like his own life, peters out inconclusively, while the *Loose Fantasies* hovers ineffectually, sometimes even ludicrously, between romance and novel. After the Civil War, the lower levels of the aristocracy cultivate yet another style in autobiography—which, as we shall see below (pp. 142 ff), again expresses their failure to come to grips with the times.[14]

Other Secular Autobiographers

Of the more than twenty autobiographies which remain to be discussed, only four were published in the seventeenth century: those of

[13] Seventeenth-century writers of the courtly school were not able to cast off the hampering influence of the romance convention; it was not until after the revolution of 1642 that the conditions for the emergence of the novel proper, with its middle-class orientation, were created. See Ian Watt, *The Rise of the Novel*, Chapters I and II.

[14] Three minor aristocratic autobiographers may be mentioned here.

Sir William Wentworth's autobiography, written 1607, gives suggestions for the prudent management of family affairs and pious advice to his children—which failed to keep his famous son from the scaffold.

The *Vita Authoris* of Mildmay Fane, 2nd Earl of Westmoreland, is a self-consciously literary Latin memoir of sixty years of the author's life, with emphasis on the Civil War and Commonwealth periods.

The autobiography of Theophilus Hastings, Earl of Huntingdon, exists in two drafts, both incomplete. It is a thoroughly pedestrian narrative, mainly about family business; but the opening statement is of some interest:

I hope you [his son George, eighth Earl?] will not interprate it an affectation that I leave you in my Cabinet [written above] | For yr private perusall | some account of my selfe since I doe it not out [of] any conceit or opinion I have of my person but because there are some things which may bee usefull for you to knowe even in the future course of yr life and will make you retain kind thoughts of your ffather when hee is in the grave (fol. 410)

None of these three autobiographies has been published; for manuscript references, see bibliography.

Bodley, Croke, Elliot, and Hobbes. In the absence of visible norms and traditions for British secular autobiography, each man was a law unto himself; the critic finds himself confronted with works in Latin hexameters (Hobbes), in the style of sixteenth-century romance, and in almost as many other modes as we have authors. For my own purposes I have divided this motley group of autobiographies into four classes, using criteria which are mainly sociological; other divisions are possible, and I would not claim that the works in each category form a literary genre or sub-genre in the usual sense of the word.

(a) *Déclassé Opportunists and Adventurers.* I include under this heading the following autobiographers: Simon Forman, William Lilly, Goodwin Wharton, Francis Markham, Thomas Raymond, Charles Croke, Adam Elliot, William Fuller, and Edward Barlow. These men seem to have been, in greater or lesser degree, 'free-floating' individuals—men who cut themselves loose from their social origins and chose, or were forced, to live by their wits. Persons of this kind became much more numerous in Britain from the later sixteenth century onward, probably because of a general increase in social mobility, and other changes in class structures, at that time (see pp. 19 ff above). The autobiographies of this group suggest that seventeenth-century society may have had more openness and flexibility than it is generally given credit for—especially in parts of society somewhat removed from the sectors fought over by the highly-organized forces of Roundhead and Cavalier.

Our first three autobiographers exploited, with varying success, the opportunities offered by astrology, necromancy, and kindred arts. Simon Forman's *Autobiography*, written at the beginning of the century, is a charmingly whimsical account of this famous charlatan's youth.[15] The style is a weird composite of romance, the Bible, and the Golden Legend; the Gospel of Saint Matthew presides at first: 'In Dei Nomine, Amen. This is the bocke of the life and generation of Simon, the sonn of William, the sonn of Richard, the sonn of ... [etc.]' (p. 1). After such an auspicious birth, Simon enjoys a visionary childhood in the country. In his dreams, floods and 'mighti mountaines and hills com rowling againste him, yet he gote upp allwaies to the top of them and with moch adoe wente over them'; he takes these to represent 'the great and mightie potentates that he had controversy with afterwards' (p. 3). He goes to school with a succession of eccentrics, one of whom uses a large stack of firewood to keep warm; not by burning it, but by carrying it up and down stairs for exercise!

[15] *The Autobiography and Personal Diary*, ed. J. O. Halliwell (1849).

Unfortunately, Simon's father dies while he is still a child and he is sent off to live with an aunt, for 'his mother, who never loved him, grudged at his beinge at hom' (p. 5). After two years of exile he is apprenticed to a cloth-merchant and new tribulations beset him: his mistress is a shrew, the housemaid will not obey Simon until he beats her, and his master breaks his promise to send him to grammar-school. But he cannot be kept down. His beating of the maid earns him her goodwill—'and many a pound of butter she yelded in the bottom after for Simon's breakfaste, which before that she wold never doe' (p. 8). He is determined to educate himself, 'for his mind was moste ardently set on his bocke', and learns the day's lessons at night from a fellow-apprentice who goes to school. After a row with his mistress Simon leaves his apprenticeship, becomes a schoolmaster at seventeen, then manages to enter Magdalen College as a poor scholar. The autobiography (it is continued as a diary) ends with Simon, ever-resourceful, benefiting from the patronage of two noble, idle, and dissolute bachelors of arts: 'and they never studied nor gave themselves to their bockes, but to goe to scolles of defence, to the daunceing scolles, to stealle dear and connyes, and to hunt the hare, and to woinge of wentches' (p. 12).

Brief as Forman's autobiography is, he is one of the first English-men whom we can know directly and as an individual. His delight in self-dramatization, his putting on of one mask after another, define his individuality rather than obscure it—having several points of view, we see him more clearly. Foreman's protean quality reflects his refusal to be bound by conventional social patterns: leaving his place of birth and his apprenticeship, he became a man without a calling—first a poor scholar and parasite, later a successful charlatan 'who combined alchemy with astrology, medicine, necromancy, and other crafts'.[16] It is unfortunate that he only carried his autobiography as far as his student days; he does not seem to have had any intention of completing or publishing the work, and his motive for writing it was, apparently, simple self-amusement. His career supports the truism that the parvenu is often a more than usually acute observer of the social scene, and especially of the roles that he himself may play thereon.

The *Life* of the astrologer William Lilly is almost as entertaining as Forman's.[17] Like Forman, Lilly was brought up in the country and

---

[16] L. C. Knights, *Drama and Society in the Age of Jonson*, pp. 206-7; quoting Herford and Simpson, *Ben Jonson*, II, 88-93. Jonson undoubtedly satirized Forman, among others, in *The Alchemist*.

[17] *The Lives of those eminent antiquaries Elias Ashmole, Esquire and Mr. William Lilly, written by themselves* (1774). Lilly composed his autobiography in 1667, at the request of his friend Ashmole.

made himself unpopular at home by his bookish inclinations and lack of aptitude for farm-work. When he was seventeen he was packed off to London to work in the house of a nouveau-riche former servant, who 'could neither write nor read; he lived upon his annual rents, was of no calling or profession' (p. 11). Lilly weeded the garden, scraped trenchers, and bided his time. After seven years his master died, and Lilly soon after secretly married his widow, a corpulent Wife of Bath who 'had been twice married to old men, was now resolved to be couzened no more' (p. 27). Now financially independent, Lilly entertained himself with fishing and sermons until, some five years later, he discovered astrology and plunged into the study of it for up to eighteen hours a day. He persevered for three years until struck by a psychological crisis of unexplained origin: 'I became melancholly, growing lean and spare, and every day worse; so that in the year 1635 my infirmity continuing, and my acquaintance increasing, I resolved to live in the country, and in March and April 1636 removed my goods to Hersham, where I now live' (p. 50). The remainder of the autobiography is mainly concerned with lawsuits, political difficulties (Lilly tried to help Charles I escape from prison on the Isle of Wight in 1648), and astrological predictions.

Because he was writing for the amusement of his friend Ashmole, Lilly emphasized the experiences of his life which would make a good story, and he seems to have shunned close self-analysis as being out of place in such a narrative. His autobiography is therefore less revealing than Forman's ingenuous account of his life, yet it has the same shrewd insights into the way of the world, set down without cant. One can only regret that Lilly's chosen form, the 'letter to a friend', led him to overload his narrative with anecdotes of slight relevance to his own development, and also to omit the harsher side of his struggle for security and respectability.

Goodwin Wharton's autobiography, which is still unpublished, is one of the most curious in the century.[18] It begins quietly enough, in a tone scarcely distinguishable from a dozen other works:

> My Life; my Deare Son being now becom most worthy of notice I thought fitt to compile it together, and resolving (with Gods assistance to continue so to doe) to leave it you you as ye greatest and best of the earthly legacies I can bequeath to you; if you sincerely make a good use of it; which if you doe, God to whose infinit marcy I comitt you will most surely blesse you, a hundred fold yett more then he hath don me: who have bin blest ten thousand times more than ether my wishes or thoughts could have reach^t: . . .

Wharton, though he was the son of a Baron, failed to establish

[18] Ms. B.M. Add. 2006-7. Wharton was a great-grandchild of Robert Cary.

himself in a career; he ran into debt and was eventually cut off by his father. In 1683, when he was thirty, he came under the influence of one Mrs. Mary Parish. With her aid he hoped to get 'some secrett power whereby I might have so good luck as to win generally att play' (fol. 33^r), and also the ability to converse with spirits. Mrs. Parish, who was suffering from a temporary financial embarrassment, was only too happy to oblige Wharton—for a consideration. She introduced him to a whole tribe of spirits or 'Lowlanders', reigned over by a King and Queen. As the autobiography continues, we realize that Wharton is more than deluded: he is insane. He becomes a full-time astrologer and spiritualist, to whom a host of spirits and angels (including Gabriel) pay regular visits.

At the end of the first volume of his massive work (289 closely-written folio leaves) Wharton reports a divine message that 'all I have herein writt . . . was by inspiration from him' (fol. 177^r). The second volume degenerates into total madness and incoherence. Though its final effect is pathetic, Wharton's autobiography impresses by its sheer massiveness; and it is a document of great interest for historians of magic and of mental illness.

The remaining autobiographers in this group were mainly men of action, in contrast to the lucubrations of Forman, Lilly, and Wharton. Francis Markham's terse and factual *Autobiography* narrates a career not unlike Wharton's, though without the latter's bizarre and ultimately insane mysticism. Markham also had the advantage of noble birth but he was a younger son and a malcontent—a man without a function. At times law student, soldier of fortune, and wooer of rich widows, his final berth was as a muster-master. He scraped a living by such schemes as buying a jewel for £50 and raffling it off among ten noble ladies of his acquaintance for £10 per ticket. Markham had little to boast about, and in an earlier age his autobiography would surely never have been written; his biographical urge seems first to have been aroused by an antiquarian interest in his descent—he wrote a history of the Markham family and probably added his auto-biography to it to complete the story. But whatever his motive, he provides supporting evidence for the hypothesis that self-concepts were changing fundamentally at this time; for his life was distin-guished only by a steady decline into social obscurity, without any of the successes that other autobiographers wrote to commemorate or celebrate.

The autobiographies of Thomas Raymond and of Charles Croke illustrate the eccentric conceptions of literary form common among secular autobiographers.[19] Both were young men in search of a

---

[19] *Autobiography of Thomas Raymond*, ed. G. Davies.

respectable career; unless one had powerful connections, this could be a difficult undertaking in the seventeenth century, when the concept of appointment and regular advancement according to merit was not widely accepted. Raymond finally achieved a modest success as clerk of the records under Charles II, but Croke was cashiered out of the army and became a professional gambler. However, both autobiographies end while their authors are still young, unsettled, and not yet inhibited by the habit of maintaining a 'public face'.

D. A. Stauffer[20] has already drawn attention to the merits of Raymond's autobiography.[21] Raymond was a sensitive, whimsical, and timorous person, prone to self-mockery and with a talent for rambling narrative which brings Sterne to mind. His 'Rhapsodie' brings together an odd jumble of anecdotes which, as with Forman, somehow add up to a work more coherent and vivid than many of more conventional mould. The fact that he was not writing for publication certainly contributed to the disjointedness of Raymond's narrative, but it also seems to have freed his imagination to wander over the misadventures of his youth without constraint. Raymond suffered from a neurotic timidity which involved him in many absurd quandaries, and which he blamed on his unhappy childhood; few self-analysts of his period show such an awareness of the importance of early experiences in the formation of personality:

> Wee were 4 children, 3 sonns and one daughter, of all which my selfe, being the second, was least beloved of him [Raymond's father], but upon all occasions (though I was not above 12 years old at his death) felt the effects of his cholor, which was of great mischeife unto me, being of a softe and tymorous complexion. And indeed thus soon began the unhappy breaches made upon my spirit, which hath followed me in all the variations and course of my life, and proved a great obstacle to the advancement of my fortunes. (p. 19)

The theme of timorousness is soon taken up again in a long account of the capture of a burglar in the house of a London lawyer with whom Raymond boarded. This incident reinforced his childhood phobias:

> This accident had soe deepe an impression on my mynde that for some yeres I never went to bed without looking under it, and in every corner of my chamber, with this good effect alsoe that I constantly sayd my prayers. I took care to secure my chamber dore and all the avenues by which I might be surprizd in the night, and I tooke my selfe to be secure in all parts of my castle but at one place where the jack weights passed up behinde a staynd cloath and was soe wide that

---

[20] *English Biography before 1700*, pp. 186-8.
[21] Published 1667; quotations are from the facsimile edition by I. M. Westcott (Oxford, 1959).

I thought some rogue might passe up at it. To prevent which (see the deepe invention of a young boy grevously tortured by feare) I gott a little tinckling bell, and fastened it to one of the lynes, assureing my selfe that they could not be much stirred but that my sentinell would presently give me the alarme. (p. 22)

But the alarm was never triggered except by a great rat that climbed the ropes. Raymond was also abnormally frightened of the moral dangers which 'younge ladds doe undergoe at their first comeing to London' (p. 23). Fortunately for him,

God was pleased in a especiall manner to protect my selfe from many greate temptations, for which I must ever blesse his holy name. One was from the lawyers sister-in-law, a very handsome younge wench and tempting above measure, becomeing at last a very light (?). Another was a man that temptd me soe as tended to the vilest beastiallity. Another that would tempt me to the stewes &c. As for drincking I have cause to aske forgivenes of God for my faults therein, and have this for my consolation, that I never loved that great and too common vice. (p. 23)

Despite these pious sentiments, Raymond's was basically a secular imagination. He seems never to have passed through the Puritan's spiritual crisis, after which all phenomena, even the most trivial, are revealed as signs of God's handiwork in the world. Whereas Bunyan is filled with terrified guilt simply by standing in a bell-tower and imagining what would happen if the bell, or even the tower itself should fall, Raymond fears for his salvation only when he has some rational occasion, such as the temptations just quoted. When he has to sleep in a garret under a rotten pinnacle of Westminster Abbey, he is afraid of being 'brayned in . . . bed' (p. 27) but does not make his exposed position the occasion of any spiritual agonizings. Though he is obsessed with lust and lechery, the instinct which troubles him is more 'the foolish blynde boy' (p. 31) than Augustine's satanic tempter; and his timorousness is directed towards thieves and murderers instead of a threatening Jehovah.

Raymond went to the Netherlands (United Provinces) with his uncle in 1632 and saw service with the Prince of Orange's forces in the Thirty Years War. His account of a foot-soldier's life is both refreshing and sobering when contrasted with conventional military memoirs by officers. We learn about hardships which the generals never mention, such as bivouacs in the rain: 'One night I had nothing to keepe me from the cold wett ground but a little bundle of wett dryed flax, which by chance I litt on. And soe with my bootes full of water and wrapt up in my wett cloake, I lay as round as a hedgehogg, and at peep of day looked like a drowned ratt' (p. 40). But in a more serious mood:

I observed how briske and fyne some English gallants were at the
beginning of this campagne, but at the latter end ther briskenes and
gallantry soe faded and clowdy that I could not but be mynded of the
vanity of this world with the uneasines of this profession. And truly,
by what I have seene and felt, I cannott but thinck that the life of a
private or common soldier is the most miserable in the world; and
that not soe much because his life is always in danger—that is little or
nothing—but for the terrible miseries he endures in hunger and
nakednes, in hard marches and bad quarters. . . . It is hardly to be
thought the devastation that an army brings into a countrie. . . . (p. 43)

He was glad to escape from the life of a soldier of fortune to which
his being a younger son had seemed to condemn him; his uncle
found him a place in the train of the English ambassador to Venice,
and his autobiography ends with anecdotes of Venetian life—some of
them, as usual, warning of 'the sad effects of filthy lust' (p. 59).

Compared with Raymond's lively narrative, Charles Croke's
Fortune's Uncertainty or Youth's Unconstancy is a pallid and conventional work. But it has some claim to interest as one of the first
secular autobiographies to be published in England. Like Digby,
Croke chose to conceal his identity behind a false name—'Rodolphus'—and to adopt a rambling, florid style deriving mainly from the
Arcadia. We see Rodolphus pursuing the career of a typical young
'homme moyen sensuel' of the mid-seventeenth century. He is a well-
intentioned but desultory student at Christ Church, fond of fencing,
robbing orchards, and running into debt. After various escapades, he
enlists in a troop of horse, where:

Rodolphus being yet very young, not exceeding 18. or 19. at most,
began to lash out there more than ever; for he soon perceived that his
years had not yet made him capable of such experimented Companions
as Life-Guard-Men; his money whilst it lasted fled merrily about, and
in less than a twelve-month his Horses head was swoln so big, that he
could not get him out of the Stable door; a disease very incident and
almost infectious among those Gentlemens Horses. (p. 32)

We appreciate Croke's ability to poke fun at himself, especially since
so few of his fellow-autobiographers seem to have been able to do so.

When Rodolphus is forced out of the guards, his father comes to
his aid by placing him in the Temple as a student; where, predictably,
'finding the Law-French, very crabid in comparison with the smooth
stile of *Pembrokes Arcadia*, or a *Scudamores Cassandra*, he was not
able to endure such harsh Lectures' (p. 33). As a last resort, his
family ship him off to Virginia as an indentured labourer; he works
as a cooper, is shipwrecked near Bristol on his return, campaigns in
Portugal against the Spaniards, and ends his story with his marriage
to 'a Gentlewoman, which the Heavens had decreed to be his' (p. 66).

Croke probably wrote and published his book in an attempt to make some money out of his adventures; and it is perhaps evidence for contemporary taste that he should choose to emphasize the literary and romantic flavour of the story at the expense of directness and verisimilitude. The popularity of the French romance in the 1660s may also have influenced him; or, finally, his choice of style may have been a psychological defence against his successive failures and loss of status—for which he tried to compensate by posing as a romantic, pleasure-loving picaresque hero. Whatever his reasons, the inverse parallel of his work to *Robinson Crusoe* is exact: Croke tells a real story like a romance, whereas Defoe presents his fiction as a real story.[22]

In Adam Elliot's *A Narration of my Travails, Captivity, and Escape from Salle* we find no romantic devices, but only a strict and literal description of events. This brief autobiography is appended to the pamphlet *A Modest Vindication of Titus Oates*, which Elliot published to defend himself against Oates's accusations that he had 'turned Turke'. He tells us something of his Cambridge days, in 1664-68, when he knew Oates; but his main narrative describes his capture by Turkish pirates, his imprisonment at Salle in Morocco, and his escape from there to a Spanish garrison. The story is an exciting one, though Elliot was scarcely motivated by the desire to examine or explore his individualism—he was under public attack from Oates, and wished to make some capital out of his escape. His narrative expounds the great hardships he endured, and his immense cleverness in tricking his master into drunkenness and evading the city guards. To disarm criticism by showing that one has led a totally blameless and admirable life was a device frequently used by seventeenth-century controversialists; but it could only inspire a bastard form of autobiography, compromised by its polemical origins.

William Fuller was also involved with Titus Oates; and, as usual, the association entangles the historian in a web of mystery and contradiction. Fuller was a professional impostor who wrote several interesting autobiographical works; but they present such a morass of lies, dubious assertions, and self-contradictions that one cannot evaluate them as literary works until further research has separated truth from falsehood. An extensive unpublished version of his autobiography, which has recently come to light, may clarify Fuller's murky career.[23]

The final autobiography of this section indicates how a few

[22] We have already noted a similar response to reality by Sir Kenelm Digby, in his romanticizing of his relations with Venetia Stanley—a woman whose promiscuity was notorious.

[23] Sold at Sotheby's to B. Dobell, June 28-29, 1965, lot 105.

members of the lowest social classes became articulate and self-aware in the course of the century. Edward Barlow's *Journal* lay unpublished and apparently unnoticed until recently.[24] He was the son of a poor and illiterate Lancashire husbandman, who sent him to be apprenticed to a cotton bleacher at fourteen years old. There Barlow broadened his ambitions in talking with an older apprentice:

> As we were thrashing in the barn, for that was the greatest of our work whilst I stayed with him, and a work which I did not greatly care for, we would often tell what a fine thing it was to travel, and how many times they that had gone a long time returned very gallant with good store of money in their pockets; which made me think that they got their money very easily with a great deal less trouble than I was likely to get any, which made me resolve not to tarry long. (pp. 18-19)

The next year, 1657, Barlow set out for London with seven shillings in his pocket to seek his fortune, and encouraging himself with a fine scorn for the rustics among whom he had grown up—'some of them would not venture a day's journey from out of the smoke of their chimneys or the taste of their mother's milk' (p. 21). Two years later he gained an apprenticeship on the 'Naseby', and for fourteen years sailed all over the world on both merchants and men-of-war. He learned to read and write, and endured the rough life of the common sailor. Barlow does not hesitate to criticize the management of the navy; he has a strong sense of working-class solidarity with his mates, and an equivalent contempt for the sometimes cowardly noblemen who were given ships to command—'but when some of these rich men come in an engagement they are afraid of venturing too far, and do love their lives with their moneys and pleasure, in which they have lived in pomp and vanity' (p. 135).

Barlow's adventures are too numerous to describe in detail: they culminate in his capture by a Dutch ship in the Straits of Banca, off the coast of Sumatra. While prisoner on the Dutch ship, he decides to write his *Journal*:

> And keeping us in the Straits two months, and I having a great deal of spare time, which I thought might be worse spent than in declaring of what I have here in this book, and thus I thought good to describe to my friends and acquaintance and to any which might take the pains to read it over, and here they may understand in part what dangers and troubles poor seamen pass through, and also of the manner and situation of most places which I have been at since I first went to sea. (p. 228)

Barlow indicates here, as in many other places (e.g., pp. 60-61), his

[24] *Barlow's Journal*, ed. Basil Lubbock (1934).

consciousness of being a spokesman for the poor and mistreated ordinary seaman—a loyalty which is in sharp contrast to his disdain for the farm-labourers and husbandmen among whom he was brought up.[25] We may note also that his resentment is expressed in direct and secular terms, without the religious and chiliastic overtones of the left-wing sects which appeared during the Civil War.

To sum up briefly the characteristics of the autobiographers considered in this section: though widely varied in their careers and temperaments, they all changed their station in life, some gaining status and some losing. Most of them made the classic journey from the provinces to London as adolescents. All, no doubt, believed in God; but religion, so far as we can tell, did not exert a dominant influence on their life-choices. Finally, although some of them achieved wealth or responsible positions none were able to establish themselves firmly as members of the upper class: in seventeenth-century Britain the absence of a regular bureaucratic elite and the fickleness of patronage made it difficult to conserve social gains. In the next section, we will be discussing autobiographers of higher and more stable social origins; their works differ significantly from the group just considered.

(b) *Gentlemen of Leisure.* I include in this class the following auto-biographers: Sir Thomas Bodley (b. 1545), Sir John Bramston (1611), Sir Christopher Guise (1618), Sir John Reresby (1634), Sir Robert Sibbald (1641), and Roger North (1653). Though solid, prominent, and respected citizens, none of these men reached high office. Several of them preferred a life of country pursuits or amateur scholarship to the turmoil of court and parliament. Their autobiographies were written in middle age or later, after they had settled down to a moderate way of life and had had time to review their past actions and take stock of their temperaments. Taken as a group, they show a bias in favour of disengagement from the social struggle: by 'cultivating their gardens' they attempted to insulate themselves from the turbulent history of seventeenth-century Britain.

Sir Thomas Bodley, though separated from his fellows by three generations or more, anticipates some of their most characteristic

---

[25] Because of their conditions of life—harsh discipline, separate quarters from officers, etc.—English sailors early developed a militant class-consciousness. Mutinies were common in the eighteenth century, long before industrial strikes began to occur. In the countryside, on the other hand, patterns of existence remained semi-feudal during the seventeenth century. Before 1700 no auto-biographies by agricultural labourers or yeomen are known; in the case of the former, at least, self-expression would have been limited by the general illiteracy of their class. Barlow himself, had he remained at home, would probably never have learned to read or write.

attitudes. His *Life* was one of the rare secular autobiographies published in the seventeenth century: written in 1609, it was issued in 1647 at Oxford as a memorial to his generosity. It is obviously a public document, recapitulating his career and justifying his decision to spend the latter part of his life in building the library which bears his name. At first his life ran in the expected channels for a young man of his class; he attended Oxford, made the Grand Tour, and entered the diplomatic service. But after having become embroiled in the rivalry between Essex and Burghley, Bodley resolved to quit the court and 'possesse my soule in peace all the residue of my daies' (p. 12). Later he was asked to accept a position as secretary to the Lord Treasurer, and refused: 'in regard of my yeares, and for that I felt my self subject to many indispositions, besides some other private reasons which I reserve unto my selfe, I have continued still at home, my retired course of life, which is now methinks to me as the greatest preferment that the State can afford' (p. 14). Bodley here draws a clear line between his public and private life; the latter he obviously considers to be no business of the curious outsider—a precept perhaps admirable as a social rule, but in conflict with modern ideas of what an autobiography should include.

Bodley's *Life* is unusually coherent for a work in the *res gestae* tradition. Though he was preceded by Whythorne, Forman, and other secular autobiographers, Bodley has a judiciousness and a feeling for the pattern of his life which they lack; one senses that he was the first British autobiographer who knew exactly what he was doing and how he wanted to do it. In retrospect, we can see that he was founding a particular genre of objective and ultra-respectable autobiography that we now tend to dismiss with impatience; yet this should not prevent us giving him his due as a pioneer.

John Bramston's *Autobiography* indicates how little the *res gestae* type of life progressed in the course of the seventeenth century.[26] Bramston, inspired by a Senecan maxim, began to write in 1685 near the end of his long life:

> Nil turpius quam grandis natu Senex qui nullum aliud habet argumentum quo se probet diu vixisse propter aetatem; which makes me call to remembrance the yeares that are passed, what I haue done, and how I haue spent (I hope not wasted) my time. That posteritie, therefore, (I meane my owne descendents,) may know somethinge of my father and my selfe . . . I haue set downe some thyngs (tho' few) done by my selfe not vnworthy. (p. 4)

This introduction is followed by nearly a hundred pages of genealogy and family anecdotes before Bramston even begins his own story.

---

[26] *The Autobiography of Sir John Bramston*, ed. Braybrooke.

Though he qualified as a lawyer and became an M.P. after the Restoration, he lived his life in the shadow of his father, who was Lord Chief Justice under Charles I. Bramston views his own life as simply an extension of the family history; by stressing the important events which he witnessed, he connects family history with *historia sui temporis*—a linking of two of the dullest genres known to literature. His work marks a dead end among the various developments of the autobiographical genre.

Sir Christopher Guise had a more introspective and fanciful nature than Bramston, though he shared the latter's preoccupation with genealogy. He begins his *Memoirs* with a discourse on the fall of the Roman Empire, English common law, and kindred subjects, then traces the pedigree of his family back to the reign of Henry III.[27] These obeisances to family piety concluded, Guise tells of his own birth and childhood. He was rather sickly, which weakness he ascribes to his wet nurse being 'indifferently antient and of a dry hott complexion and not very plentifully stored with riches, soe that itt was noe wonder if there were neglects in my attendance' (p. 112). His troubles were further aggravated when, at the age of five or six, he was sent to be brought up by his grandfather, who had become a 'greate folower and favourer of silent ministers and nonconformists' (p. 113). Guise was repressed and harshly punished by the religious hypocrites who surrounded his rich grandfather, to the effect that:

> with the ill ayre and Sir William Gises passionate hand of government and delegation of the charge of mee to such as did rather punish then correct mee, I was brought to a greate depression of spiritt and melancoly, succeeded by the measells and a great flux of reughme, which with some other ill simptomes warned my mother to take care, which she did, takeing me almost per force to live at Brockworth about the year 1623, where by her care I did agayne in part recover my health, butt never the ill habitt of melancoly wholy nor itts dangerouse effects. (p. 113)

This tracing back of adult psychological problems to their roots in childhood experience is uncommon among seventeenth-century autobiographers, though not unknown.[28] It was neither a healthy nor a

---

[27] *Memoirs of the Family of Guise*, ed. G. Davies (1917).

[28] Cf. the quotation from Raymond's autobiography, p. 137 above. Robert Burton observes that melancholy, like other diseases, may be 'engrafted, as it were, & imprinted into the temperature of the infant, by the nurse's milk' (*Anatomy*, ed. Dell (New York, 1955), p. 283). He also notes, with a humaneness ahead of his time, that 'Parents, and such as have the tuition and oversight of children, offend many times in that they are too stern, always threatening, chiding, brawling, whipping, or striking; by means of which their poor children are so disheartened and cowed, that they never after have any courage, a merry hour in their lives, or take pleasure in any thing' (Ibid., p. 284).

pleasant time to be a child, and to read extensively in autobiographies of the period is to be confronted with a veritable casebook of neuroses, especially religious ones. Frequently the harsh discipline inflicted on children by their parents seems to have been the cause of these disorders.[29]

Guise began a desultory young manhood by going up to Magdalen College, Oxford. In later life, he looked back with disfavour on these student days:

> The vice of Oxford scollars is theyr frequenting tipling houses, and comonly that liberty most taken by the most ingeniouse. I was inclined to poetry and all ingeniouse studyes, the scrapps of which dropt in att our compotations. There we censur'd and extoll'd whome we pleas'd, and the title of ingeniouse was a sugred sop that gave a good relish to all concomitant qualityes and made us swallow licentiousenesse and, by consequence, idlenesse. For who so begins to thinke well of himselfe from that time neglects to improve his stocke.[30]

After Oxford he became a student of law at the Middle Temple—where, however, he never went to a lecture and spent his time riding and reading poetry. This occupied two years, until he had to go and live with his grandfather again in hopes of a legacy. But he was soon eager to abandon his parasitic manner of life:

---

[29] Like Guise, Anthony à Wood (*Life and Times*, p. 43) and William Lilly complain of being infected with melancholy. The latter was eager to leave a home where his father 'oft would say, I was good for nothing' (*Life*, p. 10). He also endured the religious agonies that frequently darkened seventeenth-century childhood: 'In the sixteenth year of my age I was exceedingly troubled in my dreams concerning my salvation and damnation, and also concerning the safety and destruction of the souls of my father and mother; in the nights I frequently wept, prayed and mourned, for fear my sins might offend God' (p. 7).

[30] p. 116. The next paragraph gives an amusing view of sexual mores at seventeenth-century Oxford:

'*Post vinum Venus* is the old saying, and soe itt was with us, for wee being in the bloomeing time of our youth, our blouds heated with wine and prompted by the spur of our oune lazy thoughts and desires, noe wonder if we followed and courted any whome we found to be indued with the least beauty, and those tipling houses that make itt theyr businesse to draw custome by any meanes are seldome without such sirens, who are taught by all allurements to draw on expenses and yet avoyd the last act, well knowing that fruition cloyes; soe that the youth of Oxford are like to leopards, to whom Bachus shewes the face of Venus in a glass and thereby insnares them. I cannot forget how many unwilling glasses I have drunke without any advantage from those woemen; and soe doe most young men, theyr complexions naturally disposing them to hope till they grow into an unhealthy, evill and deborch't habitt, and soe are cosen'd out of theyr health and hopefull youths by such circes; and this perhaps deserves the care of publike authority.' (pp. 116-17).

I concluded to give my selfe up to mine oune inclinations and make a disguised jorney, or mascarade as the French call itt, about England, without servant, not to be betray'd, without freinds or companion, as knowing none intimately, and without other provisions then a playne freese suite and a good horse, hoping att least by this meanes to take a just measure of myselfe and try what valewe I should beare with others when I had layd aside the advantages of birth and fortune. (p. 122)

This interlude of freedom from family and class responsibilities increased Guise's self-confidence, and he thereafter applied himself more successfully to worldly business. He married twice, fought off the danger of sequestration of the family estates during the Civil War, and engaged in the usual interminable wrangles with his family and others over landed property. His *Memoirs* break off abruptly in 1659, though he lived until 1671.

Guise was a thoughtful and perceptive person, as we see in his understanding of the psychosomatic causes of his childhood diseases. His *Memoirs* mark a real advance in seventeenth-century auto-biography because, though conceived in the usually barren form of the family history, they succeed in creating a vivid portrait of the author's character instead of merely cataloguing the events in his life. Unfortunately Guise's sharp eye for character, and his attempts at giving himself a sense of identity by various experiences, were not able to overcome the central problem of his life—a problem he shared with many gentlemen of his time—that he literally had nothing to do except wait for his father to die.

In the *Memoirs* of Sir John Reresby, *res gestae* again predominate.[31] Like Bramston, Guise, and other secular autobiographers, Reresby connects his memoirs to a preceding *Family History* and states that they are 'chiefly designed' to 'posterity of his own family' (p. 286). The first part of his work, though it lacks self-insight, documents for us the preoccupations of a well-born 'angry boy'; for Bramston was addicted to seduction and single combat—often the two pursuits could be combined. The stories of his sexual adventures would nowadays be called confessions; but he is ingenuous enough to describe his encounters without either remorse or self-exaltation. His other escapades he recounts equally dispassionately, with no remorse for the triviality of the alleged slurs over which he fought so many duels (pp. 9-10).

In 1675 Reresby entered the House of Commons; from about this time on his memoirs shift into diary-form and concentrate on political events. He moderated his political ambitions after wit-

---

[31] *The Memoirs of Sir John Reresby*, ed. Andrew Browning (Glasgow, 1936).

nessing the dramatic fall of the Lord Treasurer, the Earl of Danby, in 1679:

> This confirmed me in the opinion that a middle estate was ever the best, not soe low as to be trodden upon nor soe high as to be in danger to be shaken with the blast of envie, not soe lazie as not to endeavour to be distinguished . . . nor soe ambitious as to sacrafice the ease of this life, and the hopes of happiness in the next, to clime over the heads of others to a greatness of uncertain continuance. (p. 174)

It is curious to see the bloodthirsty, almost psychopathic youth turn into a propagandist for the quiet life and the golden mean—though the seventeenth-century mind doesn't seem to have found the conversion odd.

Reresby's *Memoirs* are notable, if scarcely untypical, for their indifference to intellectual affairs. His great interests as an M.P. and landowner were money, influence, and the cultivation of people of rank; he provides a good argument for the Namierite view of English history. The work also shows how the dead hand of the *historia sui temporis* convention could blight a promising narrative, for the account of his young manhood, before he was involved in public affairs, has a vigour and directness that is entirely lacking in the account of his later life.

I suggested earlier that the autobiographers in this group are characterized by an inclination to renounce worldliness, or at least to refuse to strive for the highest (and therefore most dangerous) positions in the realm. This tendency is nowhere more pronounced than in the career of Sir Robert Sibbald, a Scots physician who in many ways may remind us of his greater colleague, Sir Thomas Browne. Though not a spiritual autobiography, Sibbald's *Memoirs*[32] begin like one with a number of quotations from Psalms, including the inevitable 'Come and hear, all ye that fear God, and I will declare what he hath done for my Soul' (Ps. lxvi, 16). He was 'a tender child', who 'sucked till I was two yeers and two moneths old, and could runn up and down the street, and speake, because my other brothers and sisters had dyed hectick; which long suckling proved, by the blessing of God, a mean to preserve me alive' (p. 51). In youth, he was serious and studious—'From the tyme I entered to the Coledge, any mony I gott, I did imploy it for buying of books' (p. 55). He went to Leyden to study medicine, supplementing the curriculum with readings in divinity and the classics; like Bramston, he developed a taste for the Stoics: 'I read Seneca and Epictetus, and some other of the stoicks, and affected ym, because of yr contempt of riches and honours. The

---

[32] *The Memoirs of Sir Robert Sibbald (1642-1722)*, ed. F. P. Hett (1932).

design I proposed to myself was to passe quietly thorough the world, and content myself with a moderate fortune' (p. 61). Despite this renunciation of ambition, Sibbald was successful enough in his profession to be appointed physician to Charles II during the latter's stay in Scotland.

In 1685 a peculiar episode endangered Sibbald's position and even his life: at the urging of the Earl of Perth, he converted to Catholicism. The scene of his final conviction shows what an impulsive and emotional decision it was:

> I knew not how it came about, I felt a great warmness of my affections while he was reading and discoursing, and yrupon as I thought, oestro quodam pietatis motus, I said, I would embrace that religion, upon which he took me in his arms and thanked God for it. That was the way, without any furder consideration, that I joined wt ym, and signified my willingness to join to the priest when he came. (pp. 88-9)

The 'rable' of Edinburgh were so enraged by Sibbald's conversion that they stormed his house and forced him to flee to London; after a few weeks he prudently repented of his conversion and was received again into the Protestant church by the Bishop of Edinburgh. The only incident worth noting in the remainder of his life was his being hit on the head by a golf-club.

Sibbald anticipates the milder and more ordered way of life of the eighteenth-century gentry; his flight from the Edinburgh mob is symbolic. Though many men of his rank may have been equally fond of Horatian *mediocritas* earlier in the seventeenth century, the turbulent history of that period would have made it very difficult to put their principles into effect. But after the Restoration, and even more so after the Glorious Revolution of 1688, men like Sibbald could expect to live peaceably, cultivate their gardens, and perhaps meditate on ways to order their past experiences. This blunting of conflicts, after a century and a half of social turmoil, may partially account for the coincidence that all the autobiographies discussed in this section— except for Bodley's—were written after 1660.

The last autobiographer of this group, Roger North, brought to the writing of his own life a talent for historical analysis already displayed in biographies of other members of his family.[33] His sense of family solidarity extended also to the declared purpose of his autobiography:

[33] Collected as *The Lives of the Right Hon. Francis North, Baron Guilford, the Hon. Sir Dudley North, and the Hon. and Rev. Dr. John North*, 3 vols. (1836); North's own *Autobiography* was edited by A. Jessopp (1887). See also the excellent discussion in J. Morris, *Versions of the Self*, pp. 39-67.

I lay it downe for a truth, Quasi Evangelicall, that the best legacy parents can leav to their children is good principles and sound bodys. And to prove it I shall alledg some few passages of my oune experience, who ascribe all the good I know and the many deliverances I have had, next to Almighty Providence, (which for ought I know wrought by such means) to the Caracter of My parents. (p. 1)

North was a sober, moral, and capitalistically-inclined child; at school he 'first perceived two great articles of happiness—liberty and the use of money' (p. 8). The latter he was soon able to enjoy by manufacturing paper lanterns, balls, and fireworks for sale to his schoolmates. He was observant as well as enterprising; the account of school society, and his place in it, marks an advance in British auto-biography by its clear and methodical self-analysis:

Here it was that I began (as I said) to have a sense of myself. I was aspiring enough, and would have been in the league with the capital boys, but had not a tour of address and confidence to be admitted, but kept in a middle order, and had my equals and inferiors, as well as superiors. I conceived a strange apprehension that I should prove a weak man, if not a fool, which shewed I aimed at more than I found I could reach, and in this despondence I had no comfort but performing exercises [i.e., school-work] without help. That did almost persuade me I should shift in other stations as well as that. I had, by the benefaction of several relations, a better cash than others, which made me an envy to the rest. (pp. 11-12)

This experience gives North occasion to note the usefulness of public schools to their students:

For there they learn the pratique of the world according to their capacities. For there are several ages and conditions, as poor boys and rich, and amongst them all the characters which can be found among men, as liars, cowards, fighters, dunces, wits, debauchees, honest boys, and the rest, and the vanity of folly and false dealing, and indeed the mischiefs of immorality in general may be observed there. (p. 12)

After school, he entered Cambridge in 1667; there his appetite 'was to natural philosophy, which they call physics, and particularly Descartes, whose works I dare say I read over three times before I understood him ... but I found such a stir about Descartes, some railing at him and forbidding the reading him as if he had impugned the very Gospel. And yet there was a general inclination, especially of the brisk partt of the University to use him' (p. 15). Two years later, North became a student at the Inner Temple. At this point of the narrative, he pauses for a lengthy digression into self-analysis and description of his pastimes. He considers the origin of his Tory bias,

149

and ascribes it to his childhood excitement at the Restoration. Then he considers his mental powers:

> Next, I have observed in myself somewhat of confusion and disorder of thought. And although I had always a forwardness to attempt anything, I never could succeed to my content. . . . For I was ever pleased to be writing somewhat or other, and striving at method and clearness, but could not attain so as to perfect any one design. . . . Now, to reflect on what may be the cause of such imperfect command of thought, as I have lamented in myself, and which I cannot describe better than by styling it an aptness to oversee,—I ascribe the main reason to the cruel fit of sickness I had when young, wherein, I am told, life was despaired of. (pp. 21-2)

He continues to analyse his supposed mental inferiority with a thoroughness and method that are not to be found in earlier seventeenth-century autobiographies. In another place, he gives his intention as to 'draw my own picture' (p. 173)—a confirmation of the impression that he has developed a more sophisticated point of view than the simple historicism of so many autobiographers earlier in the century.

Although North became rich and successful as a lawyer, he always gave credit for his good fortune to his more eminent brother, Francis North, Keeper of the Great Seal. During his brother's tenure of this office (1682-85) North was much sought after by petitioners, and he took part in high affairs of state; the effect of his experience was to make him wish to retire to the country as soon as possible: 'It hath cured me of all pining after courts, and their deceitful preferments; I have learnt that there is no condition like the private' (p. 169). Francis North died in office, and Roger then took a town house where he lived quietly and pursued his hobbies. He later became a country gentleman in Norfolk, though the autobiography breaks off before his move there (in 1696).

North's autobiography achieves a level of coherence and self-awareness which at least equals that of the average eighteenth- or nineteenth-century autobiography. The analysis of his character forms an integral part of the work, rather than being scattered here and there in chance remarks. His hobbies, especially sailing, are given a place and we are told why they appealed to him.[34] He was pompous, moralistic, and a hidebound Tory; yet he himself provides the comprehensive evidence by which we can know him for what he is

[34] See, for example, his account of an idyllic yachting expedition in 1685-88: 'For the day proved cool, the gale brisk, air clear, and no inconvenience to molest us, nor wants to trouble our thoughts, neither business to importune, nor formalities to tease us; so that we came nearer to a perfection of life there than I was ever sensible of otherwise' (p. 32).

and can judge his life as a whole. His work represents a mature stage of the dominant mode of seventeenth-century secular autobiography.

The six autobiographers just discussed have many traits in common. They were all respectable citizens, mostly from old families whose wealth was based on land. They observed decorum and moderation in their manner of life and in the way they wrote about it though, with the possible exception of Bodley, they were not writing for the general public. In religion they were Protestant with High Church leanings. Their judgements on human affairs tended to be made from a firmly moral, but not superstitiously providential point of view; in this respect they foreshadowed the eighteenth century's turn towards natural religion, and its reduced inclination to see the finger of God in all the events of everyday life. Indulging in neither the hysterical self-accusation of the extreme sectaries, nor the militant certainties of the Catholics, they preferred to follow a decent and pious middle way. Several of them had bookish inclinations, but none were professional scholars or authors; their literary styles are usually clear, unadorned, and correct, in contrast to such eccentric stylists as Forman and Raymond. All attended universities, but none could be said to have written an intellectual autobiography of the Gibbon or J. S. Mill type—this may be attributed partly to their somewhat superficial interest in ideas, and partly to the tendency for 'developmental' autobiographers to concentrate on the evolution of their religious convictions only.

Bodley excepted, the members of this group all studied law or medicine, though they were usually involved in business affairs outside their professions. They could not really be defined by their occupations, and several of them abandoned professional duties to pursue other interests—Bodley with his library, North rebuilding his country house, etc. Several of them seem to have become autobiographers by way of their interest in genealogy and their desire to commemorate their families' antiquity and importance. With such proclivities, it is hardly surprising that they were all, so far as I can tell, Tories; often their family estates were sequestered in the Civil War, and their fathers or themselves cast under suspicion. Finally, though they were in some ways bourgeois in outlook they lacked the industrious acquisitiveness typical of Whig merchants and businessmen; they were generally born to wealth and did not show conspicuous energy in adding to it. They were more likely to retire and enjoy what they had in peace. As a group, they were undynamic and perhaps rather lacking in vitality—they drew back into a comfortable private life while the merchants and speculators got on with England's business. The next section will discuss two autobiographers from this latter class.

(c) *A Magnate and a Contractor*. Richard Boyle, Lord Cork, and Phineas Pett both grew rich by taking advantage of government policy or government business.[35] Boyle was the second son of a younger brother; for lack of means he was obliged to drop his studies at the Inner Temple and become a clerk to Sir Roger Manwood, Chief Baron of the Exchequer and a somewhat shady jurist. By daring speculation, beginning with his wife's dowry as capital, Boyle amassed a vast fortune in Irish land. His *Remembrances* is a straightforward account of a successful life, almost completely objective and at times merely a catalogue of events. It is noteworthy only for being one of the earlier secular autobiographies in England, and for being the first apparently inspired by the desire to commemorate its author's rise to power and wealth.

Phineas Pett took a different road to success. Forced to leave Cambridge when his father died, he apprenticed himself in his father's profession of shipbuilding. He prospered and soon became an independent builder, though harassed by the enmity and suspicion of Fulke Greville. In 1608 came the first of several inquiries into graft in the building of warships, with Pett as one of the principal suspects; but he held his own against the 'killcows' and 'caterpillars' who accused him, and was exonerated. For the most part, his autobiography enumerates the ships that he built, the attacks on him by his enemies, and the growth of his wealth; his emotional life and even such personal events as the death of his wife get no more than perfunctory treatment. The most insistent theme of the work is his assertion of honesty in the teeth of his perennial detractors—though all outside evidence suggests that he did cheat the government. Perhaps he could not admit this even to himself; or he may not have cared to put on paper anything which might later be incriminating. In any event, his main motive for writing seems to have been self-justification. He shows remarkably little imagination in describing the great personages with whom he came in contact, being interested only in what they had to say about his handling of Navy business. If we wish to understand in depth the mentality of accumulation we must turn to such men as Ralph Josselin, on the religious side (see p. 52 above), or Samuel Pepys.

(d) *Scholars and Scientists*. Six autobiographies will be discussed here, those of Thomas Hobbes, Robert Boyle, Matthew Robinson,

---

[35] Boyle's *True Remembrances* are in *The Life of Robert Boyle* by Thomas Birch (1744); *The Autobiography of Phineas Pett*, ed. W. G. Perrin (1918).

John Flamsteed, Dr. John Wallis, and Anthony à Wood; like their authors, these works incline towards experimentation and eccentricity.[36] The most fanciful of them is *Thomae Hobbes Vita, Carmine Expressa*, a poem of some four hundred lines in Latin hexameters, which was written near the end of Hobbes' life and first published in the year of his death (1679).[37] The form of the *Vita* is basically *res gestae*, though there is some epigrammatic self-analysis, as in the famous story of his mother's terror at the approach of the Spanish Armada:

> Atque metum tantum concepit tunc mea mater,
> Ut pareret geminos, meque metumque simul.
> Hinc est, ut credo, patrios quod abominor hostes,
> Pacem amo cum musis, et faciles socios. (p. lxxxvi)[38]

Hobbes mentions his readings in English, Greek, and Latin history, and in the poets; singling out his favourite:

> Sed mihi prae reliquis Thucydides placuit.
> Is Democratia ostendit mihi quam sit inepta,
> Et quantum coetu plus sapit unus homo. (p. lxxxviii)[39]

Most of the poem is taken up with simple enumeration of the events in his life, especially his publications and controversies. However Hobbes does trace, in his dry and factual way, his intellectual influences and the development of his thought; he thereby sets a precedent among British secular autobiographers and anticipates the more substantial undertakings of Gibbon and Mill.

Robert Boyle's *An Account of Philaretus*[40] was completed before he was twenty-one, and carries its hero only to the age of fifteen. In both childhood and adolescence Boyle seems to have been a sententious little prig: his styling himself 'Philaretus' (lover of excellence) is typical. He was the younger son of the magnate Richard Boyle, a birth which he found very satisfactory: 'But now our Philaretus was

---

[36] A more conventional production is the *Life* of the great antiquary, Sir William Dugdale, written in *res gestae* style and using third-person narrative. Dugdale concerns himself almost entirely with antiquarianism and heraldry, and conceals his private life.

[37] Hobbes also wrote a prose *Vita* which is very close in scope and content to the poetic version. Both are printed in *Thomae Hobbes Malmesburiensis Opera Philosophica Quae Latine Scripsit Omnia*, ed. Molesworth, vol. I, from which I have quoted.

[38] 'But my mother conceived such fear at that time that she bore twins, myself and fear together. It is for this reason, I think, that I hate the enemies of my native land, and love peace, with the muses and good-natured friends.'

[39] 'But Thucydides pleased me more than the others. He showed me how inept democracy is, and how much more than the mob one man knows.'

[40] *An Account of Philaretus during his Minority*, in Birch, *Life of Boyle* (1744).

born in a condition, that neither was high enough to prove a temptation to laziness, nor low enough to discourage him from aspiring' (p. 19). Apart from a stutter which he claims to have acquired from one of his playmates, he had a fortunate youth, often escaping unharmed from danger; 'but Philaretus would not ascribe any of these rescues unto chance, but would be still industrious to perceive the hand of heaven in all these accidents' (p. 27). He went to Eton, where he formed a poor opinion of the humanistic studies pursued there, 'And indeed it is a much nobler ambition to learn to do things, that may deserve a room in history, than only to learn, how congruously to write such actions in the gown-men's language' (p. 30). From Eton, Boyle made the Grand Tour with an older brother. His most interesting experiences were at Florence, where he read and approved of Galileo, and extended his researches into 'the famousest Bordellos, whither resorting out of bare curiosity, he retained there an unblemished chastity, and still returned thence as honest as he went thither' (p. 45). The manuscript ends with Philaretus's arrival at Marseilles on the way back to England. Boyle was obviously a forceful and intelligent youth, but his extreme self-righteousness prevents his autobiography from being more than a psychological curiosity.

An even more self-satisfied attitude is to be found in the *Autobiography* of Matthew Robinson,[41] an ambitious and worldly clergyman. Robinson was mildly eccentric—he wrote his autobiography in the third person, claiming that its author was 'one who knew him thoroughly, and had many of these things from his own mouth' (p. 3). In form his life follows Suetonius, with fifty-four numbered divisions and two main sections, one narrating the events of his life and the other his habits and amusements. In content, the life is boastful almost to the point of megalomania. Thus, 'it would be hard to find in his times one through the whole kingdom to whose eminency nature art and fortune did so much contribute', and the village of his birth 'is famed for nothing more than that this man was born there' (pp. 4-5). Robinson was a devotee of the 'new philosophy' at Cambridge, later a fellow of St. John's, a physician and clergyman. At age fifty-four he gave up his medical practice because of ill-health and began to write an enormous work, *Annotations on the Bible*, to which his autobiography was to be the laudatory preface. His motives for writing it were suspect, to say the least, and the tone of the autobiography as a whole is invincibly complacent. He was only a moderately successful man, yet could solemnly assert that 'as to his personal manage and conduct in his own private affairs, it would appear to many men as next to miraculous' (p. 55).

---

[41] In J. E. B. Mayor, *Cambridge in the Seventeenth Century*, Part II (1856).

At three hundred years' distance it is not easy to discern precisely what degree of bad faith was employed in the composition of Robinson's autobiography; but the work remains, ironically, as a monument to the author's stupidity instead of the testament of greatness which he wished it to be. It provides further evidence of the secular autobiographer's concern for his reputation at this time, especially if he intended to publish during his lifetime; in all the secular autobiographies published during the seventeenth century I cannot recall any admission by the author of a serious misdeed or indiscretion.[42] In a morally sterner age than ours, one could hardly expect a sympathetic reception for a confession of cowardice or adultery—unless it was made in a religious idiom, and exorcized by due repentance; but the obvious disadvantages of the consequent prudent reticence help to account for the rather pallid quality of seventeenth-century secular autobiography in comparison with contemporary imaginative literature, which was not limited by any such considerations of propriety.

John Flamsteed, like many of his fellow seventeenth-century scientists, was pious and spiritually conservative; the opening of his autobiography reflects this cautious temperament:

> To keep myself from idleness, and to recreate myself, I have intended here to give some account of my life, in my youth, before the actions thereof, and the providences of God therein, be too far passed out of memory; and to observe the accidents of all my years, and inclinations of my mind, that whosoever may light upon these papers may see that I was not so wholly taken up, either with my father's business or my mathematics, but that I both admitted and found time for other as weighty considerations.[43]

His attitude to his childhood combines, in a pre-Freudian age, disdain and disinterest: 'My first ten years were spent in such employments as children use to pass away their time with; affording little observable in them'.[44] He was withdrawn from school at sixteen because of

---

[42] For example, Charles Croke conceals his dishonourable discharge from the army and desertion to the enemy during the Portuguese campaign (see *Fortune's Uncertainty*, p. viii); he admits to some youthful pranks, but they merely contribute to the attractive picture he gives of himself. Numerous examples of such whitewashing could be cited from other autobiographies.

[43] Francis Baily, *An Account of the Revd John Flamsteed* (1835), p. 7. Flamsteed's title was *Account of the Life and Labours of*.

[44] One of the most obvious differences between pre-Romantic and modern autobiographies is the much greater emphasis on childhood experiences in the latter works. Seventeenth-century spiritual autobiographers frequently deplore the sinfulness of their youth and describe childhood events in which, they think, the finger of God can be discerned; but the modern concept of childhood—and

sickness and pursued his studies of astronomy and astrology privately; the first section of his autobiography ends with a journey to Ireland to be touched (unsuccessfully) by the famous healer, Mr. Valentine Greatrackes. Flamsteed continued the autobiography to 1716 in six more sections, but these are almost entirely concerned with technical developments or with his running feud with Sir Isaac Newton. It is only in the account of his youth that Flamsteed appears as a real person—a characteristic which we have already seen in Sir John Reresby's *Memoirs*, and which can be blamed in both cases on the influence of the *res gestae* convention.

Dr. John Wallis's *Some Passages of his own Life* traces another scientific career.[45] It was written when Wallis was over eighty, in 1697, and is an unvarnished, factual narrative, though extraordinarily lucid for a man of the author's age. The chief interest of his *Life* lies in the account of a group which, from about 1645, met weekly to discuss 'what has been called the New Philosophy or Experimental Philosophy . . . which, from the times of Galileo at Florence and Sr. Francis Bacon in England, hath been much cultivated in Italy, France, Germany, and other parts abroad, as well as with us in England' (p. clxi). This group later developed into the Royal Society. For the rest, Wallis was Professor of Geometry at Oxford and a successful campus politician. He attributed his success to his philosophy of calmness and moderation during troubled times, whereby '(thro' God's gracious Providence) I have been able to live easy, and useful, though not Great' (p. clxix). It should be noted, however, that Anthony à Wood had a different view of Wallis, who roused him from his usual sullen misanthropy to active hatred:

> (Taker of all oathes, covenant, engagement. Faithful to Oliver, to Richard, to King Charles II, King James II, King William!). . . . Eat the bread of Turner, who died soon after for want of it. Would have rob'd the Civilian chest. . . . A liver by rapine in thrusting out Dr. Peter Turner from his Geometry Professor's place; Turner died for want of bread, while he occupied his place. A liver by perjury and braking statutes and oathes, in taking upon him the Custos Archivorum place.[46]

---

even infancy—as the crucial formative period of life was not widely accepted three hundred years ago. A few British autobiographers, such as Thomas Raymond and Sir Christopher Guise, show a good intuitive grasp of the ways in which adult temperament can be moulded by childhood experience, but they are exceptional. For historical surveys of changing concepts of childhood see J. H. Van den Berg, *The Changing Nature of Man*, Chapter 2, and P. Ariès, *Centuries of Childhood*.

[45] In Thomas Hearne, *Peter Langtoft's Chronicle* (Oxford, 1726), vol. I.

[46] *The Life and Times of Anthony à Wood*, ed. L. Powys (1961), p. 249.

The Individualists

So much for Wallis's cherished success in living 'easy, and useful, though not Great'! Wood's own *Life* is an entirely individual and eccentric work. He tells his story mostly in impersonal references, indistinguishable in tone from the anecdotes of Oxford which overwhelm the autobiographical material with their bulk. Wood had the magpie instinct of the true antiquarian; he accumulates in his journal a great heap of gossip. His peculiarly obsessive and curmudgeonly temperament emerges only indirectly, from the continuous railings in his journal at anyone who crosses his path: his brothers, the fellows of his college, the Presbyterians, even his friends (though few could put up with him for long). But for all the irrelevancies and formlessness of his journal, it does succeed in creating a vivid likeness of the strange personality of that scholarly misanthrope and lonely observer of the follies of Restoration Oxford.

X

Female Autobiographers

TO DISCUSS female autobiographers separately, discarding the categories previously used, is a choice which requires explanation and, perhaps, defence. This choice stems from the observation that Englishwomen of the seventeenth century lacked, because of their subservient social position, that firm identification with profession or occupation which was typical of their male counterparts. For example, most religious autobiographies were written by ministers and priests; women, who were excluded from the ministry, expressed many pious sentiments in their autobiographies but rarely adopted a consistently and exclusively religious point of view, or wrote within any particular convention of religious autobiography.[1] Similarly, female autobiographers were as a rule restricted to occasional or merely dilettantish involvement in political, intellectual, or other worldly pursuits. Often, their experience of wider horizons than simple domesticity came from identification with their husbands' careers and interests—at best, a second-hand participation.

Perhaps as a result of this relatively weak vocational interest, female autobiographers strike the modern reader as having, generally, a more 'unified sensibility' than their male counterparts: their lives seem less compartmentalized, they have a wider range of emotional responses to everyday events and more awareness of concrete realities. For example, here is a typical enough description of a deathbed by a man, Adam Martindale: 'my sister that was too proud of her face . . . became extremely ugly before she died, her face being sadly discoloured, and so swelled that scarce any forme of a visage was discernible' (*Life*, p. 18). In resorting to these dry and moralistic phrases Martindale holds himself aloof from his sister's suffering; he cannot really *see* her death because of his prejudice against her vanity and his correspondingly rigid view of what is taking place. Mary Penington, speaking of the death of her first husband, is both more emotionally involved in the scene and a closer observer of it:

[1] Exceptions to this heterodoxy may be found among Quaker women, some of whom wrote quite conventional journals.

158

at last he called to me—'come my dear, let me kiss thee before I die!' which he did with that heartiness, as if he would have left his breath in me. Come once more, said he, let me kiss thee and take my leave of thee; which he did in the same manner as before; saying now no more, no more, never no more. Which having done, he fell into a very great agony. He having but about seven days illness, of this violent contagious fever, and it not having impaired his strength but inflamed his blood and heightened his spirits, and being a young lusty man, he in this agony, snapped his arms and legs with such a force that the veins seemed to sound like catgut tighted upon an instrument of musick. Oh! this was a dreadful sight to me; my very heart strings seemed to me to break, and let my heart fall into my belly. . . . Upon which they came to me and desired me to go from the bedside to the fire, for my being there occasioned this deep perplexity; and while I staid there he could not die; which word was so great, so much too big to enter into me; that I like an astonished, amazed creature, stamped with my foot, and cried, die! die! must he die! I cannot go from him.[2]

The female autobiographer, being more concerned with intimate feelings than her male counterpart, was less likely to be satisfied with a simple record of *res gestae*.

Before turning to individual works, we should consider the six autobiographers discussed in this chapter as a group.[3] All of them wrote their lives after the Restoration, except for the Duchess of Newcastle who wrote in 1656. Coincidentally, all were born between 1620 and 1625, though it is hard to explain why such a closely contemporary group of Englishwomen should turn to autobiography as a means of expression. One naturally looks in the works themselves for a common motive for writing; but each woman gives a different reason for writing her life. Looking beyond motives to the influence of a similar environment, one finds that the six women were all of gentle birth; in fact, four out of the six had titles and a fifth, Mary Penington, was the daughter of a knight. However, only Lady Fanshawe, Lady Halkett, and the Duchess of Newcastle were royalists, and even these three wrote quite dissimilar autobiographies. The Civil War, and the religious turmoil associated with it, undoubtedly had a powerful formative influence on all the women; the vicissitudes experienced by most of them gave them unusual events to chronicle and also acted as stimulants to self-discovery—one thinks of Lady Halkett, who called herself 'the greatest coward living', facing down an unruly mob of pillaging soldiers. But the Civil War, by itself, is not a sufficient explanation of the appearance of female autobiography in

[2] *A Brief Account of my Exercises from my Childhood* (Philadelphia, 1848), p. 33.

[3] I have chosen for discussion only some of the more important female autobiographers; several other minor works by women are listed in the bibliography.

England, and other causes must be sought in the works themselves. This examination may most conveniently begin with the earliest work in the group, the Duchess of Newcastle's *A True Relation of my Birth Breeding, and Life*.[4]

The Duchess of Newcastle was not taken seriously by her contemporaries, and we can scarcely contest their verdict: she was a garrulous and self-centred eccentric, continually scribbling bad plays and worse poetry. However, she was scarcely fool enough not to realize that 'carping tongues' and 'malicious censurers' were busy behind her back; her brief autobiography was written and published in an attempt to confound these detractors. The narrative is in two parts, the first describing the careers of herself and of her relations, the second telling 'something of my humour, particular practice and disposition' (p. 208). Except for this one division, she displays no sense of literary form, bringing forth one random effusion after another.

It would be giving the Duchess more than her due to describe her as a penetrating self-analyst, but in her ingenuous way she does reveal much more about her personality than most autobiographers of her time. Moreover, her revelations show some awareness of subtle differences of temperament, as in her comment: 'as for my disposition, it is more inclining to be melancholy than merry, but not crabbed or peevishly melancholy, but soft, melting, solitary, and contemplating melancholy, and I am apt to weep rather than laugh, not that I do often either of them' (pp. 209-10). Her relentless concern with herself may eventually become tedious, but at least it ensures that we come into unobstructed contact with her, instead of being blocked by the multiple defences erected by so many male autobiographers. The line of development is unbroken from her work to a modern, subjective autobiography like Rousseau's—his kind of preoccupation with his own singularity is already implicit in the Duchess's *Relation*. The conclusion of her work suggests that it was inspired by pure egotism—she scorns to offer any of the conventional excuses for writing her own life, but stands four-square on her individual right of self-expression:

> But I hope my readers will not think me vain for writing my life, since there have been many that have done the like, as Cesar, Ovid, and many more, both men and women, and I know no reason I may not do it as well as they: but I verily believe some censuring readers will scornfully say, Why hath this lady writ her own life? since none cares to know whose daughter she was, or whose wife she is, or how she was bred, or what fortunes she had, or how she lived, or what humour or

[4] I have quoted from the reprint of this work in *The Life of the (1st) Duke of Newcastle and other writings by Maragret Duchess*, ed. Ernest Rhys.

disposition she was of? I answer that it is true, that 'tis to no purpose to the readers, but it is to the authoress, because I write it for my own sake, not theirs; neither did I intend this piece for to delight, but to divulge; not to please the fancy, but to tell the truth, lest after-ages should mistake, in not knowing I was daughter to one Master Lucas of St. Johns, near Colchester, in Essex, second wife to the Lord Marquis of Newcastle; for My Lord having had two wives, I might easily have been mistaken, especially if I should dye and My Lord marry again. (p. 213)

Ann Lady Fanshawe was more orthodox than the Duchess of Newcastle in the plan of her autobiography: she wrote for her son rather than for her own amusement, and in a spirit of self-effacement rather than of self-assertion.[5] Her introductory statement, with its concern for her son's instruction in family tradition, is similar to statements by aristocratic male autobiographers: 'I have thought it convenient to discourse to you, my most dear and only son, the most remarkable actions and accidents of your family; as well as those of more eminent ones of your father and my life. . . . I would not have you be a stranger to it, because by the example you may imitate what is applicable to your condition in the world, and endeavour to avoid those misfortunes we have passed through, if God pleases' (p. 1). We hear much of the earlier members of the Fanshawe family before Lady Ann arrives at the story of her own childhood, and in the main text of the memoirs it is her husband's career that holds the centre of the stage. Their life together was eventful, since they were married during the Civil War and had many narrow escapes from the Parliamentary forces; these exploits are described in a lively but conventional style. The feminine touch can be seen mainly in the occasional minor dramatic vignettes which interrupt the orderly exposition of *res gestae*; such an episode as Lady Ann's tiff with her husband over his concealment of state secrets from her (pp. 35-7) is sensitively re-created. Another anecdote, when their ship is preparing for the attack of a Turkish man-o'-war, shows Lady Ann's awareness of the emotional nuances of her relationship with her husband:

> This beast captain had locked me up in the cabin. I knocked and called long to no purpose, until at length a cabin-boy came and opened the door. I all in tears desired him to be so good as to give me his blue thrum-cap he wore, and his tarred coat; which he did, and I gave him half-a-crown; and putting them on, and flinging away my night's clothes, I crept up softly and stood upon the deck by my husband's side as free from sickness and fear as, I confess, from discretion; but it was the effect of that passion which I could never master . . . the Turk's man-of-war tacked about, and we continued our source. But

[5] *The Memoirs of Ann Lady Fanshawe*, ed. H. C. Fanshawe (1907).

when your father saw it convenient to retreat, looking upon me he blessed himself, and snatched me up in his arms, saying, 'Good God, that love can make this change!' (p. 64)

While quite orthodox in conception, Lady Ann's *Memoirs* show that even within the framework of *res gestae* an autobiographer can convey subtle variations in his emotional life. Her subordination of her own career to that of her husband, and her adoption of a modest, even domestic scale for her narrative, restrict her to a subsidiary place in the development of British autobiography; but her *Memoirs* are craftsmanlike, readable, and without the gross faults of dullness or insensitivity which so often mar autobiographies by men in the same mode.

The autobiography of Ann Lady Halkett resembles Lady Fanshawe's in structure, and to some extent in subject-matter, though Lady Halkett lays more stress on the emotional implications of events, and uses more directly-reported dialogue; the result is a more intimate and subjective work.[6] Lady Halkett gives no motive for writing and does not seem to have planned to publish. The detailed narrative of her role in the escape of the Duke of York from St. James's Palace in 1648 suggests that she may have written at the request of a friend or relative who was interested in her Civil War exploits; the other parts of her story could have been added to round out the narrative. In any case, she describes only the events of her adult life, passing over her childhood with the comment: 'What my childish actions were I thinke I need not give accountt of here, for I hope none will thinke they could bee either vicious or scandalous' (p. 3). The first anecdote to be presented in detail is of her courtship by a noble youth in 1644, when she was already twenty-two.

Lady Halkett's narrative comes to an abrupt end shortly after her marriage; we have no way of knowing how much more she wrote, though the work was composed more than twenty years after the date at which it breaks off. She married relatively late in life, after a wide, independent experience of the world; and she does not scruple to make her own career, rather than her husband's, the centre of interest. She emphasizes two kinds of episodes in her life: some are drawn from her participation in various intrigues and skirmishes of the Civil War, others from the experiences crucial to her emotional development, especially her three courtships. This mixing of two kinds of subject-matter produces a curious narrative, which reads like a blend of Richardson and Sir Walter Scott.

In her Richardsonian vein, Lady Halkett devotes sixteen pages to a

---

[6] *The Autobiography of Anne Lady Halkett*, ed. J. G. Nichols (Camden Soc., 1875). Margaret Bottrall discusses the work at length, and gives generous quotations, in *Phoenix*, pp. 149-60.

minutely detailed account of how the chaplain of a noble family intrigued against her while she was a guest of his patron; she reports verbatim conversations which took place more than twenty-five years before the autobiography was written, and gradually exposes the chaplain as a Tartuffe by accumulating scraps of evidence against him. Despite our heroine's case against the chaplain, however, she admits to suffering from an acute case of 'melancholy vapours' before the trouble starts, and we suspect that a neurotic over-sensitivity may have influenced her perception of the actions of each participant in her little drama. The episode appears to be a tempest in a tea cup, to which no male autobiographer would give so much importance (pp. 36-52). Yet only a year later, Lady Halkett shows herself in quite a different light. She was staying at Fyvie, in Scotland; while the master of the house was away a band of marauding English soldiers came to the door. The mistress, Lady Dunfermline, being 'great with child . . . and much disordered', Lady Halkett braved the mob of her countrymen:

> As soon as I came amongst them, the first question they asked mee was if I were the English whore that came to meet the King, and all sett their pistolls just against mee . . . I told them I owned myselfe to bee an English woman and to honour the King, butt for the name they gave mee I abhorred itt; butt my coming to them was nott to dispute for my selfe, butt to tell them I was sorry to heare that any of the English nation, who was generally esteemed the most civill people in the world, should give so much occation to be thought barbarously rude, as they had done since there comming into the howse, where they found none to resist them. . . . They heard mee with much patience; and att last flinging downe there pistolls upon the table, the major gave mee his promise that neither hee nor any with him should give the least disturbance to the meanest in the family. (pp. 68-9)

Lady Halkett's brave opposition to the soldiers shows her at her best; but the hyper-sensitive account of her troubles with the chaplain is not typical of her treatment of personal relations, which are usually described with insight and a fine sense of proportion. She appears to better advantage in telling of her three courtships, the first two of which ended in her betrayal by faithless suitors. The progress of each suit is conveyed mainly by the reporting of conversations; she does not analyse explicitly her own or her suitors' characters, but allows the narrative to speak for itself. This dramatic, rather than expository, presentation may be seen in the climax of the first courtship, when she receives a letter from her erstwhile suitor informing her that he plans to marry another:

> I was alone in my sister's chamber when I read the letter, and flinging my selfe downe upon her bed, I said, 'Is this the man for whom I have

sufred so much? Since hee hath made him selfe unworthy my love, hee is unworthy my anger or concerne'; and rising imediately I wentt outt into the next roome to my super as unconcernedly as if I had never had an interest in him, nor had never lost itt. (p. 18)

Lady Fanshawe's memoirs showed how anecdotes from the world of society and politics could be enlivened and humanized by the addition of small, but significant, details such as the feminine eye did not scorn to notice and record—the colour of the cabin-boy's cap, for example, in the passage quoted on p. 161. Her materials, however, were the staples of the orthodox *res gestae* form: the fortunes of war, politics, travel and diplomacy. Lady Halkett, on the other hand, retained the objective style of *res gestae* and some of its usual materials; but she brought in new matter with her minute and serious descriptions of everyday personal relations and domestic scenes. Without making any radical innovations in autobiographical form she widened the scope of the genre by showing how minor events, which other autobiographers passed over, had significance for her emotional development and for her moods. Her choice of subjects may have reflected simply her customary preoccupations, but few British autobiographers before her had paid such close attention to the household intrigues and drawing-room sentiments that she chronicled. Moreover, though in some respects she anticipated Richardson she wrote without his heavy-handed nonconformist moralizing: she had strong moral principles but, as a devout Anglican, left sermons to the parson. She observed human behaviour with the clear-sightedness of a well-brought-up gentlewoman who had no doubts about what was or was not socially permissible. Such a nature was, no doubt, better equipped for observation and judgement than for penetrating introspection; but with this reservation we should give Lady Halkett credit for being one of the most perceptive and skilful stylists among British autobiographers of her time.

Mary Countess of Warwick belonged to a family in which auto-biographical writing was a tradition—the works of her father, Richard Boyle, and her brother Robert have already been discussed in Chapter IX. Her own autobiography probably evolved from her habits of keeping a diary and writing pious meditations.[7] The first third of the work is about wordly affairs, particularly her courtship by her future husband, Charles Rich. However, we are given little more than the factual details of the affair, and her comments on the emotional side of their relationship tend to be flat and conventional. A few years after their marriage, the Countess retired to the country and was converted to a more devout way of life. The tone of her work

[7] *Some Specialities in the Life of M. Warwicke*, ed. T. Crofton Croker (Percy Soc., 1848).

now changes to that of a spiritual autobiography, as she turns her back on childish follies:

> I desire to acknowledge it to God's glory in changing me, and my own shame, that I was, when I was married into my husband's family, as vain, as idle, and as inconsiderate a person as was possible, minding nothing but curious dressing and fine and rich clothes, and spending my precious time in nothing else but reading romances, and in reading and seeing plays, and in going to court and Hide Park and Spring Garden. (p. 21)

We need not follow Lady Warwick's history subsequent to her conversion, for her pious reflections on the vicissitudes of her life are relentlessly dull. However, her rather unprofessional approach to spiritual autobiography is significant; a minister describing the progress of his soul in approved style would never begin, as she does, with a long and morally neutral account of a clandestine courtship. In fact, none of our female autobiographers were content to write orthodox *res gestae*, spiritual autobiography, or Quaker journal, as the case might be; they freely adapted conventional narrative modes to suit their individual tastes and preoccupations.

Lucy Hutchinson was an unusually learned woman for her time and the author of an intimate life of her husband, Colonel John Hutchinson.[8] It is unfortunate, therefore, that she did not persist with her own autobiography, but cut it short when she had barely started to describe her youth. She planned the work as a testimony of how Divine providence had influenced her life:

> in things great and extraordinary, some, perhaps, will take notice of God's working, who either forget or believe not that he takes as well a care and account of their smallest concernments, even the hairs of their heads.
>
> Finding myself in some kind guilty of this general neglect, I thought it might be a means to stir up my thankfulness for things past, and to encourage my faith for the future, if I recollected as much as I have heard or can remember of the passages of my youth, and the general and particular providences exercised to me, both in the entrance and progress of my life. (p. 2)

However, after working her way through the circumstances of her birth and parentage she seems to have had second thoughts about the whole project. She began to recall the vanities of her youth:

> I thought it no sin to learn or hear witty songs and amorous sonnets or poems, and twenty things of that kind, wherein I was so apt that I

[8] She translated Lucretius into English, and also knew Greek and Hebrew. *The Life of Mrs. Lucy Hutchinson written by herself* is in *Memoirs of the Life of Colonel Hutchinson*, ed. J. Hutchinson (1885), I, 1-26.

became the confidante in all the loves that were managed among my mother's young women; and there was none of them but had many lovers, and some particular friends beloved above the rest. Among these I have . . . (p. 26)

At this point many leaves have been torn from the manuscript and an incomplete sentence ends the work. We can only guess at Mrs. Hutchinson's reasons for abandoning what she had begun; perhaps the memories of her youth created too much pain and guilt for her to be able to continue. Her learning and her biographical talents qualified her to write an important autobiography; but her insight into what the composition of such a superior work demanded of its author may have made her unwilling to undertake it.

We may conclude this chapter with a further glance at Mary Penington's *A Brief Account of my Exercises from my Childhood*. This work has two parts, the first an account of her conversion to Quakerism and the second a letter to her grandson describing her life with his grandfather, Sir William Springett. Mrs. Penington died before the Quaker autobiography had settled into a rigid convention, and her conversion narrative has a freshness and intensity rarely found in the later journals. Her dreams, for example, have the ring of simple, unmediated truth—even when Christ himself appears in them:

I stood at a great distance, at the lower end of that great hall, and Christ at the upper end; whom I saw in the appearance of a fresh lovely youth, clad in grey cloth (at which time I had not heard of a Quaker or their habit) very plain and neat, he was of a sweet, affable, courteous carriage, and embraced several poor old simple people, whose appearance was very contemptible and mean, without wisdom or beauty. (p. 9)

This domestic and lifelike Christ is typical of the skill in character-drawing displayed by female autobiographers.

In the second part of the *Brief Account*, Mrs. Penington subordinates her own concerns to those of her first husband, Colonel Springett, whose life she narrates in eulogistic terms. Of the six autobiographers here discussed, four wrote lives of their husbands, sometimes, like Lady Fanshawe, intertwining biography with autobiography.[9] It would appear that these women became interested in self-portrayal through the experience of portraying the lives and characters of those to whom they were emotionally linked, and that their attempts to discern and record the pattern of others' lives acted as a stimulant to awareness of themselves.

[9] The four biographers are the Duchess of Newcastle, Mrs. Hutchinson, Lady Fanshawe and Mrs. Penington.

XI
Conclusion

TO CONCLUDE this study I shall summarize some general trends in
the evolution of British seventeenth-century autobiography, and
point to problems of motivation or interpretation which deserve
further study.

The Origins and Environment of Autobiography

(a) In Chapter II I emphasized two aspects of the development of
Renaissance historiography: first, the evolution of an improved 'sense
of the past' as historians gained more insight into the cultural differences that separated contemporary Europe from the ancient world;
second, the breaking of the clerical monopoly on historical writing.
These were two points of contrast between medieval and renaissance
historiography; but it would be well to note here the essential
continuity of the two traditions. In both eras the basic and similar
purpose of historical writing was didactic or exemplary. Historically-
minded autobiographers, therefore, wanted their lives to teach a
lesson to the reader, to instruct rather than delight. Herbert of Cherbury, among secular autobiographers, proclaimed that 'I have
thought fit to relate to my posterity those passages of my life, which I
conceive may best declare me, and be most useful to them';[1] Richard
Coppin put himself forward as a spiritual guide to others as he
exhorted them 'Hearken my beloved brethren, come behold, and see
the race which you are to run, the way which you are to come, and
the price that is to be won, as I will here shew unto you, by setting
before you the race that I have run, the way that I have gone, and the
price that I have won.'[2] A dispassionate analysis of intellectual
development, such as J. S. Mill wrote, cannot be expected from
seventeenth-century autobiographers: they were concerned with the
morals which might be drawn from their past actions rather than with
objective self-study. Their difference from medieval writers lay not so

[1] *Autobiography*, p. 2.
[2] *Truth's Testimony*, p. 9.

much in historical theory as in their readiness to think of their own lives as fit subjects for historical writing.

(b) *Renaissance Individualism.* After scrutinizing many renaissance autobiographies and other kinds of self-expression, I am convinced that no simple or direct connection can be demonstrated between disparate manifestations of 'individuality'; between, say, the decision of a Dürer to paint his own portrait and the decision of a Herbert of Cherbury to write his autobiography. I hope to take up in a further study the problem of the underlying cultural factors which could have influenced such decisions; at this point I will merely list a few points relevant to the present subject.

(1) Most seventeenth-century British autobiographers evinced very little interest in self-analysis or self-investigation *for their own* sakes; (2) figures like Cellini or Cardano, who may be said to have exemplified Burckhardt's 'renaissance individualism', had no real counterparts among British autobiographers before 1700; (3) both the explicit and implicit motives for writing of British autobiographers varied widely, and autobiographies were often written for purposes— vindication of the author's reputation, religious propaganda, etc.— which could have been achieved in other ways. Most autobiographies of our period were written neither as exercises in pure self-expression, nor as attempts to achieve aesthetic success according to the standards of an established literary genre. (4) Both religious and secular British autobiographies seem to have been composed, for the most part, in isolation from the autobiographical traditions of the Continent. A majority of religious autobiographies were written by poorly-educated, insular sectaries who read little beside their Bibles; secular autobiographers, perhaps because they felt no need to consult any other authority but their own experience, generally ignored such Continental self-students as Montaigne and Cardano.

These four points must be counted as evidence against the semi-mystical theory that a powerful, obscure, and widely-diffused impulse labelled 'renaissance individualism' affected all Europeans living between, say, 1400 and 1700. We cannot postulate such an archetypal and universal impulse as the cause of the rise of autobiography in seventeenth-century Britain. An equally general, but more down-to-earth, theory is proposed by Shumaker who suggests 'the substitution of inductive thought-habits for deductive' as the ultimate cause of the increase in autobiographical writing during the renaissance.[3] That such a substitution did occur, at least partially and in individual cases, and that it changed men's awareness of themselves and of their life-patterns, seems beyond question; but to explain, in any final sense, the change would require an exhaustive history of individual and

[3] *English Autobiography*, p. 29.

168

mass psychology in the renaissance which has yet to be written and perhaps, in view of the scarcity of fundamental knowledge about individual lives in the period, never can be.[4]

(c) *Autobiography and Class.* I would suggest that three general rules applied in this area. (1) Since all men were considered equal in the sight of God, but not in the sight of Caesar, a man from the lower ranks of British society could more easily and acceptably assert his own importance in the religious than in the social sphere; as a result, religious autobiographers came from all levels of (literate) society, whereas secular autobiographers were predominantly members (or hangers-on) of the aristocracy, gentry, or upper-middle class.[5] (2) On the religious side, artisans or petty traders such as Bunyan and Arise Evans were both less cautious about revealing their spiritual experiences, and more ready to publish the resulting narratives, than were members of the Anglican hierarchy or other persons with genteel backgrounds. This correlation between social status and the degree of outspokenness prevailed also, though less strictly, among secular autobiographers. (3) Because the autobiographical urge was so widely diffused in seventeenth-century Britain, the rise of autobiography cannot be linked to the fortunes or cultural habits of a particular social class. It does seem, however, that secular autobiographers were often unusually concerned with their social status, either because it had changed significantly for better or worse, or because they had perceived a shift in the relative standing of the class to which they gave allegiance.

I have not been able to establish any reliable connection between the social class of an autobiographer and his stylistic preferences, whether for *res gestae* or for a more subjective approach. One can only say that *res gestae* was, in that period, the orthodox and natural mode for *any* autobiographer to incline to; subjective works were exceptional, and were not offshoots of any particular social environment.

The problem of the roots of Renaissance autobiography is far from exhausted. It should be clear by now that autobiography is one of the most complex and varied of literary genres, and that seventeenth-century practitioners of it undertook their works for many other motives besides the basic desire for self-commemoration. We can attempt to deal with these motives through individual analysis of each work, but the task is a delicate one; as C. V. Wedgwood reminds us,

---

[4] Z. Barbu discusses some fundamental questions of methodology in his *Problems of Historical Psychology.*

[5] By 'upper-middle class' I mean, particularly, the merchants, contractors, higher-ranking bureaucrats, etc., of London.

'nothing in history is harder to establish than motive'.[6] Moreover, in trying to offer an intellectually satisfying interpretation of the origins of seventeenth-century autobiography the scholar finds that his task is made harder by the very multiplicity of the motives he collects; he finds many 'accidents', yet the nature of the autobiographical 'substance' remains elusive. We can only suggest that a solution to this problem must be sought by widening the field of inquiry to include the development of British society as a whole in the period, starting with close analysis of particular groups; Lawrence Stone's brilliant study of the aristocracy shows what can be done with modern techniques of historical sociology.

Some General Features of British Seventeenth-Century Autobiography

We should first reiterate the importance of the circumstances of composition and dissemination of autobiographies in this period. Only a minority of the autobiographies considered were published in the seventeenth century, and a small minority during their authors' lifetimes. Those members of the sects who wished to propagandize by means of personal testimony consistently published their works without delay; but outside the sects no substantial literary tradition of autobiography existed in Britain until well into the eighteenth century. Early autobiographers, therefore, could not benefit to any significant extent from mutual influence, instruction, or stimulation. The absence of a tradition, moreover, had a double effect: on the one hand, British autobiographers had little communication with other practitioners; on the other, they limited themselves to addressing small, fragmented, and private audiences—their family and descendants, close friends, comrades-in-arms, and so forth. Under these conditions, the development of the genre in the course of the seventeenth century was necessarily somewhat irregular and haphazard. Each author was free to write the kind of autobiography that seemed best to him, according to his particular aims, temperament and social position; this was a freedom especially available to secular writers, who were not bound by the constraints of sectarian doctrine. Seventeenth-century autobiographies were, as a result, so diverse that general trends are hard for us to discern; but three features may be singled out for attention: the loosening of rigid conventions of prose style, the scarcity of secular intellectual autobiography, and the tendency of autobiographers to stress practical aims at the expense of aesthetic ones.

[6] *The Reformation Crisis*, ed. J. Hurstfield, p. 109.

(a) *Relaxation of the* Res Gestae *Convention.* From the medieval period until about the third decade of the seventeenth century, virtually all British autobiographers used the organization and prose style of *res gestae*. Religious autobiographers such as Bishop Cowper and John Gerard described even their spiritual lives in a tone essentially similar to that in which they described the concrete happenings of the exterior world. Among secular works, Bodley's *Life* (1609) was typical in that it could almost as well have been written by a close friend as by Bodley himself; though an autobiography, it was neither more intimate nor more revelatory than a good seventeenth-century biography, such as Walton's life of Donne. As the century passed, autobiography came to differentiate itself more from biography, and to evolve towards a looser, more imaginative, and more varied form than simple *res gestae*.

In tracing the evolution of religious autobiography in the century, any temporal scheme has to be modified according to the changing fortunes of the various denominations. Throughout the century, Catholic and Anglican autobiographies were more objective and sober in tone than those written by members of other Protestant denominations. When this factor has been allowed for, one can say that religious autobiography in general was mainly objective and impersonal at the beginning of the century, became much more intimate, confessional, and subjective after 1640, and from 1640 to 1700 regressed, though only partially, towards its former objectivity. The connection between this advance and retreat of subjective self-presentation and the parallel fortunes of the sects has already been discussed in Chapters V and VI, and need not be further stressed.

The evolution of secular autobiography diverged somewhat from the curve just sketched for religious works. From the reticence and factual emphasis of Bodley's *Life* we traced a progressive relaxation of what might be called the 'stiff upper lip' convention, in successive generations of aristocratic autobiographers: Robert Cary, Earl of Monmouth (born 1560, fifteen years after Bodley), Herbert of Cherbury (b. 1583), and Sir Kenelm Digby (b. 1603). Digby, especially, widened the scope of British autobiography by including long descriptions of his intimate feelings and by casting his life-story in the form of a pastoral romance; unfortunately, his failure to publish the work prevented it from having any influence. In the years around 1660, other autobiographers experimented with such forms as the epistle to a friend (William Lilly), the romance (Robert Boyle and Charles Croke), and the 'rhapsodie' (Thomas Raymond). Though not all these experiments succeeded, they did show that some British autobiographers were outgrowing the limits of orthodox *res gestae*.

In the last decades of the century, there were fewer eccentric or

171

otherwise original autobiographies; this narrowing of the genre's range may have been caused by the growing influence of neo-classical ideals and norms. A measure of the century's progress can be taken by comparing Bodley's autobiography with that of Roger North, who was born about a hundred years after Bodley. North still uses *res gestae* as the basic mode of organization for his life-experiences; but he supplements the bare facts of his life with penetrating evaluations of his personality, and of the early experiences which shaped it. Despite the orthodoxy of his overall conception, North achieved a degree of personal insight little inferior to that reached by Gibbon or Mill.

In British autobiography of our period subjective or confessional passages occur more often in religious than in secular works; it would seem that few men were willing to concede to the individual sensibility an autonomous field of action, outside of religion or the external observances of the state. In a pre-romantic age, the profane creed of self-realization as the highest good did not yet hold sway, and man's relation to his God was held to be more vital than any concern with personal, secular development. Autobiographers often expressed strong feelings about their political allegiances, it is true, but being on the 'right' side politically did not guarantee salvation— politics had not yet become what they are for many in our century, a substitute for religion. Only when speaking of their religious life were seventeenth-century autobiographers free, if they so chose, to raise their tone to an 'Oh altitudo' without fear of being censured for impropriety.[7] It was in religious rather than secular autobiography, accordingly, that the greater progress away from the objectivity of *res gestae* took place.

(b) *Scarcity of Secular Intellectual Autobiography.* Spiritual autobiographies which traced the origin and development of their authors' religious convictions were common in the seventeenth century, and were undertaken even by such lower-middle-class autobiographers as Bunyan, Clarkson, and Muggleton (Chapter VI). Secular autobiographers, on the other hand, generally have little to say about the evolution of their intellectual or political beliefs. Herbert of Cherbury, for example, made an important contribution to European thought with his deistic treatise *De Veritate*; he describes the circumstances of its publication in his autobiography, but says nothing at all about how he arrived at the conclusions expressed in the treatise. Hobbes was one secular autobiographer who did trace the origin and

[7] Sir Kenelm Digby, who exalted his love for 'Stelliana' (Venetia Stanley) to a celestial level, felt compelled to defend his Platonic idealization of sexual love at great length in his *Loose Fantasies*; he also directed that the manuscript be destroyed after his death.

development of his ideas, but his exposition of his intellectual growth was brief and lacked the weighty seriousness of his major works—one may justly term his autobiography a vulgarization of his ideas. In general, most of the important British philosophers and political thinkers of the time do not seem to have felt obliged to explore closely the links between their personal histories and the intellectual systems that they constructed. This may have been because they still accepted the idea that religious belief was crucial to the conduct of their lives, but speculative philosophizing was not; secular thought was thus relegated to a position of relative inferiority.

Another explanation of the lack of intellectual autobiography in the seventeenth century may be sought in those fashionable attitudes which exalted order and the principle of subordination at the expense of personal singularity. Only an unusually strong-minded and independent person would proclaim and defend an individual philosophy derived from his particular experience; Hobbes, who thrived on controversy, was such a man, but he had few peers. Seventeenth-century intellectuals had little sense of what we now call the sociology of knowledge; not until orthodox Christianity had begun to lose its grip, in the later eighteenth and nineteenth centuries, would it become normal for an educated man to choose his own philosophy from among conflicting schools of secular thought, and to relate his choice to his character and upbringing. We see a foreshadowing of this situation in Roger North's discussion of the childhood memories which determined his later Tory bias; but he devotes little space to the question, and his work in any case was written late—it belongs as much to the eighteenth as to the seventeenth century.

(c) *Subordination of Aesthetic to Practical Aims.* Most seventeenth-century British autobiographers were rather modest in their literary pretensions; we can suggest a number of reasons for their lack of interest in formal and stylistic excellence. Most autobiographers did not write for publication, and therefore limited their literary ambitions from the start. Second, many of those autobiographers who did publish—in particular, those who adhered to the sects—made virtues of rugged sincerity, indifference to literary tradition, and plainness of style. Third, no generally-accepted norms of good autobiographical writing existed, and few successful autobiographies had been published or otherwise made available for imitation. Literary genres such as the sonnet or the drama were, by the efforts of many authors, gradually polished and developed to a high level of formal correctness; autobiography was never subjected to this kind of refining process. A sophisticated and carefully-structed autobiography, like Clarendon's, is exceptional in the seventeenth century.

Because of these special circumstances, I have usually considered each autobiography in terms of its function (i.e. the purpose which its author intended it to serve), instead of using the more conventional methods and standards of modern literary criticism. Function, in turn, can best be understood by examining each autobiographer's relation to his audience—the way in which he presents himself to them, and the devices he uses to create the particular image he desires.[8] An autobiography can scarcely be composed without assuming a role; the author 'plays his part' by selecting certain of his past actions for emphasis and omitting others, by manipulating his presentation of past episodes so as to show himself in a particular light, and by the overall tone of his narrative.[9] In the seventeenth century, most British autobiographies had a practical purpose which depended on successful presentation of an appropriate authorial role.

We may again resort to example to illustrate these principles. A didactic purpose was quite common in autobiography; Father John Gerard, for example, wrote of his adventures as a missionary in England for the guidance and encouragement of Jesuit novices training to do similar work. He depicted himself as an unworthy but devoted servant of God, who could have achieved nothing without His help. Without questioning the sincerity of Gerard's self-presentation, we may observe that it had the value of reinforcing the autobiography's purpose: by stressing his personal deficiencies, Gerard pointed a moral to those novices who read him—they too, however unworthy and full of self-doubt they might be, could accomplish great things with God's aid. Bunyan's autobiography, also didactic, exploits a dramatic posture somewhat different from Gerard's: Bunyan presents himself in an exemplary role as a 'prodigal son', one who was the chief of sinners yet repented and was received into God's favour. Seventeenth-century autobiography in Britain, far from being a lyrical expression of 'renaissance individualism', was the servant of didactic, historical, or controversial purposes. Its practitioners devoted relatively little effort to establishing autobiography as a literary genre: caught up in the turmoil of contemporary religious and social struggles, they cared more for the content than for the style of their works, and aimed at functional cogency rather than aesthetic perfection.

[8] A very few seventeenth-century autobiographies, notably those of Digby and Richard Norwood, seem to have been intended for their authors' eyes only; but even in these works the authors tended to use rhetorical devices typical of autobiographies written for larger audiences.

[9] For an extended treatment of these aspects of autobiographical writing, see Roy Pascal, *Design and Truth in Autobiography*.

Bibliography

This bibliography is divided into two parts: (1) a check-list of British seventeenth-century autobiographies, and (2) a bibliography of other works consulted or cited in the text. Where no place of publication is given, *London* is to be understood.

I

CHECK-LIST OF

SEVENTEENTH-CENTURY AUTOBIOGRAPHIES

The working definition of autobiography used in this book was given in Chapter I; in the interest of completeness, I have interpreted the definition more broadly in this list than I have in the selection of works for discussion in the text.

Under each author, I have listed first the particular edition of his autobiography from which I have quoted, or to which I have referred, in the text. Other important editions have then been mentioned briefly, together with biographical or critical notes.

In compiling this list, I have found especially helpful works by the following scholars: A. W. Brink, W. Matthews, D. A. Stauffer, W. Y. Tindall, L. M. Wright (for full references, see part II of this bibliography).

ALLEN, HANNAH. *Satan his Methods and Malice Baffled. A Narrative of God's Gracious Dealings with . . . Hannah Allen.* 1683.

AMES, WILLIAM (d. 1662). *A Declaration of the Witness of God Manifested in me from my Youth.* 1656. Quaker; see Wright.

Anon. Autobiography of a young lawyer, 1660-89. Listed in Matthews' bibliography as ms. Cambridge University Library Add. 6596, but a personal check found no such ms. with this number.

Anon. An eighteen-year-old apprentice. Brief spiritual autobiography in Doe, Charles, *A Collection*, q.v.

Anon. Autobiography of a woman (b. 1654), said to be a relative of Cromwell's. Ms. B.M. Add. 5858, ff. 213-21. Rhapsodic account of her spiritual experiences.

ASHMOLE, ELIAS (1617-92). *The Lives of those eminent antiquaries Elias Ashmole, Esquire and Mr. William Lilly.* 1774. 1st ed. 1717.

BAKER, DANIEL. Autobiography, 1690-1705. Ms. Bucks. Museum, Aylesbury. Not seen.

BAMFIELD (or BAMPFIELD), FRANCIS (1614-84). *A Name, an After-one, or A Name, a New-One, In the Latter-day Glory.* 1681. Published under the pseudonym 'Shem Acher'. See Tindall.

BANGS, BENJAMIN (1652-1741). *Memoirs of the Life and Convincement of.* 1757. Quaker; see Wright. Memoir covers 1652-91.

BANKS, JOHN (1638-1710). *Journal of the Life of.* 1712. Quaker.

BARLOW, EDWARD (1642-after 1703). *Barlow's Journal.* Edited by Basil Lubbock. 1934.

BAXTER, RICHARD (1615-91). *Autobiography.* Edited by J. M. Lloyd Thomas (abridged). 1931. First published in *Reliquiae Baxterianae.* 1696.

BAYLY, WILLIAM. *A Short Relation or Testimony of the Working of the Light of Christ in me.* 1659. Quaker; brief.

BILBY, WILLIAM (1664-1738). *Some Remarkable Passages in my Life.* Ms. Nottingham Subscription Library, Nottingham. Typescript at Dr. Williams Library, London, ms. 12.62. Written 1714; nonconformist minister.

BLAIR, ROBERT (1593-1666). *Autobiography.* In *The Life of Mr. Robert Blair,* ed. T. McCrie. Edinburgh, 1848. Written 1663.

BLAKHALL, GILBERT (fl. 1667). *A Breiffe Narration of the Services Done to Three Noble Ladyes.* Aberdeen, 1844. Written 1663.

BLAUGDONE, BARBARA. *An Account of the Travels, Sufferings and Persecutions of.* 1691. Quaker.

BODLEY, SIR THOMAS (1545-1613). *The Life of.* In *Trecentale Bodleianum.* Oxford, 1913. 1st ed. 1647.

BOYLE, MARY, LADY WARWICK (1625-78). *Autobiography.* Edited by T. C. Croker. Percy Society, 1848.

BOYLE, RICHARD. See Cork, Lord.

BOYLE, ROBERT (1627-91). *An Account of Philaretus during his Minority.* In Thomas Birch, *The Life of Robert Boyle.* 1734.

BRAMSTON, SIR JOHN (1611-1700). *Autobiography.* Edited by Braybrooke. Camden Society, 1845. Written 1685.

BRIGGS, THOMAS. *An Account of Some of the Travels and Sufferings of.* 1685. Quaker.

BUCKINGHAM, JOHN SHEFFIELD, DUKE OF (1648-1721). *Memoirs.* In *Works.* Vol. II. 1723. Fragmentary; military and political.

BRYSSON, GEORGE (*c.* 1649-after 1721). *Memoirs of Mr. William*

Veitch and George Brysson. Edited by T. McCrie. Edinburgh and London, 1825.

BUGG, FRANCIS (1640-1724?). *Pilgrim's Progress from Quakerism to Christianity*. 1698. See Wright.

BUNYAN, JOHN (1628-88). *Grace Abounding to the Chief of Sinners*. Edited by G. B. Harrison. 1928. 1st ed. 1666; augmented editions 1692, 1765. Edited by R. Sharrock. Oxford, 1962.

BURNET, BISHOP GILBERT (1643-1715). *Autobiography*. In *A Supplement to Burnet's History Of My Own Time*. Edited by H. C. Foxcroft. Oxford, 1902. Written 1710.

BURNYEAT, JOHN (1631-90). *The Truth Exalted*. In *Journals of the Lives . . . of William Caton and John Burnyeat*. 1839. 1st ed. 1691.

BURTON, HENRY (1578-1648). *A Narration of the Life of*. 1643.

CARLETON, THOMAS. *The Captive's Complaint*. 1668. Quaker; see Wright.

CARY, ROBERT, EARL OF MONMOUTH (1560-1639). *Memoirs of the Life of*. 1759. Ed. G. H. Powell, 1905. Written *c*. 1627.

CATON, WILLIAM (*c*. 1637-65). *A Journal of the Life of*. 1689. Quaker.

CAVENDISH, MARGARET. See Newcastle, Duchess of.

CHAPPELL, WILLIAM (1582-1649). *Vita Gulielmi Chappell*. In Thomas Hearne, ed., *Appendicis ad J. Lelandi . . . Collectanea*. 1770. Vol. V, pp. 261-8. Written 1641-9; first published in Francis Peck, *Desiderata Curiosa*. 1735.

CLARENDON, EDWARD HYDE, LORD (1609-74). *An Account of the Life of Lord Clarendon*. Oxford, 1759. Written 1668-72; parts included in the *History of the Rebellion*. Oxford, 1702-4.

CLARKE, SAMUEL (1599-1682). *A Brief Narrative of my Life*. In his *The Lives of Sundry Eminent Persons*. 1683.

CLARKSON (or CLAXTON), LAURENCE (*c*. 1615-67). *The Lost Sheep Found*. 1660.

COPPIN, RICHARD (fl. 1646-59). *Truth's Testimony*. 1655.

CORK, RICHARD BOYLE, LORD (1566-1643). *True Remembrances*. In Thomas Birch, *The Life of Robert Boyle*. 1734. Written 1632.

COURTHOP, SIR GEORGE (1616-85). *The Memoirs of*. Edited by S. C. Lomas. Camden Society Miscellany xi. 1907. Mainly travel interest.

COWPER, WILLIAM, BISHOP OF GALWAY (1568-1619). *The Life and Death of*. In *Workes*. 1629.

COXERE, EDWARD (1633-94). *Adventures by Sea of*. Edited by E. H. W. Meyerstein. New York, 1946. Written *c*. 1685-94.

CRAB, ROGER (1621-80). *The English Hermit, or The Wonder of the Age*. 1655. Leveller. See Hill, *Puritanism and Revolution*, Chapter 11.

CRISP, STEPHEN (1628-92). *Journal of the Life of*. In *A Memorable*

Account of the Christian Experiences of Stephen Crisp. 1694. Quaker.

CROKE, CHARLES (*c.* 1635-after 1686). *Fortune's Uncertainty or Youth's Inconstancy.* Edited by I. M. Westcott. Oxford, 1959. 1st ed. 1667. Published under the pseudonym of 'Rodolphus'; attributed to Croke by Anthony à Wood.

CROKER, JOHN (1673-1727). *Brief Memoir of the Life of.* 1839. Quaker.

CROOK, JOHN (1617-99). *A Short History of the Life of.* 1706. Quaker.

CROUCH, WILLIAM (1628-1710). *Posthuma Christiana.* 1712. Quaker.

CURWEN, ALICE. *A Relation of the Labour, Travail and Suffering of.* 1680. Quaker.

DAVIES, RICHARD (1635-1707). *An Account of the Convincement of.* 1710. Quaker.

DEMPSTER, THOMAS (1579?-1625). *Thomae Dempsteri Historia Ecclesiastica.* Edinburgh, 1829. See entry 1210.

DERBY, JAMES STANLEY, SEVENTH EARL (1607-51). Autobiography to 1650. Ms. Chetham's Library, Manchester. Not seen.

DEVENPORT, WILL. *An Account of the Work of Grace upon Will Devenport.* In Charles Doe, *A Collection*, q.v. Written *c.* 1698.

D'EWES, SIR SIMONDS (1602-50). *Autobiography.* Edited by J. O. Halliwell. 2 vols. 1845. Written *c.* 1649.

DIGBY, SIR KENELM (1603-65). *Loose Fantasies.* Published as *Private Memoirs of Sir Kenelm Digby.* Edited by Sir N. H. Nicholas. 1827. Passages expurgated by the editor are bound up in some copies; they are also printed as an appendix to E. W. Bligh, *Sir Kenelm Digby and his Venetia.* 1932.

DISNEY, GERVASE (1641-91). *Some Remarkable Passages in the Holy Life and Death of.* 1692.

DOE, CHARLES (born *c.* 1653). *Autobiography.* In his *A Collection of the Work of Grace.* N.d. (1700?).

DUGDALE, SIR WILLIAM (1605-86). *A Breif Accompt of the Parentage, and what else is Memorable of Sir William Dugdale.* In *The Life, Diary, and Correspondence of Sir William Dugdale.* Edited by William Hamper. 1827.

DUNTON, JOHN (1659-1733). *The Life and Errors of.* 1705. An erratic hodge-podge, but amusing.

EDMUNDSON, WILLIAM (1627-1712). *A Journal of the Life of.* 1715. Quaker.

EDWARDS, CHARLES (d. 1691?). *An Afflicted Man's Testimony.* 1691. Nonconformist; recital of misfortunes.

ELLIOT, ADAM (d. 1700). *A Narrative of My Travails, Captivity and Escape from Salle, In the Kingdom of Fez.* In *A Modest Vindication of Titus Oates.* 1682.

ELLWOOD, THOMAS (1639-1713). *History of the Life of.* Edited by C. G. Crump. 1900. 1st ed. 1714.

EVANS, ARISE (b. 1607). *An Eccho to the Voice from Heaven.* 1652.

EVELYN, JOHN (1620-1706). *De Vita Propria.* In E. S. de Beer, ed., *The Diary of John Evelyn.* Oxford, 1955. Vol. I. A recension of the early part of the Kalendarium (to 1644).

FAIRFAX, THOMAS LORD (1612-71). *Short Memorials of.* 1699.

FANE, MILDMAY. See Westmoreland.

FANSHAWE, LADY ANN (1625-80). *Memoirs of.* Edited by H. C. Fanshawe. 1907. 1st ed. 1829.

FARNSWORTH, RICHARD (*c.* 1630-66). *The Heart Opened by Christ.* 1654. Quaker.

FLAMSTEED, JOHN (1646-1719). *History of his Own Life.* In Francis Baily, *An Account of the Revd. John Flamsteed.* 1835. Written in seven parts, 1667-1717.

FORMAN, DR. SIMON (1552-1611). *The Autobiography and Personal Diary of.* Edited by J. O. Halliwell. Privately printed, 1849. Written 1600.

FOX, GEORGE (1624-91). *The Journal of.* Edited by John L. Nickalls. Cambridge, 1952. 1st ed. 1694.

FOX, MARGARET (1614-1702). *A Brief Collection of Remarkable Passages.* 1710. Includes *A Relation of Margaret Fell* (Fox).

FRASER OF BREA, JAMES (1639-99). *Memoirs of the Life of.* 1738. Written *c.* 1684.

FULLER, WILLIAM (1670-1717?). Fuller's many autobiographical works are full of internal contradictions; I list only the more important published works and ms.

(a) *The Life of William Fuller, gent.* 1701.

(b) A revised version of the above, published from prison. 1703.

(c) *The Sincere and Hearty Confession of Mr. W. Fuller.* 1704. A retraction of previous frauds and lies; may be spurious.

(d) *The Truth at Last.* N.d. Maintains that (c) is a fake.

(e) Ms. autobiography, longer than any of the published versions. Sold at Sotheby's, 28-29 June, 1965, lot 105, to B. Dobell.

GERARD, FATHER JOHN (1564-1637). *The Autobiography of a Hunted Priest.* Translated by Philip Caraman. New York, 1952. Written in Latin, 1609.

GODFREY, THOMAS (1586-1664). *Autobiography and Diary.* Edited by J. G. Nichols. In *Topographer and Genealogist,* ii, 450-67. Father of Sir Edmund B. Godfrey; *res gestae.*

GOODWIN, THOMAS (1600-80). Narrative of his conversion (untitled). In *The Works of Thomas Goodwin, D.D.* Edinburgh, 1861. Vol. II, pp. li-lxvii.

GRATTON, JOHN (1641-1712). *A Journal of the Life of.* 1720. Quaker.

GREEN, THEOPHILUS (born *c.* 1620). *A Narrative of Some Passages of the Life of.* 1702. Quaker.

GREENE, THOMAS. *A Declaration to the World of my Travel and Journey out of Aegypt into Canaan.* 1659. Quaker.

GUISE, SIR CHRISTOPHER (1618-70). *Memoirs of the Family of Guise.* Edited by G. Davies. 1917. Written *c.* 1662-5.

GWIN, THOMAS. Autobiography and journal. Friends' Society Library, London, ms. 77. Not seen.

GWYNNE, JOHN (fl. 1660). *The Military Memoirs of.* In *Military Memoirs of the Great Civil War.* Edinburgh, 1822.

HALHEAD, MYLES (1614-89?). *A Book of some of the Sufferings and Passages of.* 1690. Quaker. See Wright.

HALKETT, ANNE LADY (1622-99). *Autobiography.* Edited by J. G. Nichols. Camden Society, 1875. Written 1678.

HALL, JOSEPH (1574-1656). *Some Specialties of Divine Providence in his Life* and *Bishop Hall's Hard Measure.* In *The Shaking of the Olive Tree. The Remaining Works of . . . Joseph Hall, D.D.* 1660.

HALYBURTON, THOMAS (1674-1712). *Memoirs of the Reverend.* Princeton, 1833.

HAYES, ALICE (1657-1720). *A Legacy or a Widow's Mite: Left by Alice Hayes.* 1723. Quaker.

HEBDEN, ROGER (1620-95). *A Plain Account . . . of.* 1700. Quaker.

HERBERT, EDWARD, LORD HERBERT OF CHERBURY (1583-1648). *Autobiography.* Edited by Sidney Lee. 1892. 1st ed. 1764. Written *c.* 1645.

HEYWOOD, OLIVER (1629-1702). *His Autobiography.* Edited by J. H. Turner. Brighouse, 1882. Written 1661-2.

HINTON, SIR JOHN (1603?-82). *Memoires by Sir John Hinton.* 1679. Autobiographical begging-letter.

HOBBES, THOMAS (1588-1679). *Vita* and *Vita, Carmine Expressa.* In *Thomae Hobbes Malmesburiensis Opera Philosophica Quae Latine Scripsit,* edited by G. Molesworth. 1839. Vol. I. Verse life written 1672. For the early printings and translations of these two lives, see Donald Wing, *Short-Title Catalogue of Books Printed in . . . 1641-1700.*

HODGSON, CAPTAIN JOHN (d. 1684). *Autobiography.* Brighouse, 1882.

HOLLAND, HUGH (d. 1633). 'To my Mayden Muse'. Preface to his *Pancharis.* In *Illustrations of Old English Literature.* Edited by J. Payne Collier. Vol. II. Privately printed, 1866. See Stauffer.

HOLLES, DENZIL (1598-1679). *Memoirs of.* 1699. Largely *historia sui temporis.*

HOWARD, LUKE (1621-99). *Love and Truth in Plainness Manifested.* 1704. Quaker.

HOWGILL, FRANCIS (1618-69). *The Inheritance of Jacob Discovered.* 1656. Quaker.

HUNTINGDON, THEOPHILUS HASTINGS, EARL OF (1650-1701). Autobiography and family history. Bodleian Carte ms. 78, ff. 410-17. Written 1694. The manuscript is mis-bound, and should run as follows: first draft of the autobiography, ff. 410-11; second draft, 414, 415, 416, 417, 412, 413.

HUTCHINSON, LUCY (1620-71). *The Life of.* In Rev. Julius Hutchinson, ed., *Memoirs of the Life of Colonel Hutchinson.* 1885. 2 vols. Written *c.* 1670-5; first printed, 1806.

JAMES II (1633-1701). *The Memoirs of.* Translated from the French by A. Lytton Sells. Bloomington, 1962. His campaigns as Duke of York, 1652-60.

JESSEY, HENRY (1601-63). *The Life and Death of.* 1671. See Tindall, p. 29.

JOLLIE, THOMAS, *A short narrative of some passages of my sufferings these 20 yeares upon the account of nonconformity.* Dr. Williams' Library, London, ms. 12.78, pp. 145-8. Covers 1660-79.

JOSSELIN, REV. RALPH (1616-83). *Diary.* Edited by E. Hockliffe. Camden Society, 3rd series, XV. 1908.

KIDDER, RICHARD (1633-1703). *The Life of Richard Kidder D.D. Bishop of Bath and Wells Written by Himself.* Edited by A. E. Robinson. Somerset Record Society, vol. 37. 1924. Ecclesiastical *res gestae.*

KIFFIN, WILLIAM (1616-1701). *Remarkable Passages in the Life of.* Edited by W. Orme. 1823. Baptist.

KNOLLYS, HANSERD (*c.* 1599-1691). *The Life and Death of.* 1692. Baptist.

LAMPE, HENRY (1660-1711). *Curriculum Vitae.* Edited by Joseph J. Green. 1895. Quaker physician.

LILLY, WILLIAM (1602-81). *History of his Life and Times.* In *The Lives of those eminent antiquaries Elias Ashmole, Esquire and Mr. William Lilly.* 1774. Written 1667; 1st ed. 1715.

LISTER, JOSEPH (1627-1709). *The Autobiography of.* Edited by T. Wright. 1842. Written 1709.

LIVINGSTONE, JOHN (1603-72). *A Brief Historical Relation of the Life of.* Glasgow, 1754. Written *c.* 1670. Minister.

LUDLOW, EDMUND (1617?-1692). *Memoirs.* 1698. 3 vols. Military and political.

LURTING, THOMAS. *The Fighting Sailor turn'd Peacable Christian.* 1711. Quaker; shipmate of Edward Coxere, q.v.

MARKHAM, FRANCIS (1565-1627). *Autobiography.* In C. Markham, ed., *Markham Memorials.* 1913.

MARSHALL, CHARLES (1637-98). *Sion's Traveller Comforted.* 1704. Quaker.

MARTINDALE, ADAM (1623-86). *The Life of.* In R. Parkinson, ed., Chetham Society *Remains*, vol. IV. Manchester, 1845.

MATTHEW, SIR TOBIE (1577-1655). *A True Historical Relation of the Conversion of.* Edited by A. H. Mathew. 1904. Written 1640.

MELLIDGE, ANTHONY (born *c.* 1620). *A True Relation . . . of.* 1656. Quaker.

MELVILL, SIR ANDREW (1624-1706). *Memoirs.* 1918. Military.

MITCHELL, JAMES (d. 1678). Autobiography. University of Edinburgh, ms. Laing 269. Not seen. Executed for shooting the Bishop of Orkney.

MONCKTON, SIR PHILIP (1620-79). *Memoirs.* In *Monckton Papers.* Edited by E. Peacock. 1884. Civil War memoirs.

MORE, HENRY (1614-87). Autobiography. In Praefatio Generalissima to *Henrici Mori Cantabrigiensis Opera Omnia.* 1679. Vol. I, pp. i-xxiv. A partial translation of More's preface can be found in Richard Ward's *The Life of The Learned and Pious Dr. Henry More (1710),* pp. 4-16.

MUGGLETON, LODOWICK (1609-98). *The Acts of the Witnesses of the Spirit.* 1764. This is a page-for-page reprint of the first edition, 1699, with corrections.

NAPIER, ARCHIBALD, FIRST LORD (d. 1658). *Memoirs of.* Edinburgh, 1793. Court memoirs.

NEWCASTLE, MARGARET CAVENDISH, DUCHESS OF (1625-74). *A True Relation of My Birth, Breeding and Life.* In Ernest Rhys, ed., *The Life of the First Duke of Newcastle and other writings by Margaret Duchess.* Everyman edition, n.d.

NEWCOME, HENRY (1627-95). *The Autobiography of.* Chetham Society, Manchester, 1852.

NISBET, JAMES (b. 1667). *Autobiography.* In *Private Life of the Persecuted.* Edinburgh, 1827. Covenanter; written after 1714.

NORTH, ROGER (1653-1734). *Autobiography.* Edited by A. Jessopp. 1887.

NORWOOD, RICHARD (1590-1675). *Journal.* New York, 1945. Written 1639.

PATRICK, SYMON (1626-1707). *Autobiography.* In *Works.* Edited by Rev. Alexander Taylor. Oxford, 1858. Vol. IX. Written 1706.

PENINGTON, MARY (*c.* 1625-1682). *A Brief Account of my Exercises from my Childhood.* Philadelphia, 1848.

PENNYMAN, JOHN (1628-1706). *A Short Account of the Life of.* 1696. Quaker; see Wright.

PERSONS, FATHER ROBERT (1546-1610). *Memoirs.* Edited by A. H. Pollen. *Catholic Record Society Miscellany,* vol. II. 1906. Incomplete.

PETERS, HUGH (1598-1660). *A Dying Father's Last Legacy to an Onely Child.* 1660. Attempts to vindicate himself from the charge of being a regicide, for which he was executed.

PETERS, JOHN (1646-1708). *A brief Narration of the Life of.* 1709. Quaker.

PETT, PHINEAS (1570-1647). *The Autobiography of.* Edited by W. G. Perrin. 1918.

PITS, JOHN (1560-1616). *De Meipso.* In his *Relationum Historicarum de Rebus Anglicis.* Paris, 1619. Pp. 816-17. List of his deeds.

PLEDGER, ELIAS (1665-after 1712). *Autobiography and Diary.* Dr. Williams Library, London, ms. 28.4. Conversion narrative.

POWELL, VAVASOR (1617-70). *The Life and Death of.* In T. Jackson, ed., *Library of Christian Biography.* 1840. Vol. XII. 1st ed. 1671.

POYNTZ, SYDNAM (fl. 1630). *The Relation of Sydnam Poyntz, 1624-36.* Camden Society, 1908.

PRINGLE, WALTER (1625-67). *The Memoirs of.* Edited by Walter Wood. Edinburgh, 1847. 1st ed. Edinburgh, 1723.

RAYMOND, THOMAS (1610?-81). *Autobiography.* Edited by G. Davies. Camden Society, 1917. Raymond's title was 'A Rhapsodie'.

REID, ALEXANDER (1647-1706). *A Short Account of.* Edinburgh, 1825. Covenanter; minor.

RERESBY, SIR JOHN (1634-89). *The Memoirs of.* Edited by Andrew Browning. Glasgow, 1936. The nine previous editions, from 1734, are not trustworthy.

RICH, MARY. See Warwick, Lady.

RIGGE, AMBROSE (1635?-1705). *Constancy in the Truth Commended.* 1710. Quaker tradesman; minor.

ROBINSON, MATHEW (1628-94). *Autobiography.* In J. E. B. Mayor, *Cambridge in the Seventeenth Century,* part II. 1856. Written before 1680.

ROFE, GEORGE. *The Righteousnes of God to Man.* 1656. Quaker.

SALMON, JOSEPH. *Heights in Depths and Depths in Heights.* 1651. Enthusiast; see Tindall, p. 28.

SANSOM, OLIVER (1636-1710). *An Account of Many Remarkable Passages of the Life of.* 1710. Quaker.

SHAFTESBURY, ANTHONY ASHLEY COOPER, EARL OF (1621-83). *Fragment of Autobiography.* In W. D. Christie, ed., *Memoirs, Letters, and Speeches . . . of Shaftesbury.* 1859. Planned as a self-vindicatory work; includes the famous character of Henry Hastings.

SHAWE, JOHN (1608-72). *Memoirs.* Hull, 1824. Minister; Civil War in Yorkshire.

SHEFFIELD, JOHN. See Buckingham, Duke of.

SIBBALD, SIR ROBERT (1641-1722). *Memoirs.* Edited by Paget Hett. 1932. 1st ed. 1833.

SMITH, CAPTAIN JOHN (1580-1631). *The True Travels, Adventures, and Observations of.* 1630. Travel and military memoirs.

STIRREDGE, ELIZABETH (1634-1706). *Strength in Weakness Manifest.* 1711. Quaker.

SYMONDS, THOMAS. *The Voyce of the Just Uttered.* 1656. Quaker.

TASWELL, WILLIAM (1652-1731). *Autobiography.* In G. P. Elliott, ed., *The Camden Miscellany,* ii. 1853. Translated from the Latin by Taswell's grandson.

TAYLOR, JOHN (1637-1708). *An Account of Some of the Labours of.* 1710. Quaker.

THORNTON, ALICE (1627-1707). *The Autobiography of.* Edited by Charles Jackson. Surtees Society, 1875. Written after 1669. Religious.

THOMPSON, THOMAS (1632-1704). *An Encouragement Early to Seek the Lord.* 1708. Quaker.

TROSSE, GEORGE (1631-1713). *The Life of . . . Written by Himself . . . To which is Added, The Sermon preach'd at his Funeral.* Exeter, 1714.

TRUMBULL, SIR WILLIAM (1639-1716). Autobiography to 1687. All Souls College, Oxford, ms. L. R. 3. C. 20. Diplomat.

TURNER, SIR JAMES (1615-86?). *Memoirs of his own Life and Times.* 1829. Military memoirs.

VANE, SIR HENRY (1589-1655). *Autobiography.* In Charles Dalton, *History of the Wrays of Glentworth.* 1881. Vol. II, pp. 113-15. Fragmentary; apparently a memo to help in drawing up his will.

VEITCH, WILLIAM (1640-1722). *Memoirs of Mr. William Veitch and George Brysson.* Edited by T. McCrie. Edinburgh and London, 1825.

VEITCH, MRS. WILLIAM. Autobiography. National Library of Scotland, ms. 36. 6. 22. Not seen.

VERE, SIR FRANCIS (1560-1609). *Commentaries.* 1657. Military memoirs.

VOKINS, JOAN (d. 1690). *God's Mighty Power Magnified.* 1691. Quaker.

WADSWORTH, JAMES (1604-56?). *The Memoires of Mr. James Wadsworth, a Jesuit that recanted.* 1679. Stauffer: 'probably spurious'; but see *DNB.*

WALLER, SIR WILLIAM (1597?-1668). *Recollections.* In *The Poetry of Anna Matilda.* 1788.

WALLINGTON, NEHEMIAH (1598-1658). *A Record of the Mercies of God: or A Thankful Remembrance.* Guildhall Library, London, ms. 204. Not seen.

WALLIS, JOHN (1616-1703). *Dr. Wallis's Account of some Passages of his own Life.* In Thomas Hearne, ed., *Peter Langtoft's Chronicle.* Oxford, 1725. Vol. I, pp. cxl-clxxii. Written 1697.

WARWICK, MARY RICH, COUNTESS OF (1625-78). *Autobiography of.* Edited by T. C. Croker. Percy Society, 1848.

WENTWORTH, SIR WILLIAM (d. 1614). Autobiography and family history. Sheffield Central Library, ms. Strafford 40/1, pp. 22-45.

WESTMORELAND, MILDMAY FANE, SECOND EARL (1602-65). *Vita Authoris.* British Museum ms. Add. 34220. In Latin.

WESTON, FATHER WILLIAM (1550?-1615). *An Autobiography from the Jesuit Underground.* Translated by Philip Caraman. New York, 1955. Written 1611, in Latin. This William Weston is the same man as the Edmund Weston referred to in Caraman's edition of John Gerard's *Autobiography.*

WHARTON, GOODWIN (1653-1704). *My Life.* British Museum, ms. Add. 2006-7.

WHARTON, HENRY (1664-95). *Excerpta ex Vita.* In G. D'Oyly, *The Life of William Sancroft.* 1821. Vol. II, pp. 105-54. Extracts from a lost Latin original.

WHITEHEAD, GEORGE (1636-1723). *Jacob found in a Desert Land.* 1656. Conversion narrative. *The Christian Progress of that Ancient Servant . . . G. Whitehead.* 1725. Quaker journal.

WHITELOCKE, BULSTRODE (1605-75). *Memoirs Biographical and Historical.* Edited by R. H. Whitelocke. 1860.

WHITING, JOHN (1656-1722). *Persecution Exposed in some Memoirs.* 1715. Quaker.

WILSON, ARTHUR (1595-1652). *Autobiography.* In Francis Peck, *Desiderata Curiosa.* 1779. Pp. 460-83.

WILSON, THOMAS (1654-1725). *Brief Journal of the Life of.* Dublin, 1728. Quaker.

WOOD, ANTHONY À (1632-95). *The Life and Times of.* Edited and abridged Llewelyn Powys. World's Classics, 1961. Complete ed. by Andrew Clark, *Life and Times of Anthony Wood.* Oxford, 1891-1900. 5 vols.

WOODCOCK, THOMAS. *An Account of Some Remarkable Passages in the Life of a Private Gentleman.* Not seen.

II

OTHER WORKS CONSULTED

This section includes both modern critical studies and early works not falling within my definition of seventeenth-century British autobiography. I have not thought it necessary to list such standard works as the Oxford History of English Literature, *CBEL*, *DNB*, etc., though I am of course indebted to them for bibliographical and other information.

AENEAS SYLVIUS (Pius II). *Memoirs of a Renaissance Pope*. Abridged edition, translated from the Latin by F. A. Gragg. New York, 1959.

ARIÈS, PHILIPPE. *Centuries of Childhood. A Social History of Family Life*. Translated by Robert Baldick. New York, Vintage books, 1965.

AUBREY, JOHN. *Brief Lives*. Edited by O. L. Dick. 1949.

AUGUSTINE, ST. *The Confessions*. Translated by E. B. Pusey. New York, Modern Library, 1949. First English translation was by Sir Tobie Matthew (q.v., section I above), St. Omer, 1620.

BAINTON, ROLAND H. *Here I Stand. A Life of Martin Luther*. New York, 1950.

BARBU, ZEVEDEI. *Problems of Historical Psychology*. New York, 1960.

BARCLAY, ROBERT. *The Inner Life of the Religious Societies of the Commonwealth*. 1876.

BAUTHUMLEY, JAMES. *The light and dark Side of God*. 1650. Ranter tract.

BEADLE, JOHN. *The Journal of Diary of a Thankful Christian*. 1656.

BEAUMONT, AGNES. *Narrative of the Persecution of*. Edited by G. B. Harrison. 1929. A scandal involving Bunyan.

BLIGH, E. W. *Sir Kenelm Digby and his Venetia*. 1932.

BLOCH, MARC. *Feudal Society*. Translated by L. A. Manyon. 1962.

BOTTRALL, MARGARET. *Every Man a Phoenix*. 1958.

—— *Personal Records. A Gallery of Self-Portraits*. 1961.

BRINK, ANDREW W. *A Study in the Literature of Inward Experience, 1600-1700*. Unpublished Ph.D. dissertation, University College, London. 1963.

BROWNE, SIR THOMAS. *Religio Medici*. 1642. Revised edition, 1643. Written *c*. 1635.

BURCKHARDT, JACOB. *The Civilization of the Renaissance in Italy*. Translated by S. Middlemore. 1955.

BURR, ANNA ROBESON. *The Autobiography, a Critical and Comparative Study*. Boston, 1909.

CALAMY, EDMUND. *An Historical Account of my own Life*. Edited by J. T. Rutt. 1829. 2 vols. Written to 1730; introduction contains an interesting history of autobiography from antiquity to the eighteenth century.

CALVIN, JOHN. *Institutes of the Christian Religion*. Translated by Henry Beveridge. Grand Rapids, 1962. 2 vols.

CARDAN, JEROME. *The Book of my Life*. Translated by Jean Stoner. New York, 1930. 1st ed. Paris, 1643.

CELLINI, BENVENUTO. *The Autobiography of*. Translated by George Bull. Penguin books, 1956. 1st ed. 1728.

CLIFFORD, J. L., ed. *Biography as an Art, Selected Criticism 1560-1960*. 1962.

COHN, NORMAN. *The Pursuit of the Millennium.* 2nd ed. New York, 1961.

COPPE, ABIEZER. *A Fiery Flying Roll.* 1649.

COWLEY, ABRAHAM. 'Of My Self'. In *Works.* 1669.

CRUTTWELL, PATRICK. *The Shakespearean Moment.* New York, 1960.

DALI, SALVADOR. *The Secret Life of.* Translated by Haakon Chevalier. New York, 1942.

DIGBY, SIR KENELM. *Observations Upon Religio Medici* ... *The fourth Edition.* In *Religio Medici,* 1669.

DILTHEY, WILHELM. *Auffassung und Analyse des Menschen im 15 und 16 Jahrhundert.* In *Archiv für Geschichte der Philosophie* v (1892), 337.

DOUGLAS, DAVID C. *English Scholars 1660-1730.* 2nd edition. 1951.

DOWNAME, JOHN. *The Christian Warfare,* 1634.

EBNER, IVAN D. *Seventeenth Century British Autobiography: The Impact of Religious Commitment.* Unpublished Ph.D. dissertation, Stanford University, 1965.

ERIKSON, ERIK H. *Young Man Luther.* New York, 1962.

EVERITT, ALAN. 'Social Mobility in Early Modern England', *Past and Present,* 33, 56-73.

FERGUSON, WALLACE K. *The Renaissance in Historical Thought.* Cambridge, Mass., 1948.

FRÄNGER, WILHELM. *The Millennium of Hieronymus Bosch.* Translated by E. Wilkins and E. Kaiser. 1952.

FREUD, SIGMUND. 'Obsessive Acts and Religious Practices', in *Collected Papers.* New York, 1959. Vol. 2.

—— 'A Neurosis of Demoniacal Possession in the Seventeenth Century', in *Collected Papers.* Vol. 4.

—— *The Basic Writings.* Translated by A. A. Brill. New York, 1938.

GIBBON, EDWARD. *Autobiography.* World's Classics, 1907.

GILMORE, MYRON P. *The World of Humanism, 1453-1517.* New York, 1952.

GOFFMAN, ERVING. *The Presentation of Self in Everyday Life.* New York, 1959.

GOLDSCHEIDER, LUDWIG. *Five Hundred Self-Portraits.* Vienna, 1937.

GOTTFRIED, RUDOLF. 'Autobiography and Art: An Elizabethan Borderland'. In *Literary Criticism and Historical Understanding,* ed. Phillip Damon (English Institute Essays; New York, 1967), pp. 109-34.

GREENE, ROBERT. *Greenes Groats-Worth of Witte, bought with a million of Repentance.* 1592.

GUSDORF, GEORGES. 'Conditions et limites de l'autobiographie'. In Reichenkron and Haase, eds., *Formen der Selbstdarstellung.* Berlin, 1956.

—— *La Découverte de Soi.* Paris, 1948.

HALLER, WILLIAM. *The Rise of Puritanism.* New York, 1938.

HENDRICHS, DOROTHEA. *Geschichte der englischen Autobiographie von Chaucer bis Milton.* Leipzig, 1925.

HILL, CHRISTOPHER. *Puritanism and Revolution.* 1962.

HOBY, THOMAS. *A Booke of the Travaile and Lief of me Thomas Hoby.* Edited by Edgar Powell. Camden Society Miscellany, x. 1902.

HURSTFIELD, J., ed. *The Reformation Crisis.* 1965.

JAMES, WILLIAM. *The Varieties of Religious Experience.* New York, Mentor Books, 1958.

JONES, RUFUS M. *Spiritual Reformers in the 16th and 17th Centuries.* 1914.

KEMPE, MARGERY. *The Book of Margery Kempe.* Edited by S. B. Meech and H. E. Allen. 1940. Written *c.* 1436.

KILBY, RICHARD. *The Burthen of a loaden conscience: or the miserie of Sinne: Set forth by the confession of a miserable sinner.* Cambridge, 1608.

—— *Hallelu-iah: Praise yee the Lord, For the Unburthening of a loaden Conscience.* Cambridge, 1618.

KNAPPEN, M. M., ed. *Two Elizabethan Puritan Diaries.* Chicago, 1933. Diaries of Samuel Ward and Richard Rogers.

LILBURNE, JOHN. *The Christian Mans Triall.* 1641.

LUTHER, MARTIN. *Colloquia Mensalia: or, Dr. Martin Luther's Divine Discourses.* 1652.

MCLUHAN, MARSHALL. *The Gutenberg Galaxy.* Toronto, 1965.

MANNHEIM, KARL. *Ideology and Utopia.* New York, Harvest Books, n.d.

MARTZ, LOUIS L. *The Poetry of Meditation.* New Haven, 1954.

MATTHEWS, WILLIAM. *British Autobiographies.* Berkeley and Los Angeles, 1955. Comprehensive bibliography from the beginnings to the modern period, arranged alphabetically by authors.

MELVILLE, SIR JAMES. *The Memoires of.* Edited by A. F. Steuart. 1930. Written *c.* 1594; 1st ed. 1683.

MEYER, A. O. *England and the Catholic Church under Elizabeth.* 1916.

MILL, JOHN STUART. *Autobiography.* Edited by H. J. Laski. 1924.

MILTON, JOHN. *Milton on Himself.* Edited by John S. Diekhoff. 1939.

MISCH, GEORG. *A History of Autobiography in Antiquity.* Translated by E. W. Dickes. 1950.

MONTAIGNE, MICHEL DE. *The Essayes.* Translated by John Florio. Everyman's Library, 1910. 3 vols.

MORGAN, EDMUND S. *Visible Saints: The History of a Puritan Idea.* Ithaca, 1965.

MORRIS, JOHN N. *Versions of the Self.* New York, 1966.

NELSON, NORMAN. 'Individualism as a Criterion of the Renaissance', *JEGP*, xxxii (1933), 316-34.

NEWMAN, JOHN HENRY, CARDINAL. *Apologia pro Vita Sua*. 1864.

NICHOLSON, SIR HAROLD. *The Development of English Biography*. 1927.

NUTTALL, G. F. *The Holy Spirit in Puritan Faith and Experience*. Oxford, 1946.

—— *Visible Saints. The Congregational Way 1640-60*. Oxford, 1957.

OSBORN, JAMES M. *The Beginnings of Autobiography in England*. Los Angeles, The Clark Library, 1959.

PANOFSKY, ERWIN. *The Life and Art of Albrecht Dürer*. Princeton, 1955.

PARÉ, AMBROISE. *Apology*. Translated by Georg Baker. Edited by Geoffrey Keynes. 1951.

PASCAL, BLAISE. *Pensées*. Edited by Ch-M. des Granges. Paris, éditions Garnier, n.d.

PASCAL, ROY. *Design and Truth in Autobiography*. Cambridge, Mass., 1960.

PETERSSON, R. T. *Sir Kenelm Digby*. Cambridge, Mass., 1956.

PETRARCH, F. *Lettera ai Posteri*. Edited by A. Solerti. Florence, 1904.

—— *Petrarch's Secret, or The Soul's Conflict with Passion*. Translated by W. H. Draper. 1911.

PINTO, V. DA S. *Introduction to English Biography in the Seventeenth Century*. 1951.

PITTI, BUONACCORSO. *Cronica*. Edited by A. B. Della Lega. Bologna, 1905. Written 1412.

PLATTER, THOMAS. *The Autobiography of Thomas Platter, a Schoolmaster of the Sixteenth Century*. Translated from the German. 1839.

ROUSSEAU, JEAN-JACQUES. *The Confessions of*. Translated by J. M. Cohen. Penguin Books, 1953. 1st ed. 1781.

SHARROCK, ROGER. *John Bunyan*. 1954.

SHEPARD, THOMAS. *Autobiography*. Shepard emigrated to New England and died there. The first North American autobiography?

SHUMAKER, W. *English Autobiography: Its Emergence, Materials and Form*. Berkeley and Los Angeles, 1954.

SMITH, D. NICHOL, ed. *Characters from the Histories and Memoirs of the Seventeenth Century*. Oxford, 1920.

STARR, G. A. *Defoe and Spiritual Autobiography*. Princeton, 1965.

STAUFFER, D. A. *English Biography before 1700*. Cambridge, Mass., 1930.

STEINBERG, S. H. *Five Hundred Years of Printing*. Penguin Books, 1961.

STONE, LAWRENCE. *The Crisis of the Aristocracy 1558-1641*. Oxford, 1965.

189

—— 'Social Mobility in England, 1500-1700', *Past and Present*, 33, 16-55.

TACITUS. *Agricola.*

TERESA, ST. *The Life of.* Translated by J. M. Cohen. Penguin Books, 1957.

TINDALL, W. Y. *John Bunyan Mechanick Preacher.* New York, 1934.

TRAHERNE, THOMAS. *Centuries.* Edited by H. M. Margolioth. 1960.

VAN DEN BERG, J. H. *The Changing Nature of Man.* Translated by H. F. Cross. New York, 1961.

WALZER, M. *The Revolution of the Saints.* Cambridge, Mass., 1965.

WEBER, MAX. *The Protestant Ethic and the Spirit of Capitalism.* Translated by Talcott Parsons. New York, 1958.

WHYTHORNE, THOMAS. *Autobiography.* Edited by J. M. Osborn. Oxford, 1961. Written *c.* 1576.

WOODNOTH, ARTHUR. Statement of belief. In H. S. Scott, ed., *The Journal of Sir Roger Wilbraham.* Camden Society Miscellany x, 1902. 118-28.

WRIGHT, LUELLA M. *The Literary Life of the Early Friends.* New York, 1932.

Index